THE BEST EUROPEAN TRAVEL TIPS

by John Whitman

Meadowbrook
Distributed by Simon and Schuster
New York

My special thanks to these readers who have added a tip or corrected information in the previous guide: Carol Antonow, J. Bell, Jean Bullock, R. Butler, Dawn Carmack, Heather Cowap, Vivian J. Cummings, Marcia Daszko, Mike Dewey, Andrew Dorio, John A. Elling, Gwen and Davey Farrington, Sue Ferer, Tony Freeman, Albert Furtwangler, Josephine Gillis, R.L. Goodale, Leo J. Goode, Jason Gow, Jackie and Jim Haeston, Tony Harkin, Rosamond Haverstock, Joe Hodge, Jane H. Holzherr, Stephen S. Johnson, Harry O. Knowles, Glynis J. Laing, Linda D. Little, Kate MacDonald, Eloise McGinnis, Rachel McLean, Betty Mendolia, Lydia Morgan, Christopher and Marie North, Marc Parsont, Marge Ritenhouse, Marvin L. Saltzman, Floyd D. Seele, Steve Snowden, William Speck, Lynne Terrell, Gail Ann Williams, Harry P. Wilson, Kenney Wright.

John Whitman

Library of Congress Cataloging in Publication Data

Whitman, John
  The Best European Travel Tips.

  (The Best Tips Series)
  Includes index.
    1. Europe—Description and travel—1971—
—Guide-books. I. Title
D909.W536 1986 914'.04558 86-31168
ISBN 0-88166-092-2
S&S Ordering #: 0-671-63625-1

Copyright © 1980, 1982, 1985 by John Whitman

Sixth Revised Edition, February 1988

Published by Meadowbrook, Inc., Deephaven, MN 55391

BOOK TRADE DISTRIBUTION by Simon and Schuster, a division of Simon & Schuster, Inc., 1230 Avenue of the Americas, New York, NY 10020

Cover Design: Sandra Falls
Text Design: Mary Foster

Front Cover Photo ©Ivor Sharp/The Image Bank West
Back Cover Photos ©Harvey Lloyd/The Image Bank West
©Gabe Palmer/The Image Bank West
Author Photo ©Terry Dugan/Meadowbrook Press
10 9 8 7 6 5 4

Printed in the United States of America

Acknowledgments: Tips on passports and visas, pp. 12–14; credit cards and insurance, pp. 16–20; medical precautions and health problems, pp. 22–26, 210–217; travel agents, pp. 30–31; travel organizations, pp. 38, 41, 43; charter companies and clearinghouses, pp. 47–54; packing, pp. 78–79, 81, 83; and safety precautions, pp. 132–138 are reprinted from *The Best Mexican Travel Tips*, (© 1986, Harper & Row) by John E. Whitman with the author's permission.

Contents

Maps and Charts

Part I: Preparations

---

1 Travel Documents

You'll need certain documents to travel freely through Europe or to avoid potential problems. Here are some tips to make the whole process of getting these documents less costly and more enjoyable.

Passports

If you are planning a trip to Europe, you must obtain a passport. If you already have one, check the expiration date to see whether the passport will be valid for the entire length of your trip. If it will expire during your stay in Europe, you must apply for a new one.

Kinds of passports

- Each person in your party must have an individual passport. No longer is it legal for a couple or family to travel on a single, group passport as it was in the past. Individual passports give everyone freedom and flexibility — a big advantage!

- If you plan to travel in eastern Europe, ask for the special 48-page passport when you apply. It costs no more than the standard document and provides added space for the visas you will need (see p. 12).

When to apply for a passport

- If you intend to travel in eastern Europe, apply for a passport as much as six months in advance, since you will have to get visas (see p. 12). For western European travel you won't need to plan so far in advance, but make your application as soon as possible. You can pay extra to get a passport in as little as three days.

- In an emergency you can obtain a passport in one day, at a substantial fee. This service is not available to the jet-setter who decides on a whim to get a passport overnight; it is reserved for emergencies only!

Applying for a first passport

- To get your first passport, you must apply in person at the appropriate agency. So must all members of your family who are 12 years of age or older. Younger children need not appear in person.

- The passport agency is listed in your telephone directory under U.S. Government Offices. If there is no passport agency in your town, the service may be handled at a federal, state, or probate courthouse or at a designated post office. Call the listed number for hours.

- Be sure to ask the clerk about the least busy hours to come in and apply for a passport.

What to bring when you apply

Passport application: you will need to fill out a passport application in person at the appropriate passport agency.

Proof of U.S. citizenship: for proof of U.S. citizenship, come armed with a birth certificate or certified copy (look for a raised seal imprinted on the copy) or a certificate of naturalization or citizenship. If you don't have any of these, you can get by with certificates of baptism or circumcision; hospital birth records; documentary evidence from census, school, or insurance companies; or affidavits. No proof, no passport!

Proof of identity: if you're known to the clerk or if you have a certificate of naturalization or citizenship, that's all the proof of identity you'll need. Otherwise you must produce a valid driver's license, a government identification card or pass, or a witness. The witness must have valid identification (passport, driver's license, government pass, or certificate of naturalization or citizenship) and must have known you for at least two years. All identification must bear signatures and photos.

Two passport photos: you'll need two passport photos, taken within the last six months. Each should be signed as indicated on the application (the procedure changes occasionally). Note that photos taken in a photomat machine will not be acceptable. Passport photos must be 2 by 2 inches. They should be clear, front-view shots of your head and shoulders only, taken against a white background. No hats or sunglasses allowed! Prints must be on thin, nonglossy paper. Photos can be either in color or in black-and-white.

Passport photos

• Agencies no longer allow passports with a dark background, and this has caused some resentment and confusion. Be sure to have your photos taken with a white background.

• Many agencies issuing passports now offer a passport photo service as well. Be sure to call ahead to see whether such a service is available in your area. Ask what the fee will be and the cost of extra prints. Then call several passport photo shops and passport photo studios listed in the yellow pages, as well as the local branch of the American Automobile Association (AAA), for cost comparison. A separate trip might save you several dollars if you're so inclined.

• You will need two photos for your passport. You should always carry two spare copies for emergencies. And you will need extra photos for visas (see p. 12).

Passport fees

• You will be charged a standard passport fee and an execution fee for each passport. The execution fee varies from one area to the next. Call ahead to see what the total charges will be.

• When you call, ask how the payment should be made. Some offices refuse to take cash and may insist on a bank draft, money order, or check (personal, traveler's, certified, or cashier's). Avoid this situation: "What do you mean you won't take cash?" You've been warned!

Applying if you have had a passport before

• If you have had a passport during the last eight years and don't intend to make a change, apply for your new passport by mail. This will save you a trip and the execution fee. But you will pay for mailing the passport. This can now cost more than the execution fee when making an application in person.

- Call the nearest passport agency and ask them to send you Passport Office Form DSP-82, "Application for Passport by Mail." When this form arrives in the mail, fill it out, sign it, and date it. Attach your old passport, two up-to-date passport photos signed as instructed, and a check or money order to cover the passport fee.

- If your name has changed, be sure to include the original or a certified copy of your marriage certificate or of the change-of-name papers when making an application by mail.

- Be sure to send the passport by registered mail and hold on to the receipt until the new passport arrives.

- **A special note**: if you were under 18 when you applied for your old passport, you'll have to apply for the new one in person.

- Naturally, you can always apply for a passport in person if you prefer. But in that case you must pay the execution fee.

Protecting yourself and your passport

- When your passport arrives in the mail, check it for correctness before signing. If there is an error in any of the information, you must return the passport to have it corrected. Never write in, alter, or mutilate any portion of the passport, as this will make it invalid.

- Make two photocopies of information in the passport. Although this is technically illegal, these photocopies will be invaluable if your passport is lost or stolen. File one of the photocopies in a safe place and take the other with you to Europe. Don't carry it with your passport!

If you lose your passport in the United States

- If your passport is lost or stolen in the United States, contact the Passport Office, Department of State, Washington, DC 20524 **immediately.** You'll need the information that you recorded on a photocopy of the original passport.

- Canadian citizens should report lost or stolen passports to the closest Canadian passport office. You'll find one in each province.

Visas

Visas are special notations and stamps, added to your passport by officials of foreign countries, that allow you to enter and leave these countries. Most western European countries do not require visas from American visitors, except for long-term stays (over three months). However, a series of terrorist bombings in Paris in 1986 prompted the French government to tighten its visa requirements. If you plan to visit France, you should contact the nearest French consulate or government tourist office (see Appendix) for up-to-date information on visa requirements.

Eastern European countries, on the other hand, generally require visas, even for short stays.

Where to get visas

- Obtain all visas before going to Europe. Visa information is outlined in a government leaflet entitled **Visa Requirements of Foreign Governments** (Passport Office Publication M-264). You can get the leaflet from most passport agencies, and it will tell you what countries require visas. You'll then have to write the embassy or consulate of the foreign country to get a visa application form with information on fees and procedures. You'll generally have to send passport photos along with a completed application and payment for the service.

- Canadians should contact a travel agency or the nearest passport office. Visa information is outlined in the **Travel Information Manual,** which good agents should have. If they don't, ask them to order one from the following address: Travel Information Manual, P.O. Box 7627, 1117 vj Schipol Airport, The Netherlands.

Special tips on getting visas

- To get visas, you'll have to mail your passport along with the appropriate application to a foreign consulate or embassy. Be sure to use registered mail and keep the receipt until your passport has been returned.

- You are expected to include a check for the visa as well as enough money to cover **return postage.** Ask the consulate or embassy to return the passport by registered mail. Make sure you've included enough money to cover the fee for such a service.

- Always apply for visas at the foreign consulate or embassy in your city or the city nearest you. Most embassies and consulates are located in Chicago, New York, San Francisco, and Washington, DC. You'll find the addresses in individual city directories or in the **Congressional Directory,** found in most major libraries.

- In Canada, refer to the **Travel Information Manual** previously mentioned, which you'll find at many travel agencies and in a few libraries.

- If you intend to travel to areas requiring visas, allow an extra three to six weeks for each necessary visa. Obtaining visas can be a long — disturbingly long — process. You may want to start the process months ahead of your planned trip!

International Driver's Licenses

If you plan to drive at all in Europe, you should get an International Driver's License. It's required in most countries, helps you avoid hassles with the police, and occasionally gets you out of a fine.

How to get licensed

- To get a license, you must be 18 years of age or older and you must hold a valid driver's license.

- You can get a license from the local branch of the American Automobile Association (AAA) without being a member.

- You'll need two photomat photos; keep the extras. Make sure they are as similar to your passport photos as possible. Note that many branches of AAA offer a photo service, but the cost is higher than in photomats.

- You'll be asked to sign the photos.

- You may have to return or have the license sent to you. Such a license is not valid until you sign it. It's good for one year from its issue date.

Stick shifts

- If you don't know how to operate a stick shift, you should learn. Even if you reserve a car with an automatic shift, there's no guarantee that you'll get one. Furthermore, in an emergency you should be able to drive any car that's available. A competent driving instructor can teach you how to use a stick shift in six hours or less — from the basics to starting on a 45-degree incline.

International Student Identification Cards

If you're a full-time student under the age of 30, get an International Student Identification Card! It will bring reductions on inter-European charter flights (save 75 percent); on all forms of transportation; in hotels and hostels; at museums, movies, galleries, and special events; and in many shops. **This card can save you hundreds of dollars.**

To get a card

- You'll need two photomat photos (similar to the passport pose), a copy of your fee statement as proof of full-time student status, and a check for the fee made out to CIEE (Council on International Educational Exchange), 205 East 42nd Street, New York, NY 10017, (212) 661-1450; or 312 Sutter Street, San Francisco, CA 94108, (415) 421-3473; or 1093 Broxton Avenue, Los Angeles, CA 90024, (213) 208-3551.

- Or you may be able to get a card from the student office of a local university. This would be a faster way of getting the card, since it may take three or four weeks from CIEE.

Checks and Credit Cards

Each year, more than a million travelers lose cash in Europe due to theft and negligence. For this reason, you should rely on traveler's checks as a way of carrying money throughout Europe, and you can extend your purchasing power by using credit.

Traveler's checks

- Traveler's checks are available from American Express, Bank of America, Barclay's Bank, Citibank, Thomas Cook, and many other institutions.

- Normally, you'll pay a 1 percent service fee when buying these checks.

- You can purchase foreign currency traveler's checks in the U.S. For example, you can buy French franc traveler's checks for a trip to France. As strange as it may sound, these are often more difficult to cash than traveler's checks in dollars!

Fee-free traveler's checks

Offers come and go, but if you'll look around, you'll find that you can buy traveler's checks without paying the 1 percent fee. It's worth the effort.

- Auto clubs and banks often offer traveler's checks free of any fee to members or preferred customers. You may have to pay for them with cash, a cashier's check, or a bank money order.

When you buy traveler's checks

- Make sure to count them since they're usually sold in packets containing a specific amount in specific denominations. Very rarely will a check be missing, but it doesn't hurt to be sure.

- Be sure to sign them as instructed. If you lose an unsigned check, it's gone forever.

- Couples should carry individual checks. Otherwise, you'll both have to be present at foreign banks to cash them — ridiculous!

- Note numbers on a separate sheet just in case you lose them.

- Get checks of varying denominations to avoid the currency exchange rip-off. You only want to exchange the amount of money you really need.

- Buy all traveler's checks in the United States. If you buy them in Europe, your currency will go through two exchanges before being converted into checks. You might lose 5 percent of your money just on the exchange, not to mention paying an added 1 percent service fee.

- Keep a written record of all the checks you've used. The simplest way to do this is to write all the numbers down in a safe place and to strike the number of each check cashed. This will be essential information if you lose the checks!

- Don't carry this record in the same place as your checks. If your checks get ripped off or lost, you'll lose the record as well.

Letters of credit, bank money orders, or cashier's checks

- You may have heard of letters of credit. Well, forget them. Banks abroad rarely honor them — without horrendous arguments. Do not attempt to travel with letters of credit!

- The same goes for bank money orders and cashier's checks. Although perfectly legitimate, they're next to impossible to cash. Your time is too valuable to waste in dismal corridors of foreign banks.

Personal checks

- You may not believe it, but it is a good idea to take some personal checks with you. Bring about half a dozen. You'll be surprised at the hotels, restaurants, and shops that will take them. Use them only for big-bill items.

Credit cards

These are as good as gold in much of Europe. There is very little suspicion of credit cards.

- The best credit cards are American Express, Carte Blanche, Diners Club, MasterCard, and Visa.

Advantages of credit cards

- Credit cards are safer to carry than cash, because if they're lost or stolen, you have limited liability, and no liability at all if you report the loss before they're used.

- With a credit card there's very little hassle renting a car or signing in at a hotel. You don't need to carry large amounts of cash at any time to pay for these big-expense items. Your signed receipt is all that's needed — even if you choose to pay with cash later (the receipt is then destroyed).

- When you use credit cards, you have excellent records of your expenses. This is good for trip planning and for the IRS at tax time.

- Credit card companies allow you to use their money on a float — you may not have to pay the bill for a month or two. This ends up being an interest-free loan.

- Companies automatically convert all charges to dollars at the rate of exchange prevailing at the time the charges are submitted. This means you can avoid much of the currency exchange hassle by using the card frequently.

- Credit cards are easy to carry and honored in many shops, restaurants, car rental agencies, and hotels. You can get a pamphlet outlining the establishments honoring the card by requesting one from the company.

• Many credit cards allow you to get cash in a pinch. The regulations and fees for such a service change frequently, so check with your credit card company for current information.

• **Special note:** there should be no surcharge placed on any bill for the use of a credit card. If someone tries to add one, refuse to pay it.

Insurance

If you carry any insurance at all, it will probably cover part of your trip. Exceptions to this general rule and additional information on the subject are detailed below.

Accident insurance

• Check to see whether your policy is valid in Europe.

Baggage insurance

• Read your homeowner's policy. In most instances it will cover your baggage up to a specific value. But don't assume this. Ask your agent to be sure.

• If you must bring along any expensive articles, such as furs, jewelry, and cameras, pay a small fee to have a **personal articles floater** added to your policy.

• Find out whether your policy will cover new purchases made abroad for a specified grace period.

• If you don't have a homeowner's policy, you can buy special baggage insurance, which is available from most insurance companies and can be obtained directly from the airline at check-in time.

• Do some comparison shopping over the phone to come up with the least expensive coverage. Don't assume the costs will be comparable.

• To protect yourself, keep a list of all the clothes and personal belongings packed in each bag. Also note the value of each article.

• Note that even without insurance, if your bags are lost or damaged during a flight, the airline will reimburse you up to a specified limit. However, all items will be depreciated, and you may have to produce receipts.

- If you travel light and with very few valuables, all of this worry and expense is eliminated!

Car insurance

- Your car insurance is invalid in Europe. See p. 64 for full details on car insurance.

Health insurance

- **Medicare** and **Medicaid** don't cover you in Europe. However, check to see whether the law has changed recently.
- Most health policies do cover you worldwide, but you must ask to be sure. Generally, you'll have to pay for all expenses and be reimbursed when you return home.
- Carry your insurance card, your agent's telephone number, and your insurance company's telephone number when you travel. This way you can always get in touch with them for advice in an emergency. In some European countries, you will be covered, at least partially, by national health insurance; in most countries, however, you'll have to pay for all services — which is a good reason to have that information at hand.

Home insurance

- Since your home may not be covered if you are away for more than 30 days, check with your agent for advice if you plan an extended trip.

Life insurance

- If you already carry a reasonable amount of life insurance, you won't need any extra for the vacation. Flight insurance is basically a rip-off. Flying is — statistically — incredibly safe.
- Some policies are written with a double-indemnity clause for accidental death.
- If you belong to a travel or auto club, they often provide life and accident insurance to members. Check on the most recent offerings.

- Many credit card companies now offer **free** flight insurance if you charge the flight to the card.

- Some travel agencies offer **free** flight insurance to their customers.

Trip cancellation insurance

- Some flights are sold on a restricted basis and have stiff cancellation charges. If you must cancel the flight because of an emergency — such as illness or death in the immediate family — trip cancellation insurance can remove the sting.

- Note that this insurance is not valid when the illness has been in existence during the previous year.

Documents for a Trusted Friend

Following is a list of things you should leave with a trusted friend. Although your trip may go without a hitch, this simple precaution could save you an incredible amount of trouble and time.

Itinerary

Come as close to places and dates as possible. Leave exact mailing addresses (see advice on mail, pp. 187-188).

List of traveler's check numbers

You should carry a list of these numbers, but it's a very good idea to leave a duplicate list at home — just in case you lose everything, including the duplicate list.

Numbers of credit cards

Photocopy all of your credit cards as a way of keeping accurate records of pertinent information. Leave one copy with a friend.

Number, date, and place of issue of passport

You should memorize this information as soon as you get the passport. You'll need it when checking in at hotels. If you lose a passport, it will be essential information.

Number, date, and place of issue of airline tickets

If you want to get reimbursed for lost or stolen tickets with a minimum of hassle, have these numbers readily available.

2 Medical Precautions

For more medical information, be sure to read the section on what to do about problems as they come up in Europe. This is outlined in detail starting on p. 209.

Medical Documents

Most travelers don't experience major medical problems abroad. However, you should prepare for them anyway. Keeping a record of your vaccinations is a good way to start.

International Certificates of Vaccination

At one time everyone traveling to Europe was required to show proof of smallpox vaccination. The proof consisted of a doctor's signature and official stamp in a **"yellow card."** Since smallpox has been officially eradicated, such proof is no longer necessary, but these yellow cards are still available and are technically called **International Certificates of Vaccination.**

Although yellow cards are no longer necessary for travel to Europe, it doesn't hurt to have one. By having all of your immunizations listed in this official document, you have an accurate record of them. In case of an unusual outbreak of a specific disease, you can be immunized abroad and have that noted in the yellow card. This will allow you to cross the border into and out of a "disease zone." Such an occurrence is rare, but it does happen — particularly in the case of cholera.

Most passport agencies, health service offices, and medical clinics have copies of the yellow card, which is given out free of charge.

Medical Information

Never ask travel agents for medical information, since they're usually behind the times on health problems.

In the United States

Check with a **public health office,** the best being state headquarters where bulletins are kept up-to-date on disease outbreaks worldwide.

• For useful, current bulletins on disease, contact:

The Centers for Disease Control Atlanta, GA 30329 Tel: (404) 329-3311	Citizen's Emergency Center 2201 C Street N.W. Washington, DC 20520 Tel: (202) 647-5225

In Canada

The **Travel Information Offices of Health and Welfare** in Canada can give you current information and health bulletins. You'll find these offices in Edmonton, Gander, Halifax, Montreal, Ottawa, Prince George, Prince Rupert, Regina, Saint John, Saint John's, Sydney, Thunder Bay, Toronto, Vancouver, Victoria, and Winnipeg.

Inoculations

No two doctors agree on the shots that travelers should have before going abroad. However, you should follow commonsense guidelines. The longer you travel and the more remote your destination, the more protection you need.

• Many inoculations are given free of charge or for a token charge at public clinics.

• Get shots well ahead of your trip. Some must be given in series over weeks or even months.

• Some have side effects that could affect your trip if you wait until the last minute!

Cholera

• A vaccination against cholera is needed **only if** you're traveling to an area known to have it. This is rarely the case.

• Cholera shots are not totally reliable in preventing the disease and have a relatively short-term value.

Hepatitis A

• Gamma (immune) globulin can be effective in preventing hepatitis A. If you're planning a long trip, the dosage must be larger.

• Since the shot provides only short-term protection, get it only if you'll be traveling to more remote areas with poor sanitation. Backpackers and explorer types should get it.

Hepatitis B

• Hepatitis B serum is roughly 96 percent effective against hepatitis B, which can be debilitating at best, deadly at worst.

• Unfortunately, hepatitis B is becoming more common, although only 5 to 10 percent of the population in the United States has been exposed to it. In other countries the rate is much higher.

• Hepatitis B serum is given in three doses over a six-month period. It is also very expensive.

• If you plan to travel extensively in developing countries, the cost is worth it. It is doubly important if you have frequent sexual contact.

• Some doctors recommend a blood test before giving you the serum. If the cost of the blood test is low, you might save yourself a great deal of money if the test shows that you have already been exposed to hepatitis B. However, if the test is expensive, skip it. According to the laboratory that makes it, there are no adverse reactions to the serum even if you have already been exposed to hepatitis B earlier.

Polio

• All doctors agree that this is essential. You may need a booster.

Tetanus/diphtheria

• Doctors agree on this one, too. You may be due for a booster.

Typhoid

- Typhoid shots are somewhat controversial. Their value can only be related to risk, which in most areas is low. Again, if you'll be traveling to remote areas, it may well be worth the cost of this "insurance."

- Initially, you'll get two typhoid shots. After that, boosters are effective.

Getting Set to Go

A few routine steps can help take the worry out of travel if you have a medical problem of any kind. Here are some suggestions.

Medical preparations for travel

- Before going on a trip, see both a doctor and a dentist for a quick checkup.

- Have your doctor fill out the yellow card with a complete history of your immunizations.

- Get the immunizations suggested for the kind of travel you'll be doing.

- Get a prescription for a good drug to combat diarrhea.

Chronic health problems

- If you have a chronic health problem, take with you all the drugs you'll need for the entire trip. Include enough to cover a week or two extra in case of an unexpected extended stay.

- If you're pregnant, you'll want to get suggestions from your doctor before going abroad.

- If you have heart or respiratory problems, be wary of high altitude travel.

Diabetics

- Consider signing up with one of the organizations in this chapter that provide help and identification abroad — the latter can save your life.

- Carry urine-testing equipment, regular and long-lasting insulin, oral drugs or syringes, extra carbohydrates (your schedule will get fouled up), and a doctor's note stating that you are a diabetic. This note helps you explain syringes when you cross borders.

- Becton-Dickinson disposable syringes are available in pharmacies abroad.

- If you intend to buy insulin abroad, learn about the variations in strengths and how to deal with them before going.

Useful medical organizations

If you have a chronic illness or medical problem, you may be interested in contacting the following organizations for information on their services.

Assist-Card International
444 Brickell Avenue
Suite M130
Miami, FL 33131
Tel: (305) 381-9959

Intermedic, Inc.
777 Third Avenue
New York, NY 10017
Tel: (212) 486-8900

International Association of
  Medical Assistance to
  Travelers (IAMAT)
417 Center Street
Lewiston, NY 14092
Tel: (716) 754-4883

International Health Care
  Service
440 East 69th Street
New York, NY 10021
Tel: (212) 472-4284

International SOS
  Assistance, Inc.
(mailing address)
P.O. Box 11568
Philadelphia, PA 19116
Tel: (800) 523-8930
      (215) 244-1500

International SOS
  Assistance
One Neshaminy Interplex,
  Suite 310
Trevose, PA 19047
Tel: (800) 523-8930
      (215) 244-1500

Medic Alert Foundation
P.O. Box 1009
Turlock, CA 95381
Tel: (800) 344-3226

Prescription Items

A few precautions are useful here:

Drugs

- Be sure to bring fresh drugs with you. If you're not sure about the value of older medications, call your pharmacist.

- Carry enough of any prescription to last a week or two beyond your expected stay, just in case you get delayed for some unforseen reason.

- Always keep all prescription drugs in the original containers. Some of these containers are huge, so ask the pharmacist to divide the amount into two smaller containers, both clearly labeled. These are easier to carry, and you can throw them away as they're used up.

- If your drugs contain narcotics, then carry your doctor's prescription with you.

- Ask your doctor or pharmacist for the generic name of any drug you're using. Write it down. This name will probably be familiar to a foreign druggist if you lose or run out of pills.

- Never put drugs into luggage that will be checked on a plane. Always carry them with you.

Eyeglasses

- Either bring with you a spare pair of glasses in a hard case or the prescription itself. Note that a lens can be duplicated from the pieces of a broken pair of glasses (in case you forget to bring a prescription).

3 Itineraries

Determining what countries you'll visit and what spots in each country you'll see is the most obvious step in planning your itinerary. This chapter will give you many hints for planning the best trip you can have.

Where to Go

You may know from the start where you want to go; or, you may be open to any suggestion. Either way, the more care you take in picking places to go, the more fun you'll have abroad.

Basic considerations

- If you and any potential travel partner can't agree on where to go, plan to travel independently. You can still arrange to meet to do the things you **can** agree on during your trips.

- If you'll be traveling with kids, give them some say about where to go. They'll be much better travelers for it.

- If **money** is a major consideration in your plans, you may wish to restrict your itinerary to southern Europe. The least expensive countries to travel in are Greece, Italy, Portugal, and Spain. Austria, Belgium, Luxembourg, the Netherlands, and Norway are moderately expensive. Denmark, Finland, France, Germany, Sweden, and Switzerland are expensive.

- If **time** is a problem, plan your trip to the minute. If you've only got a week, you don't want to waste even an hour.

- And if your own **energy** is limited, save it by joining a tour going to the places you want to see.

Fine-tuning your choices

- Go to the library to browse in travel books and magazines (see p. 29) so you have an idea of the possibilities.

- Look at newspaper travel sections as well, especially the **New York Times** Sunday travel sections, for more up-to-date news of attractions.

- Try to get copies of newspapers from cities you might visit in Europe (newsstands and libraries may have them). Check out concerts, plays, and sporting events you may want to attend.

Sources of Information

The more you know, the better you'll plan; the better you plan, the more fun you'll have on your trip.

Airlines

- Call various airlines and ask for any free brochures or pamphlets they may have that cover different destinations on your trip.

National tourist offices

- For good general background information and some helpful tips, write to the national tourist office of each country you think you want to visit. You can ask for hotel and restaurant guides; sightseeing information; lists of gardens, castles, museums, spas; travel maps; and so on. Write two months in advance, four if possible.

- Note that tourist offices shy away from questions of comparison (Is one hotel better than another? Should we go here instead of there?). The more specific your question, the more difficult it may be for a country's tourist office to answer. Be sure to include a return address in your letter. A stamped, self-addressed envelope is not required, but often will speed up a reply. Tourist offices in both the United States and Canada are listed on pp. 227-229.

- Write to them well ahead of your planned departure date, and allow as much time as possible for a reply.

Magazines and Reports

Recommended Magazines

- **Gourmet** (for its fine restaurant recommendations)
- **Travel and Leisure** (for general travel hints)

Recommended Travel Reports

- **Passport,** 20 North Wacker Drive, Suite 3417, Chicago, IL 60606, Tel: (312) 332-3574
- **Travel Smart,** Communications House, 40 Beechdale Road, Dobbs Ferry, NY 10522, Tel: (914) 693-8300
- If you like to travel in style, check into **Passport.** If you're more interested in budget or business travel, try the reports put out by **Travel Smart.**
- To find out which of these reports suits your personality, write to each of them asking for a sample copy.

Books — Elementary and Advanced

Good Travel Books

- **Fielding** (nonbudget travel)
- **Fodor** (good general guides)
- **Frommer** (budget travel)
- **Let's Go** (student travel)
- **Egon Ronay** (good on Great Britain)
- **Michelin Red Guides** (excellent hotel and restaurant ratings)
- **Blue Guides** (minutely detailed information for experts)
- **Saltzman's Eurail Guide** (for train travel)

Specialized Books for the Travel Trade

- Plan your own itinerary (if you are so inclined) by using these specialized books: **Official Airline Guide, Official Hotel and Resort Guide,** and **World Travel Directory.** These extremely expensive volumes are used in the travel industry. You can find them in the travel section of most major libraries.
- Also very good, if quite expensive, are the reports put out by: STAR (Sloane Travel Agency Reports), 131 Clarendon Street, Boston, MA 02116. Tel: (617) 262-5000.

Mail Order Source

- An excellent source of travel books and maps is the Forsyth Travel Library, P.O. Box 2975, Dept. W, 9154 West 57th Street, Shawnee Mission, KS 66201. Send for their catalog (include 50 cents for postage).

Travel clubs

Every club broadcasts its benefits, some of which can be valuable. Check into the following clubs to see whether or not you think the benefits match the cost:

National Travel Club
Travel Building
51 Atlantic Avenue
Floral Park, NY 11001
Tel: (516) 352-9700

The Good Sam Club (for RVs)
Customer Service
P.O. Box 500
Agoura, CA 91301
Tel: (800) 423-5061

Auto clubs

You should comparison shop when looking for an automobile club. The main things to compare are membership fees, emergency road services, emergency travel expenses, accidental death and dismemberment payoff amounts, arrest and bail bond, legal defense fees, and routing maps.

• Read the fine print. Make sure the club has reciprocal agreements with auto clubs abroad.

Agents and Agencies

In the past, the traveler who walked into a travel agency could safely be assumed to be innocent — and rich. **Good** agents can find super bargains amidst the garble of airline and tour brochures. Still, it's really a customer's responsibility to do reading and research before going to a travel agent. This will make your relationship more beneficial.

• You will probably save money planning and arranging for your trip by yourself if you're a free spirit, if you're aggressive and resourceful, and if you're ready to study up on alternatives in transportation, food, and lodging.

• Even if you fit that description, an agent may know of tour packages that are so reasonably priced that you can't afford to **not** take advantage of them. So never rule out travel agencies before checking to see what they have to offer.

• If you don't want to plan and arrange for your trip yourself, a well-chosen agent can be a fine resource. Don't walk in and say, "I want to go to these 12 cities. Book me flights and rooms." If you do, you'll pay through the nose! Instead, ask for tours to match your interests and then have the agent alter them if necessary.

• In short, shop around. Compare what an agent can do with what you can do, balance the benefits and costs, and act accordingly.

What good agents can do

• They can find the cheapest airfare from A to B without making you go through the hassle.

• They can get you on a cruise or tour that matches your personality. You pay nothing extra for their service.

• They can make appropriate reservations for hotels, car rental, and sporting activities. None of these services should involve a charge.

What agents can't do

• Travel agents can't read minds. Be as specific as possible in telling an agent what you really want. The more specific, the better the chance of getting it.

Picking an agency

• Larger agencies tend to have more clout than smaller ones. It may be more personal and more convenient to go to a neighborhood agent, but what happens if something goes wrong? Find out whether or not the agency has representatives abroad, just in case something does go wrong.

• Ask the agency what kind of travel it specializes in. If it doesn't match your travel plans, ask the agency to refer you to another one specializing in your brand of travel.

• In special cases, you may want to work with agents in other cities. If the best agency for skiing tours happens to be in New York, conduct your business through the mail.

Recognizing a good agent

Good travel agents are harder to find than the American Society of Travel Agents would like to admit. Unfortunately, many of them are in the business more for low-cost travel for themselves than for caring for the interest of their clients.

On the other hand, some agents are outstanding. Most of the good ones specialize in some way: low-cost tours, luxury travel, study groups, ski vacations, incentive travel, business, etc.

- Most travel agents are members of the American Society of Travel Agents (ASTA), so be wary of those who are not. ASTA maintains a file of complaints. You can write or call them at P.O. Box 23992, Washington, D.C. 20026-3992, (703) 739-2782.

- Look for the initials CTC — for Certified Travel Consultant — after an agent's name. This designation signifies that he is a person of good reputation who has been through a specialized course.

- Find out whether someone in the agency is familiar with the specific area you plan to visit. If you find such a person, you can learn a great deal — in addition, he will be able to reserve flights, make reservations, and book you into tours as part of his general travel assistance to you.

Maps

Good maps appropriate to the kind of traveling you'll be doing can make a trip far less frustrating and more enjoyable. For most travel you can get **free** maps, which are adequate for your purposes. Detailed maps are expensive, but essential for off-the-beaten-path travel.

Good general maps (free)

- **National tourist offices:** request a free map from the government tourist office nearest you. See p. 227.

- **Travel agents:** ask any agent you deal with to provide a **free** map for your travels.

- **AAA and other auto clubs:** if you belong to an auto or travel club, have them give you a **free** map. These clubs should also provide route maps and related services. Request these as far in advance as possible!

- **Insurance companies:** if you'll be traveling by car, get **free** maps from the agent.

- **A special note:** every person in your party should have a map (see p. 167). It makes travel more exciting, makes kids feel special, divides the responsibility — and it costs nothing!

When to Go

A great deal of fiction has been written about the wonderful weather in Europe. Don't be conned by this propaganda, which is more wishful thinking than fact. The bikini-clad women in the pictures in travel brochures were photographed in the August heat, not in the dead of winter, as promoters would have you believe. The guidelines below cover the best times to visit various parts of Europe. The Climate Chart in the Appendix has more details.

Travel Seasons

- Travel to **Scandinavia** during the summer, which lasts from mid-May to early October. Not only is the weather good during this period, but you will also be able to take advantage of the long days. Just the opposite is true during the winter, which is snowy and dark — so dark that "sightseeing" becomes a joke.

- Visit **central Europe** (including the British Isles and Germany) from late April to late October, if one of your main concerns is good weather. Much of this area experiences heavy rainfall, so bring a good umbrella and the best raincoat you can afford. You'll find some of Europe's most fascinating cities in this belt, however — and if you see them during the off-season, you can take advantage of smaller crowds and lower prices.

- Winters in **southern Europe** are not as mild as some people would like you to believe. True, you'll run into sunny winter days. But don't expect to brave the chill of Mediterranean or Atlantic waters. Furthermore, summers can get so hot in the South that you will rather do what the natives do from noon until late afternoon — sleep in a cool place. Unless, of course, you're lucky enough to be on a beach by the sea — the other obvious alternative, one chosen by French, Greeks, Italians, and Portuguese, young and old.

- Some places do offer good to excellent off-season weather. In the fair to good category: the **Balearics** (Majorca, Menorca, and Ibiza) and **Madeira.** Just a little better: **Sicily.** Better yet: **Rhodes.** And the most reliable for warm winter sun: the **Canaries.**

How Long to Stay

The length of your trip may be predetermined by the time you have available for your vacation, so that you feel you have little leeway in this regard. However, if it's at all possible, try to make a trip to Europe last at least three weeks. This will give you the time to enjoy and savor the European scene.

- Subtract three days from the overall length of your trip. The first, and probably the last, day of any trip will be wasted, and you may have to spend the second day recuperating somewhat from your transatlantic flight.

• Write off at least part of any day spent traveling long distances, as from one city to the next.

• Fight the urge to see all of Europe in 10 days, and arrange to spend more time in fewer places. If you slow down, your trip will be more enjoyable.

The following simple chart indicates the minimum recommended lengths of stay in European countries. Periods are given in days, and do not include the time needed for transportation in and out of the country.

Minimum Recommended Stays in European Countries

Andorra .... One day	**Italy** .... Ten days, with four days in Rome, three in Florence, one in Venice
Austria .... Five days, with three days in Vienna	
Azores .... Three days	**Liechtenstein** Half a day
Belgium .... Three days, with two days in major cities	**Luxembourg** . One day
	Madeira .... Two days
Canaries .... Three days	**Majorca** .... Two days
Corsica .... Two days	**Malta** .... One day
Crete .... Two days	**Netherlands** .. Three days, with two days in Amsterdam
Denmark .... Three days, with two days in Copenhagen	
	Norway .... Three days
Finland .... Two days	**Portugal** .... Five days, with two days in Lisbon
France .... Ten days, with five days in Paris	
	Sardinia .... One day
Germany .... Four days, with two days in Munich	**Sicily** .... One day
	Spain .... Ten days, with three days in Madrid and Toledo combined
Gibraltar .... One day	
Great Britain Ten days, with five days in London	
	Sweden .... One day
Greece .... Seven days, with three days on mainland	**Switzerland** .. Four days
	Yugoslavia .... Three days
Iceland .... One day	
Ireland .... Three days	

How Far and How Fast

If this is your first trip to Europe, you may be inclined to travel fast and far, to give yourself a sneak preview of trips to come. It is totally natural to want to do this, and high-speed travel can be exhilarating. The trouble is, it's also exhausting and costs a bundle.

You will find that the more you try to see, the less you will really see. That's the "today-is-Tuesday-this-must-be-Brussels" syndrome. Many tours operate on this kind of plan, giving you a smattering of many cities rather than a deeper profile of several.

Planning trip mileage

- To help you enjoy your trip more fully, use the mileage chart on the following page and a map to plan your itinerary. Decide which cities you'd like to see. You might trace your route in red with a felt-tipped pen. Now add up the mileage to see just how far you plan to go.

- Divide the total mileage by the number of days you'll be in Europe. (Don't count the first and last days.)

- If you are traveling by train or car, don't plan to cover more than 150 miles per day. The same rule applies to traveling on a tour bus. Naturally, you will sometimes wind up having traveled farther than this average distance. If you consistently cover much more than 150 miles per day, however, your trip will turn out to have been too expensive and time-consuming, as well as too tiring.

- If you will be flying between two points, ignore the mileage between them — simply write off one full day. Do this for each plane trip you'll be taking. Subtract these days from the total number of days you'll be abroad (minus the first and last days). This will give you a good idea of how many days you'll have left to enjoy Europe.

- If you find that you'll be traveling too far in too short a time, admit it. Here are some options: cut down on the number of cities to be seen, extend your trip to make your travel time more enjoyable, or plan a second trip for a later date. With the possible exception of Venice, most European cities will still be there in years to come.

Mileage Between European Cities

	Amsterdam	Barcelona	Berlin	Bordeaux	Brussels	Calais	Copenhagen	Dublin	Florence	Geneva	Hamburg	Helsinki	Lisbon	London	Madrid	Marseilles	Milan	Munich	Naples	Nice	Oslo	Paris	Rome	Stockholm	Venice
Barcelona	950																								
Berlin	450	1215																							
Bordeaux	660	405	1015																						
Brussels	125	810	490	535																					
Calais	235	800	620	555	130																				
Copenhagen	590	1355	465	1185	655	780																			
Dublin	565	965	950	830	460	330	1115																		
Florence	775	730	810	815	995	880	985	1215																	
Geneva	545	490	690	440	415	470	815	1215	495																
Hamburg	290	1135	185	905	370	505	215	985	970	705															
Helsinki	1025	1865	970	1685	1185	1285	500	1615	1715	1485	720														
Lisbon	1365	725	1690	755	1245	1260	1895	1595	1455	1190	1335	2395													
London	305	690	690	570	200	70	855	260	935	540	525	1430	990												
Madrid	1145	385	1445	440	1110	945	1500	1275	1110	680	1335	2115	400	1015											
Marseilles	800	355	965	415	675	690	1060	1000	200	265	970	1735	1190	750	705										
Milan	670	650	700	740	635	510	775	950	200	230	770	1560	1430	1230	1050	120									
Munich	535	830	375	755	495	510	545	950	485	365	510	1275	1675	640	780	355	310								
Naples	1160	1055	1135	1110	1320	1145	1235	1475	440	795	1190	2040	1830	1215	1295	480	515	625							
Nice	815	420	920	515	690	790	1060	1680	325	230	1090	1785	1145	750	805	120	220	495	130						
Oslo	865	1645	805	1565	1030	1160	380	1490	1590	1370	510	445	2240	1230	1995	1615	1440	1155	1920	1660					
Paris	315	805	665	350	185	215	635	505	745	325	550	1105	1105	245	780	480	560	495	1060	465	1215				
Rome	955	825	995	970	1180	1005	1255	1590	185	650	1060	1900	1700	1075	1295	590	390	535	130	580	1780	930			
Stockholm	920	1760	865	1580	1080	1180	395	1510	1610	1380	615	105	2290	1250	2010	1630	1455	1170	1935	1680	340	1230	1795		
Venice	740	825	700	930	875	790	775	1125	170	405	815	1115	1650	865	960	550	175	325	460	370	995	690	355	1010	
Vienna	820	1155	625	1055	750	890	1030	1175	550	645	565	1305	1945	915	1700	930	505	255	955	730	1180	815	820	1200	380

4 Travel Partners and Tours

Should you make a trip by yourself, with a friend or spouse, with a group of people you like, or as part of a tour group? Should you take the kids or a baby? There's no easy answer, although the answer's often taken for granted — especially in the case of couples. The hints in this chapter should be helpful to you, not only in making your decision, but also in living with it!

Solo Travel

There are many advantages to traveling alone: you can do as you damn well please, when you damn well please, at your own pace, with or without someone else along, as you choose. In short, you have total freedom.

On the other hand, you pay for such freedom. If you go on a tour, you may be socked with a surcharge. If you're totally on your own, you will have no way of sharing bills at mealtime, in the hotel, and for personal transportation. It's all out of your pocket and only your pocket.

You may also be lonely — but loneliness can be converted into an advantage, as it will force you to get to know Europeans and other travelers.

Traveling alone and liking it

- As a loner, take advantage of short and inexpensive tours to popular tourist sights. You'll not only meet people, but also keep your costs down.

- Be willing to share the cost of a room. If you are concerned about sharing a room with a stranger, put anything of value in the hotel safe.

- When faced with the prospect of eating alone, bring a newspaper, a book, or writing paper with you to the restaurant. If you meet someone interesting, fine; if not, you will catch up on your reading.

- Go a little before or after the peak dinner hour, to avoid running into poor treatment at the hands of waiters, as solo travelers sometimes do.

Single but looking for company

- Cruises are a natural for someone looking for a travel partner.

- Probably better are resorts and tours aimed at single travelers. Following are organizations catering to single travelers:

Club Med (Head Office)
40 West 57th Street
New York, NY 10019
Tel: (800) 528-3100
        (212) 977-2100

Gramercy Singleworld
444 Madison Avenue
New York, NY 10022
Tel: (800) 223-6490
        (212) 758-2433

Mesa Travel Singles Registry
P.O. Box 2235
Costa Mesa, CA 92628
Tel: (714) 546-8181

Society of Single Travelers
4551 Glencoe Avenue,
 Suite 205
Marina del Rey, CA 90292
Tel: (213) 827-8181

Travel Companion
 Exchange
P.O. Box 833
Amityville, NY 11701
Tel: (516) 454-0880

Travel Mates International,
 Inc.
49 West 44th Street
New York, NY 10036
Tel: (212) 221-6565

Women traveling alone

Most solo travel takes place without a hitch, even for women traveling alone. Just a little common sense added to the spirit of adventure will get you by — almost anywhere! Read the section on personal safety (p. 137).

- Womantour, 5314 North Figueroa Street, Los Angeles, CA 90042, (213) 255-1115, organizes both group and individual tours for women alone.

Twosome and Family Travel

The big advantages of staying together are shared company and shared costs. A room for a couple may only be a few dollars more than it would be for a solo traveler. In many instances, the same savings apply to food and transportation. In short, it costs far less for two people to travel together than to go independently. But savings mean nothing unless you're both doing what you really want to do.

Traveling as a twosome

- If you and your partner cannot agree on the purpose of a trip, consider traveling independently. You may prefer completely different destinations, so why not go your separate ways?

- Meet again in places you'd both like to visit.

- Carry your own bags, unless you're willing to pay someone else to do it for you. It is unfair to ask a partner to carry luggage.

- Share all responsibilities with your partner. The one who has to make most of the decisions shoulders the burden for any mistakes made. That burden should be equally divided.

- Iron out all money matters before you start. Good reckoning makes good friends.

- Each person of a married couple should have control of part of the money, including "mad money" for special occasions. Each person should be responsible for handling part of the payment for everyday expenses.

Family travel

The more people involved in a European trip, the more complex the planning is going to be. You can't expect to suit all tastes at all times when working with a group.

- Make sure that each person in the family has a say in planning the trip.

- Gear the pace of the trip to that of the youngest member of the group.

- Agree that all responsibilities will be shared.

- Since each person will carry his own luggage, make sure that the size of the bag matches the size of the person.

- If children are along, allow time for numerous breaks in the itinerary: for a trip to the beach, a hike through the woods, a pause for an ice cream cone.

- Note that younger children can appreciate cathedrals, churches, and art galleries — in small doses. Children tend to be activity oriented, which means that they'd rather go to a beach than to the cathedral at Chartres — or would rather combine the two, preferably in a period of 20 minutes!

- Allow for the option of splitting up the party from time to time, so that those primarily interested in cultural attractions can have adequate time to appreciate them.

- Remember that families of all nationalities congregate in campgrounds, which makes them very enjoyable for most children.

Traveling with a baby

- When making reservations for air travel, try to schedule departure and arrival times so that they do not coincide with the baby's feedings. Avoid the peak or rush hours as well, choosing a less popular flight time.

- Contact the airline well in advance if you wish to reserve a bassinet. Ask about pre-boarding privileges.

- Bring milk if you're feeding the baby from a bottle. Ask a stewardess to warm it up when she's not busy serving drinks or meals.

- Be sure to have something for the baby to drink during takeoff and landing: the sucking will relieve the pressure that builds up in the baby's ears.

- Bring a towel to cover you during feeding and to place under the baby at changing time.

- Bring a small blanket, plastic bags for disposable diapers, small toys for the baby to play with, and a folding (umbrella) stroller. The stroller will make it much easier for you both to get around, and you can lift it into a booth in a restaurant without waking the baby up.

- Since many European restaurants welcome children at noon, but look upon them coldly in the evening, plan larger meals in the middle of the day and snacks at night.

- A helpful organization: TWYCH (Travel With Your Children), 80 Eighth Avenue, New York, NY 10011, (212) 206-0688.

- Note: if you are traveling by car, you must buy or bring some sort of safety harness that will fit into the back seat, as it is against the law in most European countries for small children to ride in the front seat of a car.

For older people

The following organizations have lots of information for older travelers.

American Association for
    Retired Persons
1909 K Street N.W.
Washington, DC 20049
Tel: (202) 872-4700

Elderhostel
80 Boylston Street, Suite 400
Boston, MA 02116
Tel: (617) 426-7788

Grand Circle Travel
347 Congress Street
Boston, MA 02210
Tel: (800) 221-2610

Younger travelers

Generally, the young have more time, less money, and more energy than other travelers — a potent combination.

• Take more money than you think you're going to need. It's cheap, but not *that* cheap.

• Pick up an **International Student Identification Card.** See p. 15.

• Try to have a vague itinerary for friends and relatives. They can get in touch with you in an emergency through:

Citizens Emergency Center
U.S. Department of State
2201 C Street N.W.
Washington, DC 20520
Tel: (202) 647-5225

• No itinerary? Then register with consulates as you make your vagabond way through Europe — if you can stand the inconvenience.

Handicapped travel

The following organizations have a way of making travel available to you:

Evergreen Travel Service
19505M 44th Avenue West
Lynnwood, WA 98036
Tel: (206) 776-1184

Flying Wheels Travel
P.O. Box 382
143 West Bridge Street
Owatonna, MN 55060
Tel: (507) 451-5005

Mobility International/USA
P.O. Box 3551
Eugene, OR 97403
Tel: (503) 343-1284

Whole Person Tours
P.O. Box 1084
Bayonne, NJ 07002
Tel: (201) 858-3400

Tours

Tours can be the answers to travelers' prayers or forms of temporary damnation. The most important question for you to ask yourself, then, is whether you are a good prospect for a tour. Loners should not take tours. Most people who are impatient standing in lines will not like tours. Impulsive, free-spirited people often regret traveling on tours.

On the other hand, people who dislike unplanned weekends, who are not very aggressive, who lead scheduled lives, and who don't speak foreign languages find tours an excellent way to travel. For those in poor health, joining a tour may be more attractive than traveling alone. In short, it's a question of personality. If you do decide to join a tour, be sure its goals and your own goals are similar.

Advantages of tours

- Tours can save you money. You're joining a group that buys everything as a block, which ensures substantial price reductions across the board.

- Tours can be prepaid, allowing you to know in advance how much the trip is going to cost. You can also put off payment by financing the trip.

- Tour packages, which cover all your major expenses, allow you to pay in dollars. In this way you avoid the currency exchange rip-off.

- Tours can be located that are tailored to individual needs or interests, from skiing to bird watching.

- Tours offer companionship for travelers prone to loneliness.

- Tours help less aggressive travelers cope with the language barrier and avoid embarrassing situations.

- Tours have clout, the ability to get you into a hotel or restaurant in peak tourist seasons.

- Tours save you time and energy by preventing potential hassles.

- Tours are organized by experts who know the most interesting sights to see. They generally hire competent travel guides in each city to help you understand its beauty, history, and traditions.

Disadvantages of tours

- Tours herd people together. To find out how you react to this experience, go to a local museum or industrial plant and take a tour with a group of people there. If it's enjoyable, you may also enjoy taking a tour abroad. If you find that this just isn't for you, avoid foreign tours!

- Tours can be hurried, impersonal, and flavorless affairs. Throughout the trip you will be bound to follow a prearranged schedule, oriented to a group and its needs. It may take the travail out of travel, but it can also wring the lust out of wanderlust.

- The normal mode of transportation for tour groups in Europe is the bus. It's convenient and usually comfortable, but it can be equally boring and confining.

- You pay for a tour sight unseen, which is something like marrying the same way. There's no real chance for a refund if things go awry.

- Tours are groups of people, people whom you may or may not like. But they'll be your companions anyway.

- The words in tour brochures are just that — words. A "first-class" hotel may end up being, well, second-rate, even in Soho!

- Most tour contracts squirm with loopholes and catches.

- Tours isolate you from contact with local people by taking care of everything for you.

- If you don't like the hotels chosen for you or the restaurants' bland fare, your complaints may fall on deaf ears.

- In some cases, you could do much better from a financial standpoint by not taking a tour. The luxury tours are a good example — Jason could have picked up a bucketful of golden fleece sheared from wealthy tour-goers!

The Tour Payment Protection Plan

Tour companies that are a part of ASTA's (American Society of Travel Agents) Tour Protection Agreement protect customers from any hanky-panky. Check with ASTA for an updated list of all companies.

ASTA
American Society of Travel
  Agents
P.O. Box 23992
Washington, DC 20026-3992
Tel: (703) 739-2782

Tour Package Checklist

If you take the trouble to consult tour brochures or agents and find answers to the following questions, you will be in a much better position to judge the quality of any tour package you're considering.

☐ Is the tour operator a member of the United States Tour Operators' Association? (Most of these operators are reliable.)

☐ How much will the tour cost altogether?

☐ Will a service charge be added? If so, how much will it be? Often you'll find that there is a service charge outlined in very fine print at the end of the brochure. Words like "extra," "optional," and "bonus" should also be red flags to you.

☐ What extra or supplemental charges will apply to you? What will optional packages cost you? How much is the advance deposit?

☐ What are the penalties for cancellation?

☐ Are substitutions allowed on the passenger list?

☐ Can the dates of the tour be changed arbitrarily?

☐ Can the schedule or itinerary be rearranged for any reason?

☐ Can the tour be cancelled? How much notice must be given?

☐ Does the tour include transportation to and from the airport? Most tours don't.

☐ Does the tour cost include the full price of airfare to and from Europe? What are the dates and times of flights? Are the flights nonstop?

☐ Does the tour price cover all airport departure taxes?

☐ Is there a supplemental charge if you want a room to yourself? How much?

☐ Which hotels will you be staying in? Get the names.

☐ Can other hotels be substituted arbitrarily? If so, get the names.

☐ What's included in the room? Bath or shower? Two beds? Get details.

☐ Where are the hotels located? Tell them to show you on a map.

☐ Are all tips and taxes included in the room price?

☐ Is there any charge whatsoever that's not included?

☐ Are all meals included in the price of the tour? Is any meal not included? If not, why not? Or if not, where not?

☐ Where will you be eating? In the hotel? In a restaurant? What restaurants?

☐ What's included with the meal? Is wine included? Is coffee included? Is dessert included? Is anything excluded? If so, how much will it cost?

☐ Do you have a choice from the menu at each meal? Can you make substitutions at no extra charge?

☐ Are all tips and service charges for meals included in the tour price?

☐ Who pays the entrance fee to museums, galleries, and events?

☐ What kind of transportation is provided in Europe?

☐ Does it include all transfers from airports and train stations? Does it include the cost of transportation to meals and nightlife?

☐ What kind of intercity transportation is provided: bus, train, air?

☐ If it's a bus, is it air conditioned or "air cooled" (a tour-brochure expression meaning that the windows can be opened)?

☐ If it's a plane or a train, what class will you be in?

☐ How many nights' accommodation is included in the tour price? Are there any nights on which the cost of a room has been left out?

☐ What is the pace of the tour? Does it leave you any free time?

☐ Does the tour spend enough time in each city to let you get anything out of the visit?

☐ Will the tour have an escort? Will the same escort be with the tour for the whole time (valuable)?

☐ Will the tour have travel guides for each city?

☐ Does the tour include insurance for accidents, health, baggage, etc.? If so, how much? Any deductible? Any exclusions?

☐ Who takes care of the baggage? Is there any extra cost? Are all tips to porters included in the cost of the hotel room?

5 Transportation to Europe

By Plane

Almost everyone flies to Europe today because air travel is faster and cheaper than ocean travel. Yet, on every flight, some passengers wind up paying as much as three or four times what others pay. Smart travelers know this and learn strategies to keep costs down.

Comparison shopping — scheduled airlines

- Spend some time on the phone getting different quotes on comparable flights on various airlines. Since the market has opened up competitively, prices do vary along identical routes.

- Watch for introductory fares or special coupon offers. As airlines open up new routes, they offer incentives to new customers in the form of reduced fares. These tend to be heavily advertised in local newspapers — so stay alert to the possibility of coming up with a once-in-a-lifetime bargain!

- Use the toll-free or 800 numbers (listed in your phone book) when you call the airlines.

Asking the right questions

- Let the person on the other end of the phone know immediately that you're bargain hunting by asking for the lowest fare from A to B.

- Ask whether there are any incentive fares.

- Find out whether there are reductions for midweek or night flights.

- Ask whether you can save money by flying to a less popular city near your final destination.

- Even after you've arranged for a flight, continue to watch for better deals. If a bargain pops up, turn in your ticket and go with the better fare. In some cases, you'll save money even if you must pay a penalty for cancelling!

- If you buy a ticket with a credit card and then have to cancel or change your travel plans, ask for a **refund receipt** when you return the ticket for credit. Note the ticket number and the date and place you bought it so that you can contact the credit card company if the credit does not show up on your bill.

Special tour rates on scheduled airlines

In most areas, there are specialized tour companies that buy blocks of seats on regularly scheduled airlines. In some cases, these seats are sold at rates far below those offered by the airline itself.

- Get familiar with the companies in your area that specialize in low-cost airfare. They tend to advertise heavily in Sunday papers.

- Call and ask them about any upcoming offerings to Europe.

Maverick scheduled airlines

After comparison shopping the major airlines, check the fares of maverick lines such as Icelandair or Virgin Atlantic. These provide an accurate barometer of prevailing low rates, which come and go, as do a number of maverick airlines.

- **Icelandair** should be listed in your phone book. It has a branch in the South listed under International Air Bahamas. If you fly Icelandair, you'll stop off in Iceland and continue on to Luxembourg City. The inconvenience may be worth the extra savings. That's for you to decide. Call the airlines for up-to-date flight information and prices.

- Prices of tickets from New York to Europe are often the lowest available. Consider checking locally with car delivery agencies. They may need someone to drive a car from your area to the East Coast. Such services generally pay for the gas.

- If you drive your own car to New York to take advantage of special low fares, you can leave your car with Auto Baby Sitters, 827 Sterling Place, Brooklyn, NY 11216. Check with them for long-term rental rates.

Comparison shopping — charters

Tour and charter companies rent planes to take passengers to specific destinations. These rented planes are called charters. In a few cases, the company actually owns the planes and virtually runs a sort of mini-airline.

- Charters often save you money because seats are usually offered at a discounted rate as an incentive to use the nonscheduled plane in the first place.

- Charters often leave at weird times and are rarely on a tight schedule, but if you're trying to save a buck, they can really make sense.

- Charters must now advertise the full price of a ticket. It can't go up or down according to the number of seats sold.

- On any contract with a charter company the escrow bank and bonding company must be clearly stated.

- Charter companies must clearly state what the itinerary will be and stick to it.

- Charter companies cannot cancel a flight within 10 days of the intended departure — they used to do this regularly, leaving passengers with no way of getting to where they were going.

- There are stiff cancellation penalty clauses on most charter airlines. You can take out cancellation insurance, available from charter companies and independent brokers.

- Two charter outfits:

GWV International
  Weekends
1170 Commonwealth
  Avenue
Boston, MA 02134
Tel: (617) 449-5450

Wainwright Travel
803 St. John's Street
Allentown, PA 18103
Tel: (215) 432-3152

Comparison shopping — clearinghouses and clubs

Clearinghouses and special airline travel clubs offer reduced tickets to countless places in the world. Basically, they pick up spaces on tours and flights that are not sold out.

- To get information on available flights and tours you pay a service fee to a clearinghouse or club. The fee is usually $35 to $45 a year.

- These clubs are geared to spur-of-the-moment travel. You may have to make up your mind to go to Europe within only a few days of the planned trip — at a discount, of course.

- Once you pay your money, there's no time to cancel. If you "get on the boat," you go!

- Also, you have to get to the point of origin of the charter, cruise, or tour that's being offered.

- Many of these clubs have a "hot line," and you may find their recorded messages long, detailed, and boring to listen to.

Discount travel clubs

Moments Notice
40 East 49th Street
New York, NY 10017
Tel: (212) 486-0503

Stand-Buys, Ltd.
311 West Superior Street,
  Suite 404
Chicago, IL 60610
Tel: (800) 255-0200

Worldwide Discount Travel
  Club
1674 Meridian Avenue,
  Suite 300
Miami Beach, FL 33139
Tel: (305) 534-2082

Money-Saving Strategies

No matter how you decide to travel, whether by tour, scheduled airline, or charter, you can usually save money by following certain strategies.

Buy tickets in the U.S.

- Buy all your tickets for transatlantic travel in the United States. If you buy tickets abroad, you'll have to pay for them in foreign currency at a preset rate of exchange, which may cost you extra money.

Buying tickets in advance

- Since only a certain number of seats are allotted for highly reduced fares on any given flight, you can save hundreds of dollars by buying a ticket far in advance of a planned trip. In short, the early bird does get the worm.

- Note that the airline cannot raise the price of a ticket once you've paid for it.

Keeping flexible about travel dates

- Be as flexible as possible in your travel plans so that you can take advantage of lower rates. What if you have to leave on a Thursday instead of a Friday or return on a Monday instead of a Sunday? Isn't it worth $100?

- Be sure to ask about excursion rates, with minimum and maximum lengths of stay. It may be that by adding or subtracting a few days from your planned trip, you can save yourself a good deal of money.

- Note that special excursion fares can be reserved in the United States, but must be paid for abroad. Travel agents neither promote nor encourage the sale of these tickets because they do not make a commission on them, but ask about them anyway.

Stopover or extension privileges

- Flights to and from minor cities within a foreign country may be no more expensive than flights to major ones. You may save yourself the price of train or plane fare to a small town by asking whether your fare would take you there in the first place — at no extra charge!

Off-season travel

The weather may not be so hot in the off-season (from November to March), but the savings are substantial.

- Note that you'll also find slightly lower fares in the "shoulder seasons" of spring and fall. Contact the airlines for exact cutoff dates for each season. Maybe you can take advantage of lower rates by changing your trip dates by no more than a week or two.

- Ask the airline whether or not a standby fare exists on the route you're planning to take. This will make sense in the not-so-popular vacation periods. Standby status is for flexible travelers, who will do anything to save a buck.

Student Discounts

- All students should contact CIEE (see p. 15) for information on inter-European plane travel. It can save you 40 to 75 percent of regular fares.

Free travel through courier services

• Approximately 900 companies use couriers between the U.S. and Europe. These companies pay for part or all of your transatlantic fare. Check with courier services to see if they're looking for runners.

Using travel agents

It costs no more to buy a ticket through a travel agent than to buy one directly from the airline. The problem is that many agents do not like working with discounted fares, because they make a commission on the total dollar value of tickets sold.

• Don't be afraid to comparison shop with travel agents. Make it clear with each one that you want to know the best deal to get you from A to B.

• A few agencies (not many) now guarantee that they will come up with the lowest possible rate or refund an overpayment you've made.

• Sometimes, a good agent will come up with a tour fare that will cost you less than comparable airfare. This is getting very hard to do now, but it does happen.

Things to watch out for

• Check and recheck all airline tickets to make sure that there are no errors.

• Count the flight coupons. Make sure that you have a coupon for each flight. If you don't, you'll pay twice for the flight.

• Check to see if you've paid for the departure tax in the ticket price. If you're not sure, ask.

Trouble-savers for booking your own flight

• Call before 7 a.m. or after 7 p.m. to get through to the airline without a long wait.

• Make a point of being very specific. Repeat the day and date several times to avoid mix-ups. Get the name of the person helping you. Mark down the date and time of your call along with the information concerning your flight.

- Try to book nonstop or at least direct flights, so that you won't have to get off the plane.

- If you do have to make connections, try to fly with the same airlines to avoid long walks and check-in hassles at the connecting airport. Airlines usually have a block of gates in each terminal; if you fly with one airline, you'll have only a short walk to a connecting flight.

- Note: airline tickets can be purchased on credit, with charges varying with repayment schedule. Compare these with rates available from your bank to come up with the best loan terms.

Picking up tickets

- Pay for and pick up tickets in advance to avoid the crush at the airport. It's a good feeling to have the ticket in your pocket, an assurance that now no one will be able to bungle your important reservation.

- When you get your tickets, be sure to check the dates, flight times, and flight numbers on them for accuracy. Read all materials closely so you know your rights.

- Count the flight coupons to make sure the number matches the total number of flights.

- Don't leave the return date blank, even if you are traveling without a set date of return. Have the clerk fill it in with an approximate date of return. For some reason, it is easier to make a new reservation when you have an already-dated, versus an open, ticket. Naturally, cancel the reservation and reschedule the return date in Europe.

Seat selection

- Find out about available aircraft and best seats at the time you pick up your ticket — not later, in the hurried atmosphere of the departure lounge. Ask to see a seating chart, choose where you'd like to be (mark down some alternates), and reserve a seat right away if you can. If you can't do so, mark down the seat choices on your ticket folder so that you can ask for them when checking in at the gate (see p. 99 for tips on choosing seats).

By Ship

Going to Europe by ship is the old-style, romantic way of getting there. In good weather it's a vacation in itself. Not only can the food and company be great, but such a trip also allows for a gradual adaptation to time changes. If you've got lots of time and enough money, going by ship is highly recommended.

But note the disadvantages. Ocean travel is very expensive for most people, costing far more than airfare. It takes time — from 5 to 10 days, depending upon the size of the ship. In rough weather, most people do get sick; even if you do not, you'll be stuck on board with people who do.

This section gives tips on both transatlantic travel and cruises (such as through the Greek islands).

Booking a cabin

Travel agents specializing in cruises are your best resource. Booking a cruise is really booking a tour — the very heart of travel agency business.

The cost

- The cost of a cruise varies dramatically by line, length of the cruise, and choice of cabin.

- If you want to travel alone (single cabin), the cost will be exorbitant.

- The higher up you get, the higher the cost. Cabins on upper decks are far from engines and noise. They also offer the best views.

- Bigger rooms (or suites) cost more because space is precious. A bath instead of a shower adds to the cost for the same reason.

- Portholes, because they offer a view, add to the cost. This is an outside, versus an inside, cabin.

Extra costs

- On some cruise ships, tips are not included in the fare. Ask to be sure.

- Any land tours or excursions to the mainland cost extra on almost all cruise ships. These can be quite expensive, especially if they include a guide and transportation.

- Wine, beer, cocktails — all cost extra. On some lines you'll get complimentary wine with a meal.

Length of the cruise

- Most cruises last one or two weeks, providing adequate time for rest.

- A few cruises offer three- and four-day voyages (the first and last days are often write-offs).

Motion sickness

- Some people get sick at the sight of sea water. See p. 216 for advice.

Special cruise tips

- The lowest-priced cabins on most cruises go first.

- Cruises are not geared to getting to know places. Europe will be a backdrop, not the main performance.

- Cruises frequently offer shore excursions during mealtimes — very annoying, but a fact. Ask about the exact schedule when booking a cruise!

- Space is critical, so rooms on luxury liners are tight, and baths minuscule.

- Bring a bottle of your favorite booze on board. This makes you less dependent on overpriced and often undersized (or watered-down) drinks.

- There are so many free snacks and edible extras on board that someone may whimsically remark that you board as a passenger, disembark as cargo.

Tipping on board

- Ask about the company policy on tipping before you buy a ticket. Tips may be included in the ticket price. If they are, the ticket is really costing you considerably less than a comparable ticket on a line where tips are not included.

- If tips are not included, tip room stewards, waiters, and other service staff for special services. The more service you ask for, the more you should expect to tip. Tips are best given immediately for such services as bringing late-night snacks.

- One very effective way of tipping: hand the room steward or waiter an amount adding up to half the tip you expect to give him altogether. Tell him exactly what you expect. And tell him that you will give him the other half of the tip at the end of the trip (the day before you disembark). This is up-front bargaining for good service. And does it work!

6 Transportation in Europe

Where are you going to go in Europe? How great will the total distance be? Are you on a tight budget or can you spend a little more? When are you going to go? How much energy do you have? Are you going to travel by yourself, as a twosome, or in a group?

Not until you have answered each of these questions should you decide whether travel by plane, train, car, motorcycle, bicycle — or by hitchhiking — makes sense for you. Each way has its advantages and disadvantages.

Basic Considerations

If you start with a few basic considerations, you will have an easier time choosing the best mode of travel for yourself.

Saving money

- If you're traveling alone, you'll have to travel by train, by motorcycle, or by thumb if you want to save money.

- If you're traveling with one or more people, you can bring the cost of car travel down to 10 cents a mile or less per person.

- If you're planning on plane travel for getting around Europe, you'll have to increase your budget, no matter how many are in your party.

Saving time

- Car travel is fine for short trips (less than 150 miles per day), but not for longer ones. It is just too time-consuming in most European countries.

- Train travel is superb for intercity trips of 300 miles or less. In fact, for short runs, a train will get you there as fast as a plane will.

- Planes are great for trips of 300 miles or longer.

- Hitchhiking is out.

Saving human energy

- Plane travel is superb, especially for long trips. (So is going by tour bus.) Train travel is also great — if you've got a seat, if the trip lasts no more than eight hours, and if you have little luggage.

- Motoring and hitching are out. Driving in Europe requires an enormous amount of energy.

Getting off the beaten path

- Car travel (or hitching) is often the only way to do it. A car offers complete mobility and freedom, and a car is an absolute necessity in Greece and Yugoslavia.

- Train travel is OK, but not great. Trains will get you to most smaller towns, but only after interminable waits and enough transfers to puzzle an electrical engineer.

- Planes? You guessed it. They're useless!

Cost Per Mile of Various Modes of Transportation	
Mode of transportation	Cost per mile
Plane	An average of 28 cents per plane mile per person.
Train	A first-class average of 15 cents per train mile per person.
	A second-class average of 10 cents per train mile per person.
Car	If you travel more than 1,000 miles per week, it will cost **less than** 32 cents per car mile.
	If you travel **less than** 1,000 miles per week, it will cost you **more than** 32 cents per mile.
	To find cost per person, divide cost per mile by number of people in car.
Motorcycle	An average of 4 cents per mile, not including initial purchase price.
Hitchhiking	No charge, unless you agree to split gas costs.

Planes

If you want to travel widely in Europe in a relatively short time and are willing to pay the high cost, go ahead and take a plane.

Advantages of plane travel

- For city-to-city trips of 300 miles or more, plane travel is the fastest way.

- It's the only way to get to some places, including many of the more popular islands.

- For a solo traveler covering great distances, it can be the most economical way to see Europe.

- You waste little precious time getting from one place to another.

- It's safe — popular misconceptions aside.

Disadvantages of plane travel

- Plane travel can be expensive, especially for shorter city-to-city trips. It's doubly expensive for twosomes and exorbitant for groups.

- Plane trips are oriented to travel between major cities.

- Plane travel can actually be slower than train travel for trips of 200 miles and less.

- You've got to spend money and time on transfers.

- You can be locked in by bad weather.

- You pass over, not through, the countryside.

Plane travel strategies

- Get all details about your plane travel worked out in the U.S. whenever possible. This includes your itinerary, confirmed reservations, and tickets for most flights.

- Have flights and flight times written on the ticket folder. It's also better to reserve a return seat on a tentative basis than to leave the return date open. If you have to change a reservation, just call it in.

- Check into stopover privileges whenever you buy a transatlantic ticket. Maybe you'll be able to see several cities en route to another one.

- Check into the possibility of adding another leg onto a ticket you've already purchased. It might be less expensive than buying a separate ticket.

- Get free brochures from the airlines that show you the seating arrangements on some of the most popular aircraft.

- Contact the airlines for information about special clubs and waiting rooms available in many airports, including a few in Europe. For a yearly fee, you can take advantage of them. These clubs are most useful for business people and other frequent travelers.

Inter-European flights

- Note: London is one of the best bases for buying inexpensive tickets to many parts of Europe, Africa, and the Middle East. Of course, you'll have to spend time finding the bargains, but they're definitely there!

- Otherwise, try to buy all tickets for inter-European air travel in the U.S. You'll save money. For some flights, you'll find that you can reserve seats in the U.S., but will still have to pay for them abroad. You can try asking travel agents for help or information on this point, but you may find that some are ignorant of European excursion fares, and some are unwilling to help because they don't make a commission on such sales.

Trains

Train travel is a sensible way to see Europe, especially if you're going from one major city to the next. It's also a low-cost, low-risk mode of transportation — but it has a few drawbacks, too.

Advantages of train travel

- You spend less money when you go by train. It is far cheaper than plane or car travel, especially for solo travelers.

- Train travel is not only safe, but also convenient, because it takes you from city center to city center with no transfer fees to pay and no weather delays.

- Train travel is less tiring than car travel.
- Going by train is the fastest way to cover short distances between major European cities, even faster than plane travel for trips of 150 to 300 miles.
- Best of all, you see the land: it can be a visual feast.

Disadvantages of train travel

- Each day on a train is wasted — unless trains turn you on.
- Since train travel is oriented to city centers, you may find it confining.
- Trains don't wait for you; you wait for them.
- Over an extended period of time, train travel becomes monotonous.
- Trains are crowded. The low price draws crowds like a bargain basement sale; the corridors are so full of so many people and packs that a trip to the WC becomes one long stutter of "Please" and "I'm sorry."

Railway passes

Some countries offer special passes for **unlimited** train travel within their own borders. You can buy these for travel in Austria, Belgium, Denmark, Finland, France, Germany, Great Britain, Greece, Ireland, the Netherlands, Norway, Portugal, Scotland, Spain, Sweden, and Switzerland.

- Regulations vary, and some of the passes must be purchased in the United States. Check with travel agents or national tourist offices (on p. 227) for up-to-date restrictions and fares.

Eurail and Youthrail Passes

The Eurailpass and the Youthrailpass are two of the most popular with American and Canadian travelers. They have been available for years from travel agents and can be an excellent choice.

Advantages of Eurailpasses

The Eurailpass offers you unlimited train travel in these countries: Austria, Belgium, Denmark, Finland, France, Germany, Greece, Ireland, Italy, Luxembourg, the Netherlands, Norway, Portugal, Spain, Sweden, and Switzerland. It covers various lengths of travel time.

- You know your overall travel costs from the start, since you must prepay them in the U.S. And you never have to exchange currency for tickets. Furthermore, you can take any train without a surcharge.

- You go first class, which is very comfortable and clean in most areas. You can bypass boring ticket lines.

- You're free to plan your itinerary by yourself — at whim.

- You won't have to explain things to the conductor in foreign languages.

- You get free extras: a free 400-mile voyage on Irish Continental Line from Cherbourg to Rosslare, free trips on Swiss lakes, free boat rides on the Mosel and Rhine, a free ferry from Stockholm to Finland. The trip from Brindisi (Italy) to Greece is free from October to mid-June and at a reduced rate in the peak season.

Disadvantages of Eurailpasses

- Although you don't have to buy tickets, you do have to make reservations for some of the most popular trains. That can mean long waits in long lines for super trains.

- You must pay a small fee for each reservation.

- The pass is not honored on privately owned railroads, which may link portions of your trip. Ask to see a map showing all available routes to avoid any unpleasant surprises.

- If you lose your pass after it has been validated, you may not get a refund. Contact the nearest Eurail Aid office for advice. Refunds are discretionary.

Where to buy Eurailpasses

- Technically, you must buy all Eurail and Youthrail passes in the United States. This is the safest and easiest thing to do if you're sure that you'll be using one.

- Some travelers have written to say that they have purchased Eurailpasses abroad from major travel agencies that requested them from the United States. They also claim that you can pick them up from national tourist offices abroad.

- The advantage of this is that you can wait and see if you really want a pass.

- The disadvantage is that it can take up to a week for the passes to be delivered.

When to buy a Eurailpass

If you intend to travel fast and far, buy one. The longer-term passes are most economical because they cut the cost per mile. Buy one if you intend to travel more than

- 1,900 miles in 15 days,
- 2,300 miles in three weeks,
- 2,800 miles in one month, or
- 4,600 miles in three months

When not to buy a Eurailpass

- Don't buy one if you'll be visiting a few major cities that are close together. You'll do much better buying second-class tickets for those few runs.

Get the most from a Eurailpass

Validate your Eurailpass at the last possible moment. Or combine it with separate, second-class train tickets to cut the overall cost of your trip. Example: you arrive by Icelandic in Luxembourg, pay for a second-class train ticket to Paris, spend 10 days there, and then use a Eurailpass valid for a period shorter than your overall trip.

Youthrail passes

The Youthrailpass, available to anyone under 26, is a variation of the Eurailpass, offering one or two months of unlimited, second-class rail travel for a set price lower than the Eurailpass.

- No longer do you have to specify the starting date of rail travel. The pass is now validated on the first day you use it.

Doing without Eurailpasses

- Even if you don't buy a Eurailpass, you can save money by buying rail tickets in the U.S.

- You can save more by traveling second class. But go first class in Greece, Italy, Portugal, and Spain, where second class can be a zoo.

Getting reserved train seats

- If you're on a tight schedule and have very little time to waste, try to make seat reservations in the U.S. whenever possible. Regulations change frequently. However, a good travel agent can keep you up-to-date.

- Be sure to ask ahead of time about any charge for this service. If the cost seems too steep, settle for making reservations abroad.

Cars

Car travel is for independent spirits who are aware that freedom has its price. It's the best way to see Europe if you want to strike out to unusual and offbeat locations. Sightseeing, picnics, looking for charming hotels, checking out unusual restaurants, getting to out-of-the-way spots — all are open to motorists.

Advantages of car travel

- You don't have to worry about reservations, tickets, and ticket lines.

- You're free to change schedules at whim.

- You're part of the living jigsaw puzzle around you.

- You can go almost anywhere.

- It's economical for a group of three or more.

- It's comfortable, convenient, and fast.

Disadvantages of car travel

- If your trip is oriented to major cities, you will do better taking a train or plane.

- Car travel is expensive, far more expensive than most Americans realize.

- Purchase, rental, lease — all cost a great deal, making car travel prohibitive for solo travelers.

- Car travel is much slower than either train or plane travel. In many countries, it can take as much time to drive one mile as it would take to drive 5 to 10 miles in the U.S.

• Car travel can insulate you from meeting Europeans.

• Finding a parking place in major European cities can be a migraine headache.

Buying, leasing, or renting a car

• Buying a car in Europe only makes sense if you plan to travel for three months or longer.

• Leasing can be a better option than rental for trips of 5 to 10 weeks. Costs are still very high, so leasing will appeal mainly to three or four people traveling together.

• Renting has the greatest appeal to travelers on vacations lasting less than a month.

Comparison shopping for cars to buy abroad

Check around to come up with the best deal. If you do some comparison shopping, you'll shave off dollars on the initial cost of a foreign car!

• You can pick up many makes of foreign cars from Ship Side Showroom at Amsterdam Airport. For information, contact Ship Side Car Delivery, Inc., 50 Chestnut Ridge Road, Montvale, NJ 07645.

• Europe by Car, Inc., 1 Rockefeller Plaza, New York, NY 10020, will send you information on buying a car abroad. Write for information on current prices and models.

• Students can sometimes get a special discount on car purchases through the CIEE (see p. 15).

• You can also purchase cars for foreign delivery from local American dealers selling the brand of car you are interested in.

Car-buying guide

• It's very important to check with U.S. Customs to make sure the car you're purchasing will pass pollution control standards, which may not be in force in Europe.

• If you intend to resell the car, ask the dealer about which models, options, and colors sell best. The best names for resale in the U.S. are BMW, Fiat, Mercedes-Benz, Porsche, Volkswagen, and Volvo.

• Plan ahead, especially for summer delivery. Order your car at least three months in advance.

- Find out the total cost, including all options, taxes, licenses, documents, and miscellaneous charges, and get it in writing. You will not have to pay major foreign taxes unless you keep the car for more than a year in the country where it was manufactured.
- Get the dealer's cost and delivery date confirmed by the manufacturer, in writing.
- Make sure your agreement is for the newest model on the assembly line. If you're buying late in the year, order the next year's model. (Get the year down in writing, too!)

Car insurance

- Most American companies will not write policies covering European travel.

- Car manufacturers do write such policies, but at rip-off prices. Be sure to ask the dealer to get you a brochure that outlines the rates before you sign any agreement.

- If the dealer has no idea of the rates, have him wire the manufacturer for them. Insist on knowing what they'll be ahead of time, to avoid hidden costs.

Car accessories

- Ask what the cost of a reflective triangle (danger sign) and first-aid kit will be. European law requres all drivers to have these, and it's often much cheaper to bring your own from the U.S.

- Always carry an extra set of car keys. Hide them in a magnetic box that will stick to the underside of your car. You'll never lock yourself out this way.

Taking delivery on a car

- Get the delivery date in writing, and have it confirmed in writing by the factory. If a car isn't delivered on that date, you have the right to ask the factory to pay for your room while you wait. They have the right to refuse, but they'll speed up delivery under pressure.

- There's no charge for delivery at the foreign plant.

- Plan to pay for the car with a certified check or traveler's checks. A sale can be completed in about an hour.

European warranties and service

European warranties and tissue paper have the same value. The former cover the car for from three to six months and include a series of so-called free service inspections, for which you get a coupon book. But only about half the listed service stations and garages honor the coupons.

- Do some garage hopping to find those that honor the coupons.
- Or be willing to pay for the "free" service for the sake of convenience.

Cars and camping

- To rent both cars and camping gear, contact Hendrik Hilde-brandt, 61 Studiestraede, Copenhagen 1554, Denmark. Cars can be delivered to Amsterdam, Brussels, Frankfurt, Luxembourg, and Oslo for a $40 charge. There is no charge for Copenhagen delivery.

Car leasing

This is really just long-term car rental with a discount, oriented to two or more people traveling together with the idea of splitting costs.

- Leasing is sensible for trips of a month or longer, but it is still very expensive. You can get information on leasing cars from the same outfits that rent them.

Car rental

- Get started on your planning early so that you can reserve a car well in advance of your arrival, especially if you will be abroad between May and September.

Base prices for car rental

The following chart shows how base prices vary by company for each country. Though the names have been omitted, companies A, B, and C do exist, and the prices listed will indicate closely what you can expect in Europe. Note that if you choose a car from a company offering the best rate and can start your trip in a low-rate country, you'll save money.

Country	Cost/ Company			Country	Cost/ Company		
	A	B	C		A	B	C
Austria	200	199	208	Italy	221	198	194
Belgium	172	175	190	Luxembourg	166	257	204
Denmark	181	207	172	Netherlands	182	200	179
Finland	248	289	254	Norway	231	224	235
France	220	248	162	Portugal	129	123	126
Germany	182	182	201	Spain	134	166	103
Great Britain	159	145	123	Sweden	256	217	208
Greece	151	170	158	Switzerland	214	288	290
Ireland	99	164	126	Yugoslavia	166	184	198

Shopping around for rental rates

- Note that base prices vary not only by company, but also by country, so comparison shop before you rent. Using the toll-free (800) numbers in your telephone book, call major car rental firms, such as Avis, Budget-Auto, Hertz, and National.

- Ask these companies to send you their free worldwide directories listing current car rental rates. You'll get fastest replies from Budget-Auto and Hertz (a few days' time). Avis takes about two weeks — and National, a month!

- Contact Europe by Car, Inc., 1 Rockefeller Plaza, New York, NY 10020, and ask for its rates. This firm also has offices in Chicago, Honolulu, Los Angeles, San Francisco, and Washington, D.C.

- Note that airlines offer fly-and-drive tour packages, combining airfare and the cost of car rental in Europe. These are couple oriented. You can get information on such packages from travel agents and airlines.

- Explore auto club discounts for members.

- Students should check with the CIEE (see p. 15) for rental discount information.

Rental Taxes and Additional Fees

The base price is just that. You'll notice how the base price is augmented by taxes at the following rates:

Austria	20 percent tax plus a 1.2 percent contract fee	**Italy**	18 percent tax plus 12 percent gas tax
Belgium	25 percent tax	**Luxembourg** .	17 percent tax
Denmark	22 percent tax	**Netherlands** ..	19 percent tax
Finland	19.05 percent tax	**Norway**	20 percent tax
France	33.33 percent tax	**Portugal**	8 percent tax
		Spain	5 percent tax
Germany	14 percent tax	**Sweden**	23.46 percent tax
Great Britain	15 percent tax	**Switzerland** ..	no tax
Greece	20 percent tax	**Yugoslavia**	15 percent tax plus a $3 tank-filling charge
Ireland	10 percent tax		

If you plan to pick up your car in one city with the intention of leaving it in another, you'll pay a fee in many instances. Ask about these charges when making a car rental reservation.

Rental pitfalls

- Do not plan to rent a car on any **island** where it's impossible to take out full insurance on the car. Instead, avoid potential legal hassles by hiring a taxi daily.

- Never rent a car in **Great Britain** if you intend to cross the Channel with it. To avoid stiff surcharges and premiums on insurance, leave the car in England and rent another car on the Continent!

- When they're available, Italian gas coupons are only given for vehicles with non-Italian license plates. During such periods of availability, rent your car outside of Italy (see pp. 165-166).

Motorcycles

You can go anywhere on a cycle — up rutted mountain paths or over to an old, abandoned Moorish castle that's stranded miles from a main road. You're always close to the earth, the smell of mimosa trees or manure, the colors of bright-red poppy fields or pastel-pink Portuguese walls, and the sounds of clicking tracks and buzzing mosquitoes or grape flies. It's an exciting sensation.

Advantages of motorcycle travel

- You can park a cycle almost anywhere.

- The gas costs are extremely low, since you'll get from 60 to 90 miles to the gallon.

- You can pass long lines of traffic anywhere, in the city or at borders.

- There's no doubt about it — it's an exciting way to travel!

Disadvantages of motorcycle travel

- The once-low initial cost of a bike is now very high.

- All mothers and lovers are afraid you'll fall. You will. But the odds are 50/50 that you'll survive the scraped knees, twisted feet, and close shaves.

- Motorcycle touring appears glamorous in the movies and on television. In real life, it can be dirty, tiring, cold, annoying, and frustrating. Have you ever changed a bike's tire and taken it off its rim by yourself? If not, you don't understand motorcycles, their absolute unreliability, the exhaustion of riding, and the experiences you're in for.

- That's not all: you're at the mercy of the weather, and a bike is easy to vandalize and easy to steal.

- The rational conclusion would be never to buy a bike. Fortunately for motorcycle manufacturers, emotions run stronger than logic at times.

Buying a motorcycle abroad

- Buy a prestige bike for high resale value.

- Order the cycle for foreign delivery months in advance, since the supply may not cover the demand.

- Be willing to pick it up at the factory.

- Read the sections on buying and driving cars abroad (pp. 161-174) for other helpful hints.

- Remember that a cycle takes thousands of miles to break in (something you should point out when you sell it).

Motorcycle options

- Don't get a tank lock. When you're cold and exhausted, you don't want to have to undo your coat to look for a key. And tank locks rattle.

- Try to replace the side kickstand with any other kind. Side kickstands are useless since they sink in sand and tar. (If you do have a side stand, you'll have to carry a board with you!)

- Equally useless is the average rear view mirror that comes with the bike. If it's the kind that you can loosen with just a quick turn of the hand, have it immediately replaced with a good one — one that won't jiggle loose after 20 miles and then smash as it flies off onto the pavement.

- Although crash bars that protect your legs are sometimes called sissy bars, that's a misnomer. When you dump, you'll know why. Get them!

- The electric starter is worth every extra cent you pay for it. There's nothing worse than trying to kick-start a bike that is cold, wet, or overheated.

- Pay extra for a luggage rack.

Other motorcycling equipment

- Wear a helmet. The law requires it.

- A tinted bubble that covers your whole face is much better than goggles. Dust stings; bumblebees and fat bugs explode when they hit your face; and rain is unbearable at normal driving speeds (60 to 80 miles per hour).

- Always carry spark plugs, since they foul constantly.

- Carry spare light bulbs.

- Use plastic laundry bags to protect the contents of your pack from getting soaked when it pours.

- Bring a pair of sunglasses with hardened lenses for low-speed driving.

- Bring or buy abroad hooked rubber straps to keep your pack from flying around.

Special clothing for motorcyclists

- Since bike-riding can be cold even on a summer night, think about bringing a down-filled parka or comparably warm jacket.

- Buy the best rain gear available, since you will be miserable if it leaks. It should snap closed around the sleeves and pant cuffs. Rain gear should be brightly colored (yellow or orange) to glow in the dark. Make it double as a windbreaker in clear weather.

- Bring heavy, comfortable boots. Combat boots work perfectly.

- Wear leather gloves to protect your hands from the cold and from the blisters you'll get as you work in the clutch and front brakes, which are always stiff on a new bike.

Hitchhiking

Hitchhiking is known as **auto-stop** in Europe. It is accepted in some countries and loathed in others. The accompanying chart will give you a good idea of what success to expect in each country. (See also pp. 178-181.)

Advantages of hitchhiking

- Hitchhiking is as cheap as "free" can be. It offers total freedom — with one hitch: you've got to hitch a ride. So the only thing that can break down is you.

- Hitchhiking is also the best way to meet Europeans because it's a direct and immediate appeal for help.

- Hitchhiking is a sport, and like all sports it reveals inner qualities in its participants. It's also an art, demanding skill, intelligence, and patience.

Disadvantages of hitchhiking

- Hitchhiking is time-consuming, tiring, and potentially dangerous — especially for women traveling alone.

- Furthermore, it doesn't always work, as hitchhikers soon discover in southern Spain. You've got to be tough, patient, and wily to make it work.

Prospects for Hitchhiking in European Countries	
Austria ....Good.	**Liechtenstein** Does it matter?
Belgium ....Very good.	**Luxembourg** ...Very good.
Denmark ....Excellent.	**Netherlands** ....Very good.
France ....The worst (especially in the South).	**Norway** ....Tough.
	Portugal ....Fair.
Germany ....Excellent.	**Spain** ....Lousy.
Great Britain ..Excellent.	**Sweden** ....Good.
Greece ....Poor.	**Switzerland** ....Good to very good.
Ireland ....Excellent.	
Italy ....Good (despite hostility).	**Yugoslavia** ......Fair, but getting worse.

Gear for hitchhikers

- Use backpacks with metal frames. They distribute the weight evenly, are great for walking, have convenient zippered compartments, take more abuse, don't get dirty quickly, and are harder to steal than most other packs.

- Or use a pack made of leather and canvas. This kind takes up less space, rips less often, and never suffers from frame damage (because there is no frame to be damaged).

- Make sure the straps of the pack won't cut into your body or tear off. Check the stitching carefully.

- Bring a large poncho to cover both you and the pack in heavy rain.

- Pack a sleeping bag (down compresses the most, but comparable synthetics stay warmer when wet) and a thin foam pad.

- You'll also need a water container, a flashlight, some insect repellent, a Swiss Army knife, some soap in a plastic container, and matches.

- Carry most of your funds in traveler's checks or plan to use credit cards. Carrying cash is risky.

- You can buy gear abroad. Try Kaufman's (throughout Germany), Black's of Scotland (London), or Galleries Lafayette (Paris).

7 Lodgings

Variety in places to stay — that's what Europe has to offer. And that's part of its charm and challenge to Americans not used to quite so diverse a choice.

Varieties of Lodgings

B & B (Bed and Breakfast): You'll find these small family hotels and boardinghouses throughout Great Britain. You'll get a comfortable, small room and usually a very good breakfast for a set price that is usually inexpensive. You don't need reservations in most of these places. Look for "B & B" signs posted out front.

Boardinghouses: Boardinghouses **(pensions, pensiones)** come in all categories, from luxurious to dismal, in every country in Europe. Generally, you rent a room without a bath. You eat in a central dining area. In some cases, you'll be expected to stay at least three days or so. The price you pay includes however many meals you agree to eat. Prices range from inexpensive to moderate. You normally don't make reservations for these accommodations.

Castle Hotels: Many castles in France, Germany, and Great Britain have been converted into unusual hotels varying from ultradeluxe to quite uncomfortable. You can get information on castle (château) hotels from both the Austrian and French National Tourist Offices (see pp. 227-228). A brochure is also available from Gast Im Schloss, D3526 Trendelburg 1, Germany. Lufthansa, the German airline, often stocks good brochures on castle hotels. The important thing to remember: both cost and comfort vary enormously among castle accommodations (some even serve as youth hostels).

Gîtes: In France 25,000 privately owned residences are now available for one-week stays. Lists are posted in county halls **(préfets)** or in the **French Farm and Village Holiday Guide** from Unipub, 343 Park Avenue S., New York, NY 10010. A catalog listing similar spots is available from the French Experience, 390 Fifth Avenue, Suite 407, New York, NY 10018. Note that there is usually a two-week minimum stay in July and August.

Historic Inns: Great Britain is world famous for its atmospheric inns, some dating back to medieval times. Comfort varies from inn to inn, but rates are uniformly reasonable. For a brochure and map, contact the British Tourist Authority (see p. 227). In Switzerland, you can find many comparable historic inns, and a booklet will be sent to you free upon request from the Swiss National Tourist Office (see p. 229).

Home Exchange: To exchange your home with a foreign person, contact:

Vacation Exchange Club
12006 111th Avenue,
  Suite 12
Youngtown, AZ 85363

International Home
  Exchange
250 Bel Marin Keys
Ignacio, CA 94947

Hotels: Most tourist offices will send you booklets or pamphlets giving addresses and telephone numbers of hotels throughout each country. Note that they will contain no subjective comments, just facts on cost and conveniences. To come up with a good hotel, it's best to collect and cross-reference information from friends, guide books, and travel agents. (See also pp. 108-120.)

Kroer A **Kro** (plural: **Kroer**): This is a Danish country inn, often filled with the kind of atmosphere you'd travel thousands of miles to enjoy. And the food is often tops. These inns are quite expensive but still offer good value. You'll find them throughout the country. For a list of some of the most interesting, contact the Danish National Tourist Office (see p. 227).

Mission Hotels: Throughout Scandinavia, the mission hotels offer modest, comfortable rooms at reasonable rates — reasonable for Scandinavia, that is. The only catch: no drinking is allowed. These hotels are very popular, and you'll want to reserve a room well in advance from May through September.

Paradores: The Spanish government has supported the construction and maintenance of inns throughout Spain, some of which are starkly modern, while others are filled to the brim with native ambience. The **paradores** offer excellent value, comfortable rooms, and good regional cooking, and are located in areas of historic or cultural interest. Get a list from the National Tourist Office of Spain (see p. 229). Make reservations as far in advance as you can, especially during the peak season.

Pousadas: These are Portugal's version of Spain's **paradores,** and very fine at that. Both countries have regulations on maximum stays, and you should make reservations as far in advance as possible. Even during the off-season, the **pousadas** and **paradores** can be packed!

Private Homes: Renting a room in a private home **(privat Zimmer, sobe)** can be a fascinating and relatively inexpensive experience. As you would guess, there are so many rooms available all over Europe that it's impossible to give any overall conclusion except for this: they usually give you good value, and people respond to you according to your warmth and openness.

Pubs: That's right. Throughout Great Britain and Ireland you can find rooms in pubs. Note that these have unusual hours, so that you can be locked out of your room unless you ask about closing times in advance. Fun, good value. Don't try to reserve such rooms in advance.

Relais de campagne: These country inns offer excellent atmosphere, idyllic settings, comfort, and some of the best cooking in Europe. Most of them are located in France, but others are scattered in Belgium, Great Britain, Italy, and Sweden. For full information, contact the French National Tourist Office (see p. 228). Note that these are quite expensive, especially when it comes to quality cuisine.

Rentals: Many homes, villas, and apartments are available for rental in Europe. Contact tourist offices abroad for information, or write Vacation Exchange Club, 12006 111th Avenue, Suite 12, Youngtown, AZ 85363.

Romantik Hotels: A group of Austrian, German, and Swiss hotels offering family-owned-and-operated inns to travelers. Each is atmospheric, comfortable, and reliable concerning its kitchen, which usually specializes in regional cooking. Many of these inns are located off-the-beaten-path for a true glimpse of another culture. Prices range from moderate to expensive, but are always good values. For information contact Lufthansa, the German airline, or the German National Tourist Office (see p. 228). You can also write directly to the central office of the group: Romantik Hotels and Restaurants, 8752 Gross-Weldheim, West Germany.

Rorbu: Nothing more than fishing shanties, open to foreigners on the coast of Norway throughout the summer season. Cost varies from nothing to next-to-nothing. For the adventuresome. For information, contact the Norwegian National Tourist Office (see p. 229).

Student Hotels: Don't confuse these with hostels. Student hotels are quite distinct. If you're a student or living on a student's budget, get in touch with the CIEE (see p. 15) for details on the assortment of student hotels and dorms in Europe.

Villas and Apartments: At Home Abroad, Inc., 405 East 56th Street, #6H, New York, NY 10022; Chez Vous, 220 Redwood Highway, Suite 129, Mill Valley, CA 94941; RAVE, 500 Triangle Building, Rochester, NY 14604; Swiss Touring USA, 5537 North Hollywood Avenue, Milwaukee, WI 53217; Villas International, 71 West 23rd Street, New York, NY 10010.

Xenia: These comfortable hotels are located throughout Greece and are supported in part by the government. For information on these fine hotels, contact the Greek National Tourist Office (see p. 228).

Youth Hostels: Hosteling is one of the least expensive ways to get by in Europe. It's very simple, modest, dormitory-style living in most instances. See Chapter 11 for tips on hosteling and where to write for information.

YMCAs and YWCAs: The Ys in Europe are much better than their counterparts in the U.S., and they give you very good value for your travel dollars. For information, contact YMCA, 101 North Wacker Drive, Chicago, IL 60606; or YWCA, 726 Broadway, New York, NY 10003. Or call any local branch.

Room Reservations

Reservations are not necessarily essential for enjoyable travel, but they certainly can help, especially for brief trips. A poorly made reservation may be worse than none at all, however. Here are some tips on doing it right.

When reserving a room makes sense

- Have a reservation for the first night abroad. Since you'll be exhausted when you arrive in Europe, you won't want to look for a room.

- Make reservations if you want rooms of great charm or value, especially during the peak season.

- If you're on a short trip with little time to waste, have reservations for every night abroad. You can't afford the hassle or the time involved in looking for rooms on your own.

Problems with reservations

- You may have to pay a fee for room reservations or else foot the cost of cables and phone calls.

- You're usually renting sight unseen. Unless you have great confidence in your "source," you may end up disappointed.

- You'll end up paying for higher-priced rooms or paying the highest price a room will rent for. Reservations take away all your bargaining power and make it very difficult for you to shift from one room to another.

- Reservations tie you down. If you're on a short trip, this will make no difference, but when a trip stretches to three weeks or longer, a reservation schedule can begin to feel like an ill-fitting shoe on a 10-mile hike.

Avoid getting bumped by hotels

Many hotels routinely overbook by 10 to 15 percent. Unless you've got a confirmation in writing, you could be one of those bumped.

- Make reservations as far in advance as possible. Note that some hotels in major cities fill up six to nine months in advance.

- Get your reservation confirmed in writing. If you know that you'll be arriving at a hotel after 6 p.m., make sure that the hotel knows this. And have this late arrival time noted on your room confirmation slip.

- Pay a substantial deposit on the room. With money in the bank, few hotels will worry about your showing up.

- If you make reservations through a travel agent, choose one with clout — preferably one with many offices abroad, so that you will have someone to call if things go awry.

- If you get delayed unexpectedly, notify the hotel. Few hotels will rent your room if you have contacted them.

Travel agents' reservations

- Most agents charge nothing at all for making room reservations, unless doing so involves a special service, such as phoning or cabling (their commission is paid by the hotel).

- Ask the agent whether you'll be charged for cables or phone calls — or for anything, for that matter!

- If the agent insists that there is no charge at all, ask whether a surcharge will be added to your hotel bill abroad.

- If the agent says that no such commission need be paid, ask for a letter typed on the agency stationery stating this in straightforward terms. If a hotel in Europe then tries to stick you with a surcharge, produce the letter and refuse to pay it.

Airline reservation services

- With enough advance notice, airlines will gladly reserve a room for you at any destination or stopover point, both of which are stated clearly on your ticket. They charge no fee for this service.

Credit card reservations

- Note that with some credit cards you can get a confirmed room reservation in major hotels throughout Europe. Call major credit card companies for current information on making confirmed room reservations.

Making your own reservations

- Larger hotel chains with many branches abroad have toll-free (800) numbers listed in the phone book. All you have to do is dial the number and make a reservation. Be specific about dates and ask them to send you some sort of confirmation in writing. Also ask for a reservation or confirmation number.

- You can write directly to hotels listed in guidebooks. If you use business stationery, request information on business discounts (up to 30 percent).

- Send your letter by airmail, and tell the hotel to reply by airmail. Include international reply coupons (available in main post offices) to cover the cost of the hotel's airmail reply.

- Most hotels will reply with a request for a deposit to show good faith. An international money order will do the trick. Sometimes just a check is good enough.

- Another method that's expensive but effective: call the foreign hotel during local business hours. Ask for the front desk, where you'll probably find someone who can speak English. Talk very slowly and very clearly. Repeat the dates of your intended stay several times. Ask for a written confirmation. And be sure to get the name of the person with whom you're talking.

8 Packing

What to take, how to pack it — two of the most basic questions of travelers! Read this chapter to simplify the process of finding answers.

Traveling Light

Traveling light means less hassle and less frustration. But the advantages don't stop there.

Advantages of traveling light

- If you'll travel light, you'll save money at every turn, on porter or extra taxi charges. You can handle your luggage yourself — easily.

- Traveling without bags allows you to take inexpensive public transportation. You can hop on buses, trams, and subways to avoid stiff taxi fares.

- If you travel light, you can bargain with clerks in hotels over hotel rates. With several bulky bags you're stuck, no matter what the rates are. With just one piece of luggage you can move on.

- You never miss connections waiting for bags to be spewed out of the belly of a 747. You're the first through customs, the first out — saving hours of frustrating waits in baggage claim areas.

- You never lose anything. You've got your luggage with you. You're not dependent on anyone, whether competent or incompetent.

- All of this adds up to less stress, less worry, and a sense of freedom — your attitude will reflect this feeling.

How to travel light

- Do it like the pros — stewardesses, travel writers, experienced business people, correspondents — get by with one piece of hand luggage. If you can't carry it on a plane, it's too large. If you can't carry it for a mile without setting it down, it's too heavy.

- It's natural for you to feel somewhat skeptical about traveling with only one piece of carry-on luggage. Questions will pop into your mind: "Can I really get by on only a few clothes?" "Won't I be embarrassed by wearing the same outfits over and over?" "Can I get by in more formal places with less-than-formal clothes?" "What do I do about climate changes?" "What happens if something gets stained?"

- If you choose your clothes wisely, you'll have no problem at all. The reaction to this style of travel is always the same: "Are you ever smart!" As long as you're clean and comfortably dressed, you'll exude an aura of contentment and confidence. Europeans judge you more by this attitude than by your clothes!

- Leave electrical items at home. They're heavy, bulky, and can be damaged by varying voltage.

- Pack only items you need to survive — the essentials. I met one person who considered a toothbrush the only item essential for travel!

- Make each item serve as many purposes as possible. A bathing suit or bikini can pass as underwear. A one-piece woman's swimsuit can be converted into a dress by adding a wraparound skirt of the same material. Shampoo can wash not only hair, but also the body — think versatility.

- Go for comfort first, style last. The two need not be mutually exclusive.

- Make sure all clothes are light, easy to wash, and quick drying. Test them before you leave. Pick up heavier items for special needs abroad.

- While traveling, wear your heaviest clothes whenever possible.

Use light luggage

- Travel with one small carry-on bag or backpack. Either should be able to fit under the seat of a plane.

- Try a nylon, canvas, or vinyl bag, which will be relatively inexpensive, feather light, and soft-sided — avoid frames of any kind! You want a bag that is light, pliable, and durable.

- Get a bag with a shoulder strap, to make carrying easier. It should also have some small outer compartments for odds and ends, from toilet articles to an umbrella.

Garment bags

If, no matter how hard you try, you can't get the things you'd like to take with you into one small bag, carry a garment bag onto the plane and hang it in one of the coat compartments.

- You'll pay half the price for the same bag if you shop for one in discount outlets. You can get a high-quality bag for around $20.

- Garment bags can also be made at home. Patterns appear in women's magazines and can be found in many fabric shops.

- The bag should have some outer pockets for odds and ends. These should have snap or zipper closings.

- It's much easier to carry the bag if it has a shoulder strap. Most do.

- **Note:** airlines are now discouraging the use of garment bags by stuffing them in compartments in the rear of the plane. As a result, you have to wait for all the passengers to disembark before getting your bag.

When you can't travel light

- Never carry one huge bag. Split the contents into two lighter bags for easier handling.

- Think about using a luggage roller. They do stick in cracks, but will make lugging baggage much easier, except on stairs.

- Think about taking a backpack. If you've ever worn one, you know how much easier it is than carrying a suitcase. No one will think you're crazy — just smart.

- Store your bags in lockers at airports and train stations whenever possible, to leave you free to do some sightseeing without dragging bags around with you.

- Remember that hotels will store bags if your flight or train leaves late at night, well past checkout time.

- Don't overpack! You can't collect insurance on baggage damages if your bags are really stuffed.

Dress in Europe

- Dress is casual in most areas of Europe. No one expects you to dress up, except in fancier restaurants, hotels, and night spots.

- Formal dress, black tie or blue suits, and comparable dress for women, is extremely rare — suited to business or diplomatic occasions, a few casinos, and "dress-up" nights at deluxe restaurants.

- Generally, even in stuffy places, you can get by with a sports coat and tie with equivalent dress for women. The average tourist can slide by with simple, casual clothes — nothing stylish at all.

Dressing for the weather

- Worry more about the weather than how you'll look. Try to match your clothes to the altitude (much cooler), the season (southern Europe sizzles in the summer), and the place (who needs long pants on a beach?).

- The weather chart on p. 230 tells you the average temperature and rainfall in many areas. Match your clothes to the month during which you'll be traveling.

Tips for women

- Keep makeup extremely simple while traveling.

- Leave your valuable jewelry at home. You can buy inexpensive silver- and gold-imitation jewelry in countless stores and street stands. Only experts can tell it from the real thing.

- Remember that strong perfumes and cosmetics can make you sun-sensitive. So can some antibiotics (see p. 217).

- Samples of beauty products are light, small, and easy to carry. Collect them for short trips.

- A denim skirt is more comfortable than jeans. It has all the advantages and more — it doesn't stain easily, doesn't show wrinkles, and it breathes.

- Carry a flat, large purse for all your odds and ends — a folding umbrella, a camera (best kept out of sight), a snack — you name it. Keep your makeup case and your money in a wallet or change purse. These fit nicely into the larger purse.

- One of the most versatile items to pack is a **long,** cotton beach robe. Not only can it be used on the beach as a cover-up or beach blanket, but it also can pass as either casual or elegant dress. It's extremely easy to keep clean, weighs very little, and packs tight with little wrinkling — absolutely fantastic!

- Keep your shoes comfortable. Forget style. Shoes can be very casual. Many young and old travelers wear nothing but tennis shoes for the whole trip. Visiting ruins, climbing steep stairs, walking on cobblestone streets, strolling along a beach — these are activities that require comfortable, casual shoes. No one cares in the least whether you're fashionable or not (except in discos and elegant restaurants).

Basics of Packing

Use the rolling technique to keep clothes wrinkle-free and accessible in a small bag.

- Lay slacks or pants out on a flat surface (such as a bed) with the leg seams together. These will serve as a base.

- Fold such things as a T-shirt, sweater, turtleneck, or shorts in half lengthwise, with sleeves together. Lay these out evenly on both the top and bottom portion of the slacks.

- Roll the clothes into a loose ball, working from the pants legs up and slip the ball into a plastic bag.

- Clothes in a plastic bag slip in and out of luggage very easily. The plastic also protects them from dust, dirt, and any liquids that might spill accidentally.

- You just unroll the ball to get to whatever item you need later on.

Packing toiletries

- Put all liquids in plastic bottles. Place each bottle in a separate plastic bag so that your luggage won't get soaked if it leaks.

- To prevent leaking: gently squeeze the bottle as you put on the top to create suction. Seal the top with tape for full protection (just for plane flights).

- As you use up your toothpaste and other creams in tubes, roll tubes up tightly so that they will take up less space. Carry two small tubes of such products instead of one large one, if you'll be traveling extensively.

- Keep all toiletries in one place, like in a makeup case, so that you can get to them easily at any time.

Packing larger suitcases

If you've decided not to travel light, here are two tips:

• Plastic bags keep clothes from getting wrinkled. Slide each shirt, jacket, or skirt in a separate bag. Lay the clothes flat or folded once into the suitcase. The film of air retained between the plastic and clothes will keep them wrinkle free. Jackets and coats can be kept on hangers so that you can whip them out of the suitcase in their plastic wrap and hang them immediately in a closet. The plastic used in average dry-cleaning establishments is just fine.

• You'll have to check bags, so strap them closed. Mark each with bright tape, a decal, or a bumper sticker. This will save you time identifying them at the baggage carousel.

Packing garment bags

• Hang a number of clothes on no more than two hangers. If you use too many hangers, the bag will become bulky and hard to handle.

• Light plastic hangers with rounded corners work best. They don't rust, jab you with pointed ends, and they help keep clothes in their original shape.

• You can stuff an incredible number of small items into the bottom of a garment bag. The temptation to do so can result in a heavy bag!

Protecting and carrying valuables

The best way to protect and carry valuables such as a passport, plane tickets, traveler's checks, and money is to make or buy a secret pocket that slides under your clothes against your hip. It is attached by loops directly to your belt (see p. 133).

Companies specializing in travel items

You can buy travel odds and ends from the following companies, which specialize in such merchandise: Traveler's Checklist, Cornwall Bridge Road, Sharon, CT 06069; TravLTips Mart, Ltd., 163-09 Depot Road, Flushing, NY 11358.

Traveler's Checklist

A trip should start off relaxed, so pack well in advance of your departure. If you do, you will have a chance to check and recheck what's packed and to remember things you've overlooked.

Use this checklist to help you pack. It's an exhaustive list — choose those things that will be essential to your enjoyment of a European trip.

☐ **Adaptor.** Since currents vary from country to country, you'll need an adaptor to use with your electrical items. Adaptors are found in shops specializing in travel. My recommendation: do without electrical items completely!

☐ **Address book.** Don't leave home without a small, light, thin address book to fill with the names of new acquaintances and to refer to if you write home. Absolutely invaluable!

☐ **Alarm clock.** Take one only if you have important meetings abroad and don't want to rely on hotel wake-up services (which is smart). You'll find tiny travel alarm clocks on the market. Some watches also have built-in alarms.

☐ **Alcohol.** Take a quart of your favorite brand into Scandinavia, where prices are exorbitant. Don't bother when going to other areas, unless you have a penchant for bourbon (a rarity abroad).

☐ **Antacid.** Everyone should carry a few tablets. If you've got chronic problems, take all you could possibly need.

☐ **Aspirin.** A must. Take along one of the small plastic or metal boxes that contains at least a dozen tablets. Or put some into a small, easy-to-carry pillbox.

☐ **Band-Aids.** Bring a few. They're light and take up little space.

☐ **Bathing suit.** Bathing suits can double for underwear if they're easy to wash, quick drying, light, and comfortable. Fifteen minutes in the sun is all it takes to dry out a suit after swimming or washing. If you're skeptical, test the idea before you start a trip. Pick suits that don't bind or have tight elastic belts.

For a bathing suit that can be converted into a dress by adding a wraparound skirt: McCall's Pattern No. 6337.

☐ **Bathrobe.** Not essential and easily replaced by an overcoat or trench coat. Leave it at home!

☐ **Belt.** Men should bring one reversible or money belt. Women can easily replace belts with scarves, which are far more versatile and lightweight.

☐ **Birth certificate.** Essential for long-term study abroad. It must be translated into the foreign language. A notarized copy will be helpful if you lose your passport.

☐ **Birth control pills.** Bring extra, just in case you stay longer than you expect.

☐ **Black tie.** For the upper .1 percent (casino crowd).

☐ **Blazer.** A great idea. It should be made of tightly woven material, stain and wrinkle resistant, and dark colored. Spray it with water repellent to prevent stains.

☐ **Blouse.** Take two at most — one light colored, one dark (or print). They should be lightweight and easy to wash.

☐ **Boots.** Bring either one pair of boots or one pair of shoes, but not both. They should be broken in and very comfortable. You can always buy beautiful boots and shoes abroad, if you run into a special occasion demanding elegant footwear!

☐ **Bottle opener.** One of the most useful and easy-to-forget items! Get a Swiss Army knife with an opener on it.

☐ **Bra.** Bring no more than two. Substitute a bikini top if possible.

☐ **Calamine lotion.** Great for relieving the itching of insect bites and bee stings, but rarely needed.

☐ **Calculator.** A thin, ultralight model for currency exchange and bargaining.

☐ **Camera and film.** Great to have, but a hassle. Bring only if you're serious.

☐ **Camping carnet (the camper's "passport").** Essential for campers (see p. 124).

☐ **Can opener.** Absolutely essential, if you'll be shopping in grocery stores for picnics. Some Swiss Army knives come with these. Get a good one.

☐ **Cards, playing.** Easy to forget, but a wonderful way to while away the hours on planes and trains.

☐ **Chapstick.** Essential. The very things that cause chapped lips are also the most enjoyable: eating, drinking, kissing, and outdoor activities, all of which result in a loss of essential lip oils. Chapstick and tinted lipsticks with moisturizers contain both petroleum jelly and sunscreens to make them useful all year 'round.

☐ **Coats.** Bring one only. (See Raincoat, Trench coat, Overcoat, and Poncho.)

☐ **Collapsible cups.** Lightweight, easy to use.

☐ **Comb.** Essential.

☐ **Corkscrew.** Get a Swiss Army knife with one of these on it.

☐ **Credit cards.** Increasingly helpful, with many travel advantages.

☐ **Cufflinks.** Take shirts that don't require them. Just a nuisance.

☐ **Cummerbund.** The same.

☐ **Curling iron.** Can you get by without one? If not, make sure it's the lightweight, flat, plastic kind. (See Adaptor.)

☐ **Currency.** Bring $50 dollars in small American bills to avoid the currency exchange rip-off. Carry only the amount of cash you can afford to lose.

☐ **Decongestant.** Prone to earaches on planes? Take a decongestant before flying.

☐ **Dental floss.** Easy to forget. An unusual use: it cuts through cheese easily, making perfect thin strips for a picnic! It can also replace thread (very strong, durable).

☐ **Deodorant.** Take a small stick — not an aerosol can (such cans may explode on planes).

☐ **Desenex.** Bring one small tube, if you're susceptible to athlete's foot.

☐ **Dinner jacket.** Hardly a necessity for most travelers. A dark sports coat is usually acceptable attire even in stuffy places.

☐ **Dress.** Take one at most. It should be wrinkle resistant, easy to wash, and easy to dress up or down. Dresses of double-knit cotton T-shirt material are excellent.

If the dress gets clingy on the trip, hang it in the bathroom while you take a shower or bath. The steam will be absorbed to prevent static electricity.

☐ **Dress shirt.** Rarely needed and easily replaced with a nice white shirt.

☐ **Drugs.** Take as many prescription drugs as you'll need for the entire length of the trip, plus enough for a week or two to spare. Carry prescriptions with you if you remove drugs from the original containers. And be sure to learn their generic names, in case you lose them.

☐ **Ear plugs.** If you're sensitive to noise, these are just great on planes and in noisy hotels. Get the easy-to-mold kind, like *Flents.* I'd suggest that all travelers carry ear plugs, just in case.

☐ **Electric razor.** No, don't take one. It's nothing but a hassle. If you have to, try the battery-operated models. Small, light travel kits consisting of a compact safety razor and blades make a lot more sense.

☐ **Eurailpass, BritRailpass.** It's safest and easiest to buy them in the U.S. before you leave. (see p. 59).

☐ **Evening bag.** Not necessary, but nice at times. Maybe you should buy one abroad.

☐ **First-aid kit.** Required for auto travel abroad (see p. 64)

☐ **Fishnet shopping bag.** Very smart to have. Light, compact, useful. Highly recommended.

☐ **Flashlight.** All motorists and travelers in Greece, Ireland, Portugal, and Yugoslavia should have one. So should campers in any country. Bring spare batteries.

☐ **Garters.** Only if you can't do without.

☐ **Girdle.** Likewise.

☐ **Glasses.** One spare pair of both sunglasses and prescription glasses.

☐ **Gloves.** Only when necessary, as for off-season travel and when traveling by motorcycle.

☐ **Hairbrush.** Essential.

☐ **Hair dryer.** Another gadget requiring an adaptor. Women for centuries got by without them. Can't you? (see Adaptor.)

☐ **Hair conditioner.** If you use it, bring it with you, because it's hard to find in Europe. Make sure it's in a plastic container, tightly sealed, and placed in a plastic bag. Or carry travel packets given away as samples or as bonuses in hotels.

☐ **Hair spray.** Get by without it, if possible. Take a small plastic container with pump, if not.

☐ **Halter.** Useful as a T-shirt or bra (or both).

☐ **Hangers.** Plastic or inflatable hangers work great. Many hotels do not provide them or have the kind that cannot be moved around — useless for washing clothes.

☐ **Hankies.** Use disposable tissues instead. Buy some as necessary in Europe.

☐ **Hat.** Highly recommended is a cloth or khaki fisherman-style hat, deep enough to stay on your head in heavy winds, with a wide brim to protect you from rain or sun. Spray it with water repellent. It may be frumpy looking, but it will do the job!

☐ **Health certificate.** Needed only for extended foreign study. It must be translated into the foreign language.

☐ **Heater, immersible.** A very clever gadget that heats up water quickly, but needed only for long-term travel. You can usually get water hot enough for tea or hot chocolate by letting the faucet run. (See Adaptor.)

☐ **Helmet.** Required of motorcyclists, who will get fined for disobeying the law if they don't wear them. Get a helmet with a bubble to protect your face from rain, sleet, and bugs.

☐ **Hostel card.** All hostelers should have one (see p. 122).

☐ **Insect repellent.** Only necessary for campers and ardent bathers. Get the strongest stuff available, in small plastic containers.

☐ **International driver's license.** Don't leave home without one if you intend to drive in Europe (see p. 14)

☐ **International student identification card.** Every student should take along one of these for travel in Europe (see p. 15).

☐ **Iron.** Don't bring one. Instead, take clothes that are wrinkle resistant or wrinkle-proof.

☐ **Jacket.** Fine for casual travel, but don't bring one if you're taking an overcoat.

☐ **Jeans.** Accepted almost everywhere, even in sophisticated places. Europe has gone casual, imitating the millions of youthful American vagabonds. Simple is best, and jeans typify the trend.

Jeans make excellent ski pants if you spray them with water repellent.

☐ **Jewelry.** Leave it at home. Or wear simple, all-purpose jewelry that you'll never take off. Scarves are much better and more versatile as a way of adding fantasy to your wardrobe.

☐ **Knapsack.** One of the smartest ways of carrying weight, if you can't force yourself to travel light. Also a very good item for trekking. Only in the more expensive hotels would knapsacks be frowned upon.

☐ **Knife.** Essential. Get a good Swiss Army knife with a bottle opener, can opener, corkscrew, scissors, and tweezers. With recent airline restrictions you may have to buy one abroad if you travel light (knives may not be allowed in carry-on luggage).

☐ **Laces.** Change the laces on your shoes or boots before going to Europe. This way you won't have to take along a spare set.

☐ **Laundry soap.** Get a few travel packets.

☐ **Lighter.** Take one if needed. Or take several. Lighters make great gifts, especially in Portugal.

☐ **Lomotil.** A very strong medicine that works wonders for diarrhea and requires a prescription from your doctor. Get some and bring it!

☐ **Magic marker.** Ideal for making signs if you'll be hitchhiking. It should be permanent ink, which won't run in the rain.

☐ **Maps.** Get the best available, in a light and easy-to-handle form. Free maps are sent out by tourist offices. If you're a member of travel or auto clubs, they'll often provide maps free of charge. Highly detailed maps are available in bookstores abroad.

☐ **Mirror.** One tiny pocket mirror is enough.

☐ **Money clip.** Not necessary and a come-on to crooks.

☐ **Moleskin.** Dr. Scholl's adhesive felt — better for blisters than Band-Aids.

☐ **Nail clippers.** Easy to carry and worth bringing.

☐ **Nail file.** The same.

☐ **Nail polish and remover.** Can you get by without it? If not, put polish in a plastic bag. It's simply disastrous when polish leaks on your clothes. Note that remover comes in tiny travel packets — easy to use and carry.

☐ **Nasal spray.** Great for hay fever victims. Also good if you're prone to earaches on planes.

☐ **Needle and thread.** Bring one needle and a little thread (off the spool). If you have trouble threading the needle, dip the thread in nail polish. To shield the point during your trip, poke the needle into half a dozen twist ties.

☐ **Nightgown.** Almost all experienced women travelers replace a nightgown with a T-shirt.

☐ **Nylons.** Bring no more than two pairs of nylons or kneehighs per travel week. If nylons get baggy, just dip your hands in warm water and rub them from the ankles up.

To stop a run: use a dab of nail polish.

In desperation: if the opposite legs of two pairs of panty hose have been damaged, cut them off. Then wear both as if they were one pair.

☐ **Overcoat.** If you take an overcoat, get one made of tightly woven material that doesn't pick up lint, doesn't stain easily, and doesn't wrinkle. Take one coat that best matches your style of travel. Spray the coat with water repellent so that it can double as a raincoat; it can also be used as a bathrobe when you trip down the hall to take a bath. It makes a good blanket in a freezing train compartment: wrap it loosely around yourself like a straitjacket to trap your body heat and keep you warm.

You may want to have a button-down flap or zipper sewn on the inside pocket.

This will protect anything placed there from pickpockets and keep things from falling out accidentally. You may also want to sew in extra pockets — a very simple technique to increase what you can carry on your body.

☐ **Pajamas.** Totally unnecessary. It's this kind of thing that's got to go if you're going to travel light.

☐ **Panties.** You can substitute a bathing suit for one pair. Since they're so light, you can bring several pairs — all nylon for fast drying.

☐ **Pants.** Don't carry more than two pairs, one of which should be jeans. The other pair should be easy to wash and dark-colored to hide stains.

☐ **Paper clips.** Bring a few. If you have a visa, place a clip on that page of your passport to make it easy to find.

☐ **Passport.** If you forget this, forget the trip. **Carry your passport with you at all times and guard it with everything but your life!** You'll need it when exchanging currency, cashing traveler's checks, picking up mail at **poste restante** (general delivery) or at American Express, signing in at the hotel, and whenever the police ask to see it. If you're involved in a traffic accident abroad and are not carrying your passport, you may end up in the clink.

☐ **Passport wallet.** A good way to carry a passport, currency, credit cards, papers, etc.

☐ **Pen.** One of the most useful items abroad. Bring one or two.

☐ **Photos.** Photomat photos can be used in a number of ways — for an international driver's license, for study abroad (identification papers), ski-lift passes, etc. It's a good idea to carry a few extras.

☐ **Plastic bags.** Bring along the size and number appropriate to your style of travel. Possible uses: to hold bottles containing liquids, to carry soiled or damp clothes (such as a swimsuit), to protect clothes from the rain (as in backpacking), to sit on at picnics or spectator sports, to hold food while in a car (plastic keeps banana and cheese odors contained).

☐ **Plastic flask.** A gem, to be filled with water, booze, fruit juice, or whatever. Great for long plane rides when you don't want to rely on the whim of a stewardess, and especially good for car and train travel. Also a good way to avoid the high liquor prices in hotels (who doesn't drink in a room these days?). Don't leave home without one or two flasks!

You may prefer metal to plastic. Metal stands up to abuse and doesn't absorb odors.

☐ **Poncho.** Although this is a good replacement for an overcoat, the latter will prove more versatile.

☐ **Purse.** Don't be timid! Carry a huge purse with room to spare. Forget about style. It should have tight-fitting clasps to prevent spills and thwart thieves.

Within a larger purse you can use smaller cosmetic cases for odds and ends. These keep things from getting jumbled together in one large mess.

☐ **Radio.** Leave it at home. If that's not possible, bring a minuscule transistor radio with a few spare batteries. Sell it before returning home. Every maid you meet will want it. Do not play your radio on a plane, because it can interfere with instruments!

☐ **Raincoat.** Replace this with a trench coat or overcoat, both of which can be sprayed with water repellent.

☐ **Rain gear.** Essential for backpackers, hitchhikers, and motorcyclists. Get the best money can buy with rugged seams, snap-tight cuffs, and a durable hood.

☐ **Razor.** Take one with a few extra blades. Minuscule travel kits are on the market.

☐ **Rollers.** Can you make it without them? Can you change your hairstyle to make them unnecessary? If your hair gets a little messy, use the standby technique of covering it with a scarf. If you do bring rollers, here's a tip for a quick set: roll dry hair, cover with damp towel for five minutes, remove it, and let hair dry.

You can get free or inexpensive washes and sets in many foreign beauty schools. Ask the concierge to look them up in the foreign telephone book.

☐ **Rubber baggage tie-down straps.** The best way to hold gear on a motorcycle.

☐ **Rubber or nylon braided clothesline.** Inexpensive, light, and useful. Great for hanging up wet clothes in limited spaces.

A note: never let foreign maids see them, or they'll take them from you. Technically, you're not supposed to do laundry in hotel rooms (but everyone does).

☐ **Safety pins.** Bring a few. Use them to keep your pockets closed to protect your wallet.

☐ **Sandals.** Buy an inexpensive pair abroad when needed.

☐ **Sanitary products.** Take tampons and a few minipads. Also available in Europe at pharmacies.

☐ **Scarves.** Just like gold to women travelers, because they're stylish, lightweight, compact, and versatile (they can be used as belts, skirts, and even shawls). Scarves replace jewelry, transforming one outfit into many.

You must cover your head with a scarf in most Roman Catholic churches in Europe.

☐ **School transcript.** Students who wish to study abroad must have a school transcript with a seal imprinted on it. It must be translated into the foreign language.

☐ **Scissors.** The small travel scissors prove useful, but are not indispensable.

☐ **Seeds.** You may think this item's for the birds, but packaged flower seeds from home make a great gift, a wonderful way to say thanks to a foreign host. Since they're lightweight and easy to carry, think about bringing some.

☐ **Shampoo.** Bring as little as you can get by with in a plastic container. Little packets from beauty shops and hotels are ideal for travel.

☐ **Shirt.** Two at most. They should be easy to wash and dry. Dark colors are best.

☐ **Shoes.** Take one pair of your most comfortable walking shoes. Don't bring shoes that need polishing. You don't want to worry constantly about how they look, and you want to avoid the hassle of having shoeshine boys tagging along behind you.

You can replace shoes with boots, but don't take both. Make sure they're comfortable.

Women's shoes should be comfortable and durable. Do not worry about how they look. When you travel, you can overlook style. If you need an elegant pair of shoes for a special occasion, buy a pair in Europe.

Do not wear high heels. Much of the enjoyment of travel comes from walking ancient streets and visiting hard-to-reach sights. High, thin heels are forbidden in many museums and castles, because they damage the floors!

☐ **Shoe polish.** If you follow the advice under "Shoes," this becomes an unnecessary item.

☐ **Shorts.** Replace with a bathing suit in resort areas. Elsewhere, put on pants, skirt, or dress. In Europe, shorts are for tennis courts only.

☐ **Shower cap.** If needed, get the light plastic kind found in hotel rooms. It scrunches down to nothing. On the other hand, you can wrap your head in a towel like a turban and do without a cap.

☐ **Ski jacket.** A good replacement for an overcoat if you'll be hitchhiking, skiing, or cycling. Make sure it's down filled or made with top-quality down substitute (like Polargard).

☐ **Skirt.** Bring one at the most. It must be easy to wash, dark colored to hide stains, and wrinkle resistant.

A long, print skirt with a drawstring or elastic waist can be worn higher, like a muumuu. And it makes a nice bathrobe. Create one yourself from Butterick Pattern No. 5387. For a skirt-dress combination, try Butterick Pattern No. 6140.

☐ **Slacks.** You need no more than one pair. Some come with drawstrings — very useful for fluctuating weight!

☐ **Sleeping bag.** If you'll be camping out, get the best and most compact you can afford. A bulky item that should be carried only if necessary.

☐ **Sleeping pills.** Get a few from your doctor to help you with jet lag.

☐ **Sleeping sheet.** Required in hostels. You can make or buy one (see p. 122).

☐ **Slippers.** Unnecessary. If you disagree, get the fabric kind that fold into a tiny package.

☐ **Slip.** No more than one, if any at all.

☐ **Soap.** Take small, individually wrapped bars — the kind you find in hotels. Tuck them into a plastic soap dish. Some hotels offer soap, some don't.

Liquid soap may be more manageable than bars and

can be found in plastic containers. In a pinch, use shampoo or shaving cream for soap: both work well.

Empty film containers with rubber tops make excellent containers for powdered soap and detergent.

☐ **Socks.** One pair to wear and one for a spare — of synthetic material. Both wool and cotton hold up well, but are difficult to wash and take a long time to dry. That's why synthetics are better for travel.

Many hotels do not have stoppers in the sink. A sock works well as a replacement.

To wash socks quickly: put them on your hands like surgeon's gloves and scrub them with a bar of soap.

☐ **Spare keys.** All motorists should have one set of spare keys, best stored in a small magnetic box that can be hidden anywhere on the car.

☐ **Sports coat.** Only necessary if you plan to dress up occasionally — that is, if you'll be staying in nicer hotels and going to fancier restaurants. Take one that's lightweight, but not a wash-and-wear jacket, which will end up looking like a used handkerchief after two days.

Tweed is one of the better materials, because it's tough and rarely looks like it needs cleaning, even if it really does. Corduroys are OK. So are some double knits.

Choose a dark color. It's going to be stained at some time during the trip, so let the stains disappear in a dark brown or blue sea of color.

Spray the coat with water repellent. You'll get rained on for sure, and the repellent will fend off dirt as well.

The inside pocket should have a button-down flap or a zipper to lock in its contents. This can be added at home or inexpensively at a dry cleaner's specializing in simple garment repairs and alterations. If you forget to have this done, use a safety pin to fasten the top of the pocket.

☐ **Spot remover.** This should be unnecessary if you travel with easy-to-wash clothes. But if you must, **Goddard's** is one of the best.

☐ **Stamps.** Colorful American stamps — the lightest, least expensive, most appreciated, simplest gift to carry for foreigners you meet.

☐ **Stole.** Another .1 percent item.

☐ **Studs.** The same.

☐ **Suit.** Unnecessary, except when on business trips. An attractive sports coat can replace a suit almost everywhere.

☐ **Suntan lotion.** If needed, bring one small plastic bottle or buy some in Europe.

☐ **Sweater.** One at most, none if possible. If you take one, wear it to save precious packing space.

☐ **Tape.** Occasionally helpful, but not indispensable.

☐ **Tent.** If you'll be camping out, bring a light one. And be sure to try it out before taking it to Europe.

☐ **Tickets.** Easy to forget, but don't!

☐ **Tie.** One at most. Spray it with water repellent. This will make it easy to remove any stains!

☐ **Toilet paper.** Tuck a small wad into your purse or wallet. Refill as necessary. This may seem comical — it isn't, as you will find out.

☐ **Toothbrush and paste.** Bring a small tube and replenish as needed.

☐ **Towel.** A real hassle to carry, but many European hotels give you miniature versions of the real thing.

☐ **Tranquilizers.** Get a few from your doctor, just in case.

☐ **Traveler's checks.** Most money should be carried in this form (see p. 15).

☐ **Trench coat.** Take either one trench coat or one overcoat — but don't take both. Trench coats should have removable linings. These linings make good pillows.

If your coat has a flimsy pocket, replace it with a deep and solid one. This will give you added space and protection. The pocket should have a button-down flap or a zipper. Add extra pockets, if you have the time. They'll come in handy.

And be sure to spray the coat with water repellent, which will protect it from stains and rain.

☐ **Triangle danger sign.** Required by law for motorists in Europe (see p. 64).

☐ **T-shirt.** You'll probably live in it. You can also sleep in it.

☐ **Tucks.** Available at drugstores, Tucks will be of interest to hemorrhoid sufferers.

☐ **Turtlenecks.** Not recommended, because they're hard to wash and dry slowly. However, they do not wrinkle.

☐ **Tweezers.** A good little item that takes up very little space and often comes in handy. Some Swiss Army knives have tweezers on them.

☐ **Umbrella.** Bring one that folds down to less than 14 inches long. If you shop around, you'll find one for a steal. Put the umbrella in one of the outside pockets of your carry-on bag.

☐ **Underwear.** Use the new, synthetic-fiber underwear: easy to wash, quick drying, and very colorful. Underwear can easily be replaced by bathing suits.

☐ **Velcro.** Replaces buttons nicely.

☐ **Visas.** Necessary for long-term study abroad and for travel in eastern European countries (see p. 12).

☐ **Washcloth.** Do they exist in Europe? If you must have one, bring it along!

☐ **Watch.** Toothpaste will help clean a fuzzy crystal.

☐ **Wet Ones.** These pre-moistened cloths, available in drugstores are not necessary but are nice.

☐ **Windbreaker.** Good in the Mediterranean areas and anywhere along the Atlantic. Can be used in place of a shirt. Or simply buy what's known as a wind shirt.

☐ **Woolite.** Bring a few travel packets, if you have any woolen items along.

9 Final Steps

Few travel books will tell you about steps you can take to give yourself peace of mind while away from your home or apartment. An important part of the relaxation you deserve on a vacation depends upon these precautions. With more than 2 million burglaries a year in the U.S., it's a reasonable concern.

Home Security Checklist

☐ Cover or screen garage windows so that a potential burglar will not know if your cars are gone. Bring tools inside from the garage.

☐ Set timers on lights to turn them on and off at varying intervals.

☐ Put valuables and important documents in a safety deposit box.

☐ Never talk about upcoming trips with strangers.

☐ Get an engraving pen and I.D. number from the local police and mark your valuables. Put "Operation Identification" stickers on doors and windows.

☐ Make sure basement windows are locked or protected with grilles.

☐ Place removable drop bars on sliding glass doors.

☐ Never leave spare keys in their "secret" hiding place while you're gone.

☐ If you leave your car at an airport parking lot while you're away, don't leave a house key on your car keychain.

☐ Leave window shades and blinds in different positions, the way you would if you were at home.

☐ Get the post office and newspaper to stop delivery a day before you leave.

☐ Ask a neighbor to pick up any letters, packages, or papers that may get through.

☐ Have a lawn boy continue to keep up your garden and lawn.

☐ Ask your neighbor to park his car in your driveway — occasionally.

☐ Have him fill up a garbage can or two with his trash from time to time.

☐ Set the bell of your telephone at its lowest ring so that any potential burglar will not hear it go unanswered from outside the house or apartment. If you have plug-in style phones, unplug them for the same reason.

☐ If your trip has been announced in a local paper for any reason, hire a house sitter. Burglars use these announcements as one of their main sources of information.

☐ Never leave notes outside the house.

☐ Steal the most valuable items from a potential thief by carting TVs, radios, stereos, guns, and so on, to the house of a neighbor or friend.

☐ Make sure your insurance policy is paid for and up-to-date.

Plant Care While You're Gone

No one wants to spend weeks, months, or years growing beautiful house plants, only to return to a withered mass of brown mold or leafy splinters. To avoid these losses, use a plant sitter, especially if you'll be gone three weeks or longer.

Using a plant sitter

• Give the sitter a key and basic instructions on care.

• Put an identifying mark or a reminder note on each plant needing special care (misting, infrequent watering, etc.).

Doing without a plant sitter

If you'll be gone less than three weeks, you can get by without a plant sitter.

• Remove all dead leaves, flowers, and buds.

• Place a plastic bag on the bottom of your tub and cover it with several layers of newspaper.

• Spray the paper with water until it's thoroughly moist.

• Cover the paper with another sheet of plastic and sprinkle it with water as well.

• Soak plants thoroughly, allowing excess water to drain completely before setting them on the plastic.

• When all your plants are in the tub, cover them with a plastic sheet and tape it in place. Poke some holes in it to let air circulate.

• Leave the bathroom shades up (or turn on the light if there are no windows).

• If you have more plants than your tub holds, or in the case of huge plants, group them away from direct sunlight and follow the same general procedure to trap humidity after a thorough soaking and draining. Poke holes in your plastic coverings to ventilate plants.

The Last Few Days

The way you handle the minor details of any trip in the last few days before going abroad could make a major difference in averting problems.

Three days before your flight

- Reconfirm your flight reservation, according to the procedure outlined on your ticket.

- Get the name of the person you are speaking to and note the day and time you call.

- If you should get bumped from your flight, this procedure gives you grounds for legal action.

- More importantly, this call will usually drastically lower the odds of your being bumped at all.

The day before your flight

- Check to make sure no mail or papers are delivered.

- Take the pets to the place where they'll be staying.

- Check through the things you'll be taking (see pp. 84-93).

- Make a list of what's in each bag. If a bag gets lost, you'll be able to identify its contents exactly. When the bag is opened after three days, you and it can be reunited quickly.

The day of your flight

- Call the airport to ask whether your flight will be leaving on time. If you are a member of a tour, you'll usually be informed about any delays, but if you are an individual traveler, this would be rare indeed.

- Turn down the heat in your house (if it's possible).

- Water the plants for the last time.

- Make sure the house is secure, all windows and doors locked.

Getting to the airport

- Figure out how long it takes to get to the airport. Then allow an extra 45 minutes for delays and traffic jams.

- Add another 30 minutes for Friday and Sunday nights or for either Los Angeles International or New York's JFK.

- Now add another hour if you intend to register items with customs (see p. 98).

- To avoid the congestion around the terminal, park in one of the more remote parking lots. If you are traveling light, you won't mind the walk!

At the Airport

All you want to do is get to the airport, check your luggage, walk through the security check, and board the plane with a minimum of delay and hassle. Today, that's asking quite a lot.

Checking bags

Over a million bags are lost per year. The best way not to lose luggage is to travel so lightly that you never have to check anything!

- Check in with time to spare. Most luggage that's lost is checked in less than a 30 minutes before flight time. **Never use curbside baggage-check service if you're running late.**

- Put your name, address, and phone number on a sticker inside the luggage. Lost bags are opened after three days if they haven't been claimed. The sticker on the inside will get your bag back to you, particularly if you include a note with a dated itinerary.

- Remove tags and stickers from past trips. They make handling difficult.

- At check-in, watch to make sure that each bag is tagged and placed on the conveyor belt. Never assume that either step has happened.

- Keep your claim check in a safe place — or have it stapled to your ticket folder. You'll need to show it to claim your baggage.

Protecting your belongings

- Lock and strap every bag. Straps keep bags from popping open, even under grueling conditions, and they discourage pilfering, an increasing problem.

- Never pack cash, documents, fragile items, furs, jewelry, medicine — anything valuable or hard to replace — in your checked baggage. These should always be carried onto the plane. Baggage containing expensive items is sometimes "lost" on purpose. Furthermore, the airline will not reimburse you for such things.

- Baggage insurance, available at a set price per $100 of declared value, can be purchased to cover more expensive items. Note that it rarely pays off at full face value. Leave expensive things at home!

- Never leave bags unattended anywhere for any reason. Ask someone you trust to watch them or take them with you — even to the WC.

Registering valuables

It's best to register valuable items before you get to the airport, but if you forget, do it there. Otherwise, when you come back to the U.S., you may have to pay duty on items that you did not actually purchase in Europe.

• You'll find registration booths in international airports as a part of the Customs Department.

• You'll be asked to fill out a small white form with pertinent information, including a description of the article and serial numbers when applicable. **You must have the items with you in order to register them!** The official will check over the information, verify it, stamp the form, and give it to you as proof that you had these items before going abroad. The slip is valid for all future trips, so don't throw it away.

• If you have items to register, allow yourself an extra hour for the process. Occasionally, the booths are closed — it's inexcusable, but true.

Boarding a plane

It all used to be so simple. All you had to do was tie a string on your finger and point yourself toward the plane. It's not quite so easy nowadays. To get on a plane, you need a ticket, a boarding pass, and in most cases a seat-selection card.

• If you don't have your ticket yet, you'll wait in line.

• If you have to check baggage, you'll wait in line.

• However, with a ticket in hand and bags either with you or checked, you can proceed straight to the boarding gate. If you arrive too late, you may lose your seat.

Security and customs

To get to the gate, you'll have to pass through a security check. In a crowded airport, this can take 45 minutes or longer.

• If it's obvious that you're in danger of missing your plane, go right to the front of the line and calmly explain your predicament to security personnel.

• Under no circumstances should you make joking remarks about hijackings, bombs, or drugs!

- If you get hassled for carrying a Swiss Army knife, have them put it in a package to be given to the stewardess on your flight. If they refuse this courtesy, have them put it in an envelope to be sent to your home.

- On some international flights, you'll pass through a customs inspection, which may add another 30 minutes' delay. Start for the gate as soon as possible.

At the boarding area

- Unless you already have a seat assignment and boarding pass, you'll wait in line at the counter at the boarding area. You'll be given both at this time.

- Until you have a boarding pass in your hand, you essentially have nothing — except a contract that gives you specific legal rights. In short, you can still be bumped.

- When the plane is ready for boarding, the flight will be announced. If you do not board the plane when you're supposed to, your seat can be given to a standby.

Seat assignments

- Ask for a seat away from the galleys, partitions, or toilets.

- Choose an aisle seat if you have long legs. If not, choose a window seat.

- If you are traveling with one other person, reserve the window and aisle seats in a three-seat section. Few people select middle seats unless a plane is fully booked. If someone should sit down there, just switch seats with him so that you and your friend can sit together. If no one shows up, it will be easy for one of you to find a single seat while the other person sleeps. This way you can guarantee yourself at least a few hours of slumber.

- Find out whether there are any infants traveling on your flight. Stewardesses like to seat parents with young children in the first row of seats behind the partition nearest the galley; so if you relish peace and quiet on a long flight, choose a seat far enough away from that first row.

- If you're traveling alone, be the last person to board. Look for a block of three unoccupied seats. If you board late enough, most stewardesses will allow you to sit anywhere.

- If they go by the book and force you to take an assigned seat, agree. You can move as soon as the cabin door is locked.

Problems with Flights

This section gives you information about problems that you may run into when flying and strategies to help you cope with them.

Lost airline tickets

- Whenever you buy an airline ticket, write down the ticket number, date and place of purchase, and method of payment. Carry this information separately from your ticket — perhaps on the same piece of paper as your list of traveler's check numbers.

- If you lose a ticket or have one stolen, **immediately** go to or call the refund department of the airline from which you bought the ticket. You'll be asked to fill out a refund application.

- If you want to replace the ticket, you'll have to buy a new one, using the original form of payment. (If you paid for the original ticket with a credit card, your account can be credited immediately for the lost or stolen ticket. If you paid with cash or by check, you will be reimbursed only after a 120-day waiting period. This is one big advantage of using credit cards!)

- You're liable for the loss should the ticket be used illegally during the 120-day waiting period.

- You may be given a card to send in for a refund after the waiting period is over. If you don't send it in, you will not get the refund.

- In short, treat airline tickets like cash and expect nothing but grief if you lose one!

Getting bumped by airlines

Your plane ticket is a legal contract with an airline. It guarantees your right to the flight, under specific conditions.

- An international ticket is valid only if you reconfirm your flight within 72 hours of departure. Always get the agent's name when you reconfirm a flight.

- You must arrive at the airport within the time limit specified on your ticket. If you do not confirm your flight or if you arrive late, the airline can sell your seat to another person (bump you from the flight) — legally! If you do reconfirm your flight and arrive on time, the airline cannot legally sell your seat. However, airlines do so — about 150,000 times a year.

Voluntary and involuntary bumping

Nowadays, airlines ask for volunteers to be bumped for a sum of money that varies with each airline and situation. If there are not enough volunteers, then some people will be bumped involuntarily. This could include you.

- If this happens to you, ask for a written statement outlining compensation for being denied boarding. Depending upon the value of your ticket, you'll be paid a minimum to a maximum amount as denied boarding compensation (DBC). This money is yours for the inconvenience caused you by having been bumped.

- Note that DBC is only paid to passengers bumped from flights that actually take place (not canceled or delayed flights). It's meant only to discourage overbooking, which airlines do to survive.

- If an airline cannot get you to your original destination within two hours of the original scheduled arrival time for a domestic flight, or within four hours for an international flight, the DBC must be doubled, and the airline still must get you to your destination.

- Naturally, it's to your advantage to work out all problems with the airline on a fair, even-handed basis.

Taking it to court

You are under no obligation to accept DBC, since you can take the matter to civil court. The odds are against you there, however. And it's an unbelievable hassle.

- Don't accept DBC if you plan to take your case to court. Once you accept the compensation, the affair is closed. You have no further legal redress.

- Be sure you have a case before you act. The airline does **not** have to pay DBC if the government takes over a plane (very rare), if a smaller plane is substituted for the original aircraft (occasionally happens), if you have not reconfirmed your flight, or if you check in later than the time specified on your ticket.

Flight cancellation

If your flight is canceled, the airline should get you on the next available flight. It will do little good to complain about the cancellation.

- Note that each country has its standard of what's expected in this situation. As long as you're being treated the same as other passengers, don't make a scene.

Changes of fares

Once you have paid for and received a ticket, you cannot be charged more money to board a plane within the U.S. However, in Europe you may be forced to pay whatever fare is applicable on that day.

• Be sure to ask the airline what its policy is when purchasing a ticket for international flights.

Flight delays

• When a flight is delayed after initial boarding has started, the airline is obligated to provide meals, lodging, transportation, and a free phone call to each passenger.

• If you have not started to board a plane and a delay is announced, you have no legal right to demand compensation of any kind. Nevertheless, most airlines will provide necessary amenities to stranded passengers.

• You will usually be given a voucher for a set-price meal and, in extreme cases, even a free hotel room.

• If the airline does not volunteer such things, don't hesitate to ask — and be polite, firm, and fair in your request.

Changing travel dates

Most discounted tickets require passengers to fly within specific time periods, with no changes allowed. If you try to make a change, the airline may ask you to pay full fare. This rule can be overridden for humanitarian reasons, and it's up to the airline to decide what that means in any given case.

• Note that you can take out special insurance to cover changes in travel plans caused by illness or death in the family.

In-flight precautions

• Never leave money, valuable papers, or your passport unattended at any moment on a plane. They should be carried on your person at all times — even when you go to the bathroom! And this advice goes double for when you get off the plane during a stopover.

• Get up and stretch occasionally; it will keep your body relaxed.

- Water and juice served on board will not be enough fluid to prevent dehydration, which is one of the factors leading to jet lag. Bring a flask or bottle of cold water or juice to drink on the flight. (The water on board is usually lukewarm.)

Disinfecting aircraft

- If you're allergic to ragweed, you can get very sick from the pyrethrin insecticide sprays that are occasionally used in planes during a flight.

- If you see spraying, immediately warn the flight attendant of your allergy.

- Cover your nose with a wet cloth.

Jet lag

When people cross a number of time zones, they experience something known as jet lag. The condition, a foul-up of the natural body rhythms, varies from mild to dangerous, depending upon the person and his or her physical condition. People with strong internal clocks (who wake up each morning at exactly the same time without an alarm) tend to have marked jet lag.

- Any person 50 or older who has diabetes, high blood pressure, or either pulmonary or arterial problems should consult a doctor before crossing many time zones. Jet lag has recently been linked to heart attacks.

- Jet lag symptoms: fatigue, irritability, anxiety, headache, insomnia, and hunger in the middle of the night.

Avoiding jet lag

- Go to bed early for three or four days before flying abroad. This will prepare your body for the time change to come.

- Don't make a marathon of any trip. Break long trips into smaller segments, taking advantage of stopover opportunities.

- A simple solution: take a morning flight abroad, which will allow you to recoup in about 12 hours. Night flights are more exhausting and require about 24 hours of cold storage (according to doctors). Unfortunately, night flights are the most common.

- If possible, take a weekend flight and allow for one day of rest.

- Drink lots of nonalcoholic fluids to reduce the effects of jet lag.

Strategies for night flights

- If you have to fly at night, sleep through the entire trip. If you have to take a sleeping pill, do it. Don't try booze — martini poisoning combined with jet lag can be lethal (almost).

- Use pillows and blankets (in the compartment above your seat) to get comfortable and warm.

- Take off your shoes and loosen all tight-fitting clothing.

- Use ear plugs and eye masks. (Who cares what you look like? They work!)

- Draw the shades and tell the stewardess not to bother you, not even for snacks and meals.

- If you can't sleep, go easy on food.

Once you arrive

On arriving in Europe, plan to go right to bed, even if it's still light out. Get as much sleep as you can without worrying about getting in tune with the new time schedule.

- If that's impossible, at least go to bed early.

- Eat sparingly for two days as your body becomes accustomed to new mealtimes.

- Businessmen should never rush off to meetings without enough rest to get them physically and mentally prepared for tough decisions.

Anti-jet-lag diet

The Argonne National Laboratory claims that a special three-day diet will help your body quickly adjust to a new time zone. For a free copy send a self-addressed, stamped envelope to Argonne National Laboratory, 9700 South Cass Avenue, Argonne, IL 60439.

Part II: The Trip

---

10 Arriving in Europe

It's a fairly straightforward process getting from the airport to the hotel, but things can and do go wrong. The hints in this section deal with customs, obtaining foreign currency, handling luggage, and finding a way to your hotel.

Foreign Customs and Currency Exchanges

Most people are a little bit nervous going through customs, and that's natural. However, anyone who seems overly nervous or who makes jokes may find himself going through a customs check.

In some airports you'll find two gates set aside for incoming passengers. One is marked "Nothing to declare." Naturally, if you have nothing to declare, you simply walk through the gate and out to the real world. Of course, you can still be stopped for a spot check. But normally, a person carrying very little baggage sails through customs!

Common customs questions

- Never volunteer information while going through customs! You'll seem suspicious if you do.

- Customs officials can ask you to tell them the exact amount of money you're bringing in and in what form you've got it. If you're low on money, tell them you plan to stay only a week or so in the country, and that you plan to stay with a friend (have a name and address ready). But only say these things if they ask.

- Always tell officials that your reason for travel is pleasure.

- Say that all belongings are for your personal use, unless it's obvious that you're bringing in a gift.

- Never go through customs with illegal drugs, not even a small amount of marijuana. Do not carry more than a quart of liquor or a carton of cigarettes.

• Remove all film from its boxes to show that you have no intention of reselling it. You can usually avoid paying duties on large quantities of film for your personal use in this way.

Getting foreign currency

• Note: the rate of exchange is usually poor at airports and other locations where travelers are most dependent on the service.

• Exchange only enough to cover costs from the airport to your hotel (usually $20 is enough).

Luggage Handling

Your luggage presents you with many possibilities for trouble. Of course, the lighter you travel, the less the likelihood of snags — but here are a few helpful ideas to avoid them.

Getting a porter

Once you're through customs you can hire a porter (though porters are a vanishing breed). Most travelers nowadays can get by without them, though.

• In order to assure a fair price, ask the charge per bag before the porter picks any of them up.

• If you're handicapped or have any serious medical problems, ask the airline for help in getting from the airplane, through customs, and on your way to your hotel.

Losing luggage

It's frustrating to lose luggage. If you've followed the advice of never packing irreplaceable items in bags you check on to the plane, however, you'll be relatively calm in your dealings with the airline. And that's the best way to be.

• Report the loss to the airline representative immediately. Be polite but vocal about the loss, and note the representative's name.

• If the airline can't find your bags after checking the plane and baggage area, file a written claim notice immediately. Give a detailed list of the contents of the lost luggage.

• Make sure you get a copy of the claim and do not surrender your claim checks, the only proof you have that the airline has indeed lost your bags. If the airline insists on keeping a claim check, get a written receipt for it and the name of the person who takes it from you.

Making do when your luggage is lost

- Ask the airline representative for an overnight kit and emergency funds to purchase essential clothes and toiletries. Even if the luggage is found, you can keep the kit and anything you've purchased with the money (but be fair in your demands).

- Ask the airline to deliver your bags to your hotel in town if they are recovered shortly.

- If the airline loses your luggage permanently, you'll be paid a set amount per pound by the airline, usually no more than $700. The exact reimbursement plan is on your ticket.

- You'll be paid more than that if you've taken out extra luggage insurance (see p. 18).

Dealing with damaged luggage

- If there is any sign of damage to your bag, check the contents immediately.

- If you find damaged goods, immediately file a claim with an airline representative. Make sure you get a copy of the claim form. You'll be reimbursed for damage done to the bag or its contents.

- **Any** bag that is overpacked will disqualify a claim.

Getting from Airports to Hotels

You'll almost always find relatively inexpensive local transportation to take you from an airport to the center of a town or city.

Finding cheap transportation

- Go to the airline counter, the information booth, or the local tourist office and simply ask for the most economical way to get into town.

- Several people can sometimes split the cost of a taxi and come out ahead. But most of the time local buses will offer the best value.

- If you want to take a taxi, ask the airline or information clerk for the approximate cost of the trip and about tipping practices and percentages.

- When you enter the bus or taxi, show the driver the name and address of your hotel and be sure he can take you to your destination.

11 Hotel Strategies

In this chapter, you'll find helpful tips on everything from getting settled in a hotel to staying in boardinghouses and youth hostels. The information may help make your stay in Europe an experience truly worth remembering.

Arriving at a Hotel

Getting settled in a hotel may or may not take long. Many things can go awry. Here's how to avoid problems.

Bringing bags into a hotel

Whether you use public transportation or a taxi, you'll eventually arrive at the steps of your hotel. Taxi drivers normally do little more than remove the bags from the car and set them on the curb.

- If the driver carries your bags into the hotel, you should tip him as you would a hotel porter. Normally, whoever is behind the desk will see you struggling and come to your aid, if the cabby doesn't.

- Do not leave bags unattended on the curb while you search for someone to bring them into the hotel.

Checking into a hotel

At the front desk, give the clerk your name and the dates of your reservations. You will then be asked to fill out a police form. If you've memorized the number, date, and place of issue of your passport, filling out this form will be easy.

- If the clerk asks for your passport so that he can fill out the form for you, tell him you'd rather do it yourself.

- If he insists, give him half an hour to return it (a little longer in Portugal, where the local police may need to see it). Under no circumstances should you surrender it for any longer — it's your document, and you need it!

- While you're checking in, ask the clerk for stationery or matches — something with the hotel's name and address on it. It may sound ridiculous, but almost everyone forgets the name and address of one of their hotels at some time during a trip!

Hotel costs and services

Check-in is the time to get everything straight on costs and services. Avoid conflicts by asking questions right away.

- Is the cost of breakfast, or any other meal, included with the room price?

- Will there be any additional service charges?

- What's the tax on rooms and services?

- Are there any additional charges for laundry, local calls, television, etc.?

- How much does a bath cost?

- Does the hotel supply towels with the bath?

Checking out your room

If the porter shows you to your room, tip according to the amount of luggage. If there's anything wrong or you want to change rooms, let the desk clerk know right now!

- Check the room for noise. A room near a subway or railroad, overlooking a main boulevard, next to the elevator, or by a bathroom is hard to sleep in.

- Check the smell: does the room smell fresh and clean?

- Check the posted price on the wall or on the back of the door. Does it match the one quoted to you in the lobby?

- Check for hot water — it can be a luxury in a small hotel. Do the faucets drip?

- Check the heat: if you'll need it, make sure the system is working. This can be difficult, since some hotels shut off heat during the day. Ask whether a space heater is available.

- Check the bathroom (or shower) and the WC. Many superb small hotels don't have baths or showers in individual rooms — accept this and the subsequent savings!

- Check the bedding. If you must have an American-style pillow, make sure one is available (they're often stuffed in closets or bureaus). Ask about extra blankets if you'll need them.

Getting bumped despite written confirmation

Many hotels overbook by 10 to 15 percent to make up for no-shows and then bump the overflow. Unfortunately, if you don't have a **written** confirmation of reservations, you have no legitimate grounds for complaints. But if you do have such confirmation, here's what to do if you're bumped.

- Insist that the hotel come up with a room. Also insist that they pay your cab fare from the hotel to a new hotel if you must move.

- If the management refuses to do anything, create a small scene. No hotel likes a scene in its front lobby! The very least the hotel should do is to pay your way to the local room-finding service (see below).

Getting bumped without written confirmation

Unless you have a written confirmation, you can expect no sympathy. A telephone conversation or a voucher may be helpful, but neither is enough. That's why you should insist on written confirmations.

- Stay calm and polite. Ask the clerk to help you to find a room. He or she will often make many phone calls to help a stranded tourist.

- Failing that, get directions to a room-finding service (see below).

Reservation Services

The big advantage of traveling without reservations is the overall freedom it gives you. Many people prefer to travel in this fashion. When you arrive in a city without a reserved room, you can almost always get one from a reservation service.

Tourist information offices

When you arrive in a strange city without a room reservation, go directly to the nearest tourist information office. These are located in railway stations, airports, docks, and in the center of cities and smaller towns. If you don't know where the tourist office is, the clerk at the nearest hotel can tell you.

- Many of these offices have a room-finding service or can direct you to one. They are generally open from 9 or 10 a.m. to 10 or 11 p.m., though they may close on holidays and Sundays.

- You're always served on a first-come, first-served basis. Time will pass more quickly if you bring a snack and something to read while you wait.

- When you're served, tell the clerk what price range you want. Note that the cheapest rooms fill up fast in peak seasons and may not be available. It will take anywhere from 10 minutes to two hours to book a room.

- Ask about the fee structure for booking and determine how much it will cost before you book a room.

- When a room is found and booked, ask the clerk to mark its location on a free map that the tourist office will have. Write down its full name and address as well — partial information or unknown locations spell trouble.

- For members of racial minorities: discrimination is virtually impossible when you use room-booking services.

Other booking services

- **American Express** offers a room-finding service on a fee-paid basis. So do many other large travel agencies. However, most of these deal in higher-priced rooms.

- **Airline offices** often have books listing good, moderate-to-expensive hotels. If you have a ticket through an airline, you can often get room-finding information and help.

- **Student offices** can locate rooms for those who qualify either by age or student status. You can get lists of foreign student offices from the CIEE (see p. 15).

- **YWCA/YMCAs** and **youth hostel organizations** can also be of help (see pp. 122-123).

Finding Your Own Room

The alternative to having an agent or a tourist office clerk book a room for you is obvious — book one yourself! The big advantage of this approach over the others is that you get to see the room (and the hotel) before you rent. That advantage pales in extremely crowded cities during the peak season, but the fact is that you often do better on your own than when others book for you. It's quite easy and can save you a bundle if you know a few basic principles and techniques.

Hotel rates

- In general, the larger the hotel, the higher the rates. "Name-brand" hotels are especially expensive.

- Almost all hotels in Europe have a wide variety of rooms that vary from abysmal to great. Even in large and overly expensive hotels, you may find a bargain.

- The more Americans in a hotel, the higher the rates. Americans are just not bargain-hunters when it comes to lodgings. The British, Scandinavians, and Germans tend to be more skillful travelers — watch for them in smaller hotels offering more for your money.

- Hotels grow progressively more expensive as they get close to the heart of the city. Near the airport, railway station, or docks of main cities, you'll also find inflated rates.

- During festivals, pilgrimages, sporting events, fairs, and conventions, all rooms are overpriced — if you can find any at all — even on the outskirts of town.

Hotels in outlying areas

On the fringes of larger cities, you'll find the kind of small hotels that make a trip to Europe memorable. True, you will have to commute to city centers for sightseeing, but it will be worth your while to check out these hotels for several reasons.

- Hotel rates in outlying areas are low!

- These hotels are not what every American has seen or visited, and are more typical of the area you are in.

- You may have to forgo television or a private bath, but you'll meet Europeans more readily.

- Many hotels in outlying areas are far from bright lights and traffic, so you'll sleep better there.

Using a travel guide to find lodging

- Use the guides listed on p. 29 to help you find lodging. Travel guides are most useful for the off-season, from late September through April.

- Buy a guide that lists telephone numbers along with the hotel descriptions.

- If you want to avoid the expense of making many calls, go to an area that's thick with listings. Then check that area out on foot. Often this will lead you to a gem that's not even listed.

- To get a room in a crowded city, your timing must be right: the earlier you try, the better the odds are.

Room-hunting preliminaries

- Never judge a hotel by its exterior or lobby. Smaller, less expensive hotels may not put money into appearances but may still offer comfortable, charming, clean accommodations.

- Go into the hotel and ask the person at the front desk if a room is available. (See p. 114 for ways to get past a "No Vacancy" sign.) Ask for room rates. If one's open in your range, ask to see it. If none are open, ask whether a nearby hotel has rooms and rates that suit you.

- If there's a room open in your price range, look at it before renting it (see p. 109). Then you can begin to bargain.

Bargaining on room rates

Once you find a room you like, you'll want to come up with the best price possible. Although it goes against the American grain, bargaining in various ways is acceptable throughout much of Europe. Naturally, it's only effective in an area with many open rooms, and for that reason it's done more successfully in the off-season.

- Remember that you can play a big part in determining the price of the room.

- Begin by being flexible. Tell the clerk that the room is great, but that it's too expensive for you. This will often bring the price down.

- Or be blunt: tell the clerk that you like the room and will pay such and such an amount — a lower, but still fair, price. This also works frequently, but you have to have the right temperament to try it.

- Or be hesitant: a clerk can sense this. He'll often respond by showing you a room that's just as nice but costs less.

- If you find a hotel you like in which the cheaper rooms are filled, ask whether you can rent a more expensive room for one night and then move to a cheaper one the next day. This puts the clerk in the position of weighing a cost reduction against the bother and a cost of cleaning an extra set of sheets. Sometimes a clerk will agree to give you the more expensive room at a lower rate to avoid moving you at all.

Room-rate discounts

- You should get a room-rate discount in most countries during the off-season. Rates posted in a room vary from a minimum (off-season) to a maximum (peak season). Insist upon the lower rate in the off-season!

- You should not have to pay as much for a double bed as for two twins in comparable rooms, since the hotel saves money on the number of sheets it has to wash.

- Always ask about discounts for prolonged stays (usually three days or longer). If none exist, the hotel will tell you so. You can then either accept the standard rate or shop around.

- Ask if the hotel offers weekend discounts, especially at hotels in larger cities appealing to business people.

- Try to rent a room without breakfast included, since continental breakfasts will cost you several dollars. During the peak season many hotels refuse to do this, but in the off-season most of them give in.

Beating the "No Vacancy" sign

It can be frustrating at times, this process of finding a room on your own. It's particularly frustrating when you see **"No Vacancy"** on every door (**"Complet," "Besetz," "Occupato"** — dirty words when you're looking for a room). When things look very bleak, try some of the following techniques to help you come up with a room.

- Tell the clerk that you stayed in this hotel once before and want very badly to stay here again. When he tries to remember your face, tell him how much you liked the hotel and the town. He may sense that you're lying; if he's got a good memory, he'll be sure of it. But he'll smile, try to find you a room in the hotel, or call one of his friends in a hotel down the street.

- When you walk up to the clerk and the first thing you hear is "How long do you intend to stay?" you've got to answer, "A week," or there may suddenly be no vacancies. Short stays cost hotels more in overhead.

- At about 11 p.m., walk into the lobby of a small hotel, hand the clerk a piece of paper with the hotel's name scribbled on it, tell the clerk that André Papillon (make up any name) recommended the place to you, and ask him if there might be a room available. At this point the clerk may take the gamble of giving you a room reserved for someone else. The hotel collects double, and you have a room.

- In desperation, try a taxi driver. The word **hotel** is an international one. The driver may just steer you to a nearby spot. More than likely he'll take you for a ride, but the ride as a bribe sometimes pays off.

Miscellaneous charges

Watch for miscellaneous charges. Unless you understand them in advance, you'll end up paying far more than you planned.

- Prices for hotel rooms are sometimes quoted on a **per person** basis, especially in Italy and Spain. Get the price straight to start with: "Is that per person or the total price of the room?"

- Avoid having the hotel set up tours or arrange for nights on the town. Naturally, this is a legitmate part of their business, but you'll save money if you only use them when you really can't get tickets or tour seats yourself.

- If you make long-distance phone calls from a hotel room, you can legally be socked with a surcharge that may be as much as 40 percent on any bill. Therefore, before making such calls, find out about possible surcharges. If they seem steep, make your call from the central post office.

- If there's a charge for hotel parking, just leave your car in the street under a light. Be sure to remove all your belongings from the car and lock it.

Room and board

The term **full room and board (pension complet)** means that you're staying in a hotel and eating all meals there. **Half room and board (demi pension)** indicates that you're skipping either lunch or dinner at the hotel. Most European hotels offer good rates for both full and half room-and-board arrangements.

- If you're eating meals at your hotel, see whether there is a discount for full or half room and board. Make sure any discounts you opt for show up on your final bill.

- Some hotels will even force you to have meals there before they will rent you a room. In the peak season you may have to submit to this racket, intended to jack up the price of government-controlled room rates.

- Many hotels will not offer room-and-board discounts unless you stay for a minimum of three days. But they won't tell you this in advance, so ask about it.

- If you do stay on a room-and-board basis, find out whether there is an extra charge for anything, such as wine, dessert, or coffee.

- As unbelievable as it may sound, you must pay an extra charge in some hotels for **not** eating breakfast. So you really end up paying a surcharge for not getting out of bed and going down to breakfast.

- In resort areas, many luxury hotels have agreements for reciprocal lunches and dinners for guests staying on room-and-board terms. Ask the clerk at the front desk for information on such arrangements.

Idiosyncrasies of European Hotels

Half the pleasure of travel comes from discovering the difference between "them" and "us." However, some differences come as a shock. Here are some bridges for cultural gaps in hotels.

The front desk

- Get the clerk's name when you check in. Ask for all prices to be written down on a slip of paper to avoid confusion about rates at check-out time.

- Don't assume that your name is easy to spell or read. Write it down for the clerk.

- Ask as late in the day as possible for a morning wake-up call. With luck you'll be leaving it with the person responsible for calling you in the morning, and your message won't go astray.

Elevators

- The elevators in most hotels do not work like Swiss watches. The clunk when you push the call button means it's heard you. The whine means it's on its way. The second clunk means the maid has intercepted it on the third floor and it will now head in the opposite direction.

- Once you've cornered the elevator, you must shut the outer gate tightly before closing the inner door and pushing the floor button. If the gate isn't closed, the elevator won't work — no matter how much you swear.

Bath Rooms and showers

Although the trend in Europe is toward the American-style hotel room that includes a tub or shower, many European hotels have detached rooms for bathing.

The room with the shower or bath is always separate from the toilet (WC). Both may be at the end of the hall, but they could also be four floors up, tucked under the slanted roof where only cats and bats can live.

You often have to get a key for the bath or shower room from the clerk at the front desk. The clerk will ask the maid to bring you a towel.

- Ask the owner about the best time to take a bath. Some hotels arrange hours for their guests so as not to disturb sleep.

- You pay extra per shower or bath unless you've agreed that it's included in the price of the room.

- There are public baths in most cities. You'll also find them in many train stations.

Hot and cold water

- In small hotels with a central water heating system you may be out of luck (and hot water) if you don't time your bath or shower properly.

- The red spot on a faucet means hot, the blue means cold. After five minutes of running the red spot without getting warm water, assume the plumber was color-blind or, more likely, the hotel is out of hot water.

- Quite a few hotels have individual gas water-heating units for the shower or bath. When you turn on the hot water faucet, the unit will burst into flame, heating only the water you'll need.

- The water will be scalding. The trick for getting the right temperature is to turn the hot water on full and turn the cold water on — gently, or you'll end up with a cold stream shooting at you. The code of the road in the bath room is that cold water has priority over hot.

- One out of 10 small European hotels has broken pipes.

Toilets

- Toilets are generally labeled "WC" (water closet) and are intended for both sexes if they're not otherwise designated (watch out for **"signori"** and **"signore,"** for men and women, respectively, in Italy).

- Many toilets do not have a light switch. As soon as you lock the door, the light will go on.

- If the light doesn't go on, the switch may be on the outside of the toilet.

- Light a match or two in smelly toilets. You won't notice the smell.

- Most toilets have some form of toilet paper: real stuff, pieces of newspaper, a kind of dark crepe paper, magazine pages. Some don't have any — a good reason to carry some tissue in your purse or wallet.

- In some parts of Europe, toilets are no more than holes in the floor with two tile steps to squat on. You'll feel like an experienced traveler after you've visited your first **steppe!**

Bidets

You'll find bidets in many European hotel rooms and WCs. If you care to experiment with these toilet-shaped porcelain fixtures for your personal hygiene, do so. (Europeans can't believe that Americans do without them in their bathrooms!)

- Otherwise, use them for sponge baths, for hair washing, or for hand washing clothes.

Mattresses and bedding

- If you're the kind of person who doesn't have to jump to sink a basket, ask to see the bed in a room before renting it. You may have to settle for a double bed on which you can lie diagonally.

- You'll run into a mattress every now and then that gives you a spinal tap for no extra charge. Just toss it on the floor and sleep there.

- In some countries, you'll find pillows that look like short, rolled-up rugs. If you don't like them, check in the closet or bureau drawers for American-style pillows **(oreillers).** If you can't find any, ask the front desk for some. If they don't have any, you're stuck.

- Many European hotels substitute wedge-shaped bolsters under the mattress for pillows. If you don't like these, just pull them out and look or ask for American-style pillows.

- Pat the feathers in the down quilts you'll find in Germany, Austria, Italy, and Scandinavia until they spread out evenly under the thick white cover. Then toss the comforter up and down a few times. This fluffs up the feathers. You place the whole thing over you, covering most of your body.

- If you want to slide two beds together to make one, place the box springs side by side, but always place the mattresses **across** them. If you don't, someone will disappear during the night.

Lights

The lights in the hall can be a problem in some hotels, since they'll only stay on for a minute after you push a button on the wall. This conserves electricity but forces you to grope for that button if you don't want to trip and fall down the stairs.

- You may want to carry a small flashlight and beat the system.

- Turn off the lights in your room when you leave, or Frau Weber, with characteristic wit, will say, "So you think this is Christmas?"

- If you want strong lights for reading, you may have to carry a high-wattage bulb with you.

Guests

Hotels are strict about inviting guests to your room. The landlady will look at you and your new friend heading up the stairs and say, "Excuse me. You paid for one person, not two."

- If you are expecting, or hope to find, a partner, pay for two from the start.

- In most countries it is illegal for unmarried people to share a room. The restriction is almost universally ignored as long as the bill has been properly paid.

Maids

The maid will do everything possible to wake you up. If your door isn't locked, she'll open it, say the equivalent of "oops!" then slam it closed. You can avoid this by locking the door when you go to bed and placing a "Do Not Disturb" sign (if there is one) on the outside knob. Some experienced travelers carry such a sign with them for hotels poorly supplied with such vital amenities. But this won't stop the maid from jabbering with other maids in the hall, coughing, laughing, singing, telling jokes, and making other cleaning-maid sounds — which are not very subtle ways of letting you know that it's time for her to make your bed.

- Unless you put small things in a drawer or in your luggage, they may disappear. They're usually not being stolen, but are being thrown away.

Laundry

Placards in most hotel rooms say that it's illegal to do laundry in your room; virtually every traveler ignores this warning, once burned by outrageous laundry service prices. Hand washing your clothes saves time as well. (Hotel laundries take three days!) Besides, today's fabrics are practically maintenance-free.

Washing clothes in your room

- Roll clothes in a towel to collect excess moisture and speed drying before you hang them. (But don't wring out drip-dry clothes.)
- Be sure to bring a braided rubber clothesline from which you can hang wash to dry.

Hanging clothes to dry

- Never hang your laundry out a window to dry. That will cause an international incident, either with the maid or with the management itself.
- Don't lay wet clothes on a stained wood surface, since they'll bleach the wood and end up stained themselves.
- Try not to swamp a room with dripping water. Place plastic over a newspaper in any area prone to water damage.
- Separate the back portion of any wet clothing from the front.
- Smooth to eliminate wrinkling.
- Button the two top buttons of a shirt and set the collar in the correct position.

Wrinkles, lint, and stains

- To get rid of wrinkles in shirts, skirts, slacks, or dresses after they are dry, hang them in a steamy bathroom.
- Or, run any moist item over a hot light bulb — acts like an iron.
- Use any kind of tape to pick up lint off clothes.
- Soak blood stains in cold water to remove them.
- Sprinkle salt or soda on wine stains and talcum powder on grease stains to help absorb and remove them before washing.

12 Alternatives to Hotels

There is a wide variety of accommodations available in Europe. If you're on a budget or if you prefer a more intimate experience than hotels can offer, boardinghouses, youth hostels and other youth-oriented accommodations, and camping (or simply sleeping out) will give you plenty of options to consider.

Boardinghouses

Boardinghouses **(pensions)** are as common as hotels in Europe. They offer most of the advantages of hotels and the added element of personal attention. They provide rooms and meals at reasonable prices.

The rate in a pension varies according to the room-and-board plan being offered. The full pension **(pension complet)** arrangement includes all meals plus a room, while half pension **(demi pension)** covers the room, breakfast, and either lunch or supper.

Boardinghouse rates

- Note that the basic room rate generally includes the cost of breakfast and the price of a bath; but you'll have to work this out in advance.

- Have the price of the room written down on a slip of paper and hang on to it. Or pay ahead of time. This way any misunderstandings, hidden service charges, and surprise taxes will surface before you move in.

- If you plan to stay in a boardinghouse for more than three days, ask about long-term rates. The difference may really surprise you.

Food at boardinghouses

Meals are generally served at a common table where you'll get to know the other boarders.

- You are not expected to tip the cook or maid, although a token tip would be in order when you leave.

- If you want to affect the quality of the cooking, honestly tell the cook what you think of different dishes, either verbally or in sign language.

- Never start off with a full pension **(pension complet)** agreement. You want to be able to eat out at local restaurants as well. If a boardinghouse insists that you eat all meals there, look somewhere else for a room.

Youth Hostels and Youth Accommodations

There is a network of more than 2,000 hostels in Europe, including camps, castles, lodges, huts, villas, ships, and schools. They're interesting because the people who stay in them are real adventurers.

The American Youth Hostels (AYH) association issues youth hostel cards, which you must have if you're planning to hostel your way around Europe. Costs vary according to your age. You can get information from any local branch or the central office: American Youth Hostels, 1017 K Street, N.W., Washington, DC 20001, (202) 783-4943. All mail should be directed to AYH, P.O. Box 28607, Central Station, Washington, DC 20038.

Technically as an American, you can't get a youth hostel card abroad, but many Americans get around this by giving a foreign address.

Basics of hostels

- Check ahead if you're about 25 or older, since some hostels impose age limits to keep room available for youths.

- Bring a sleeping sack (like a sheet), which you can make yourself or pick up from the Metropolitan New York Council, 75 Spring Street, New York, NY 10012. Some hostels insist that you have such a sheet, while others provide them or let the rules slide. Sleeping arrangements are mostly dormitory-style set-ups on simple cots.

- Save money by trying out the communal dining rooms. The meals are filling and sometimes quite good.

- If you find that a certain hostel restricts its space to foot travelers, park your car around the corner and hike in.

Ground rules for hostels

- You help with the cleaning.

- Neither smoking nor radios are permitted in the sleeping area.

- Alcohol is allowed only with meals in France, Italy, Portugal, and Spain.

- There's a three-day limit on stays (unless there's lots of room).

- Lights go out by 10 p.m., and you get up by 7 a.m.

- Hostels often close from late morning to late afternoon — so get there early to register for the coming night!

- Many hostels will take reservations for the next day. All it costs is the price of a phone call.

- If you want to reserve a room in advance, write to the hostel requesting a reservation. Enclose one night's fee and enough international reply coupons to cover an airmail reply.

Inexpensive, youth-oriented rooms

- If you're young and on a budget, take advantage of the many youth-oriented facilities available, which include student hotels, dormitories, and the many YMCA/YWCAs throughout Europe.

- Get information on these facilities as far in advance as possible, making reservations by mail in time to beat the summer rush!

- For information on facilities abroad, contact the YMCA, 101 North Wacker Drive, Chicago, IL 60606; YWCA, 726 Broadway, New York, NY 10003; or any local branch of these organizations.

- For information on student hotels and dormitories, contact the CIEE (see p. 15).

- Note that facilities in Europe tend to be better than those in the U.S.

- Note, too, that you will find better facilities in central and northern Europe than in the South.

Camping

Camping is geared to a loose, free-flowing style of travel that is not compatible with limited time. If you've got the time, however, you'll find that European campgrounds are well organized, often offering facilities that include showers and grocery stores. You'll find them everywhere, even in major European cities.

International Camping Carnet

- Get an International Camping Carnet, the passport to camping abroad, that entitles you to small reductions in fees. Contact the National Campers and Hikers Association, 4804 Transit Road, Building 2, Depew, NY 14043, (716) 668-6242.

- If you forget to pick one up in the U.S., ask for one at an automobile association abroad.

Camping equipment

- Know your outfit before traveling abroad, which means trying it out in the U.S. before you leave. Nothing's worse than a so-called waterproof tent that lets the rain in or a mosquito net that's worn through. If you camp out before going to Europe, you'll find out quickly what gear you're missing (or what miserable gear you've got).

- Bring the minimum gear: sleeping bag (down, or comparable synthetic), plastic sheet, tent, warm clothes, bug spray, and flask.

- Bring a good knife with a corkscrew and bottle opener. A Swiss Army knife is excellent.

- Plan to use a butane stove and a large, refillable cylinder of gas. Buy these abroad.

- Travel by car, not by truck or trailer. Can you imagine taking a trip to a fjord in a car pulling a trailer?

Camping etiquette

- Always ask permission to camp on someone's property.

- Avoid using fires; they are illegal in almost all areas.

- Leave the campsite spotless.

- Note that in Europe, saying thank you and goodbye to your host, with a handshake, is **minimal** good manners.

Sleeping Out and Other Tactics

Thousands of young people travel throughout Europe each year without spending a cent for a hotel room. While this practice is officially discouraged by most police departments, it's nevertheless tolerated in most countries. Be cautious in eastern Europe, though.

Sleeping out

Sleeping out is a cinch in most rural areas. It has some advantages over sleeping in campgrounds, where you have to pay an entrance fee for the privilege of being surrounded by a milling crowd. You become a part of the spot you've chosen: the farmer waking you up could either ask you to leave or invite you to have breakfast with him!

• Try to find as isolated and protected a spot as possible.

• Be prepared to end up with two cat's eyes peering down at you over a flashlight in the middle of the night. Be polite, show your visitor your passport, offer him or her a cigarette.

• Consider paying the small entrance fee for a campground when you are in a city. It's harder to sleep out in urban areas.

Alternatives to sleeping out

• Try the train station: it's the warmest, safest place to sleep for free in cities. The police will wake you up if you're lying down; but if you can sleep sitting up, you've got it made.

• Don't count on getting the police to put you up in a cell for the night if you can't find a room in a crowded town. Usually, the police will not want you around, since many unpleasant things can happen in jails.

• If you have a Eurailpass, try sleeping on trains. This is less comfortable than some know-it-all travel writers insist (they've never done it). If you try it, be sure to pull out the leg support (if there is one) from underneath your seat. Always take your shoes off if you put your feet on a train seat.

• For men only: if you have friends in the army, try to stay in the barracks with them. Although this is quite illegal, it will save you a wad. Someone always pulls night duty, which will leave a bunk open for you.

• In a pinch, try restaurants, bars, or even rooftops of small hotels (great idea in Greece). The cost is usually just a token charge.

Staying with Europeans for free

If you get along well with a European, it's possible that you'll be invited to stay in his or her home. Bring a small token gift (a bouquet, American stamps or books, Kennedy coins) when you arrive. And remember the saying, "Fish and visitors stink after three days."

- Keep addresses of people you meet during your travels. You'll enjoy an area much more if you have a contact there. You'll often be asked to stay for a night or two as a courtesy.

- Keep your needs to a minimum. In some areas the heat will be lower than you're used to. Simply put on a sweater.

- Hot water is expensive to heat. Many Europeans consider a daily bath both unnecessary and bad for your health (many doctors agree). So follow the bathing patterns of your host.

13 Money Matters and Safety

Foreign Currency

One of the realities of foreign travel is the necessity to exchange American money for foreign currency. You'll need your passport for each exchange. Money-changers charge a fee for their service. **Each time you exchange money, you lose money.** The more exchanges, the greater the loss.

Rates of exchange are posted at banks, in American Express and other travel offices, and at money-changers' offices. Rates fluctuate daily.

Exchanging currency

- Study foreign currency and coins until you are familiar with all the denominations you'll be dealing with. Just as in the U.S., size and value may not be related — small coins may be worth more than larger ones.

- If the foreign country's monetary system is not clear to you, have someone explain it. This will save you money in the long run!

- Find out the banking hours and dates of bank holidays of the place you're visiting.

- Don't make fun of foreign currency in public, even if some of the coins will float on water or the paper money would pass as newspaper.

- Never ask how much a foreign currency is worth in **real** money. It's just as real as American currency.

Getting the best deal on currency exchanges

- Most banks in the U.S. offer a very poor rate of exchange on all foreign currency transactions.

- The following organization claims that it will charge a small fee for each transaction and will accept credit cards for payment. Contact it three weeks ahead of your planned trip for current exchange rates (please let me know if you have any problems).

Texas Foreign
  Exchange, Inc.
1130 Travis
Houston, TX 77002
Tel: (713) 654-0999

- Avoid exchanging money in airports, train stations, and hotels. Wherever exchange is most convenient, it's most costly.

- Exchange only about $20 — enough to get you to your hotel — when first arriving abroad.

- Never exchange money at the border between two countries, for the same reason.

- Know the current rate of exchange before you go shopping. Some shops **always** give a better rate of exchange than banks as a way of encouraging shoppers to return (a kind of built-in discount). Others try to rip you off.

Where to exchange money daily

- Exchange your money in reputable banks or in traveler's check offices.

- Exchange traveler's checks at their own name-brand offices in order to get the most favorable rates.

- Don't deal with money-changers. Although their rates vary from favorable to unfavorable, they offer a less favorable rate of exchange overall.

- If saving money is more important to you than saving time, check several banks before you exchange currency. Rates sometimes vary from one bank to another, and the right choice can save you 2 to 4 percent.

How much to exchange

- Most banks and traveler's check companies charge a set service fee per transaction. Thus, the person who exchanges small amounts frequently gets burned. **The minimum anyone should exchange on a routine basis is the most he or she can afford to lose.**

- You'll sometimes get better rates of exchange for larger amounts, usually over $100.

- Unless you intend to return to a country, never carry coins across a border, since most banks won't exchange them. Note that you can exchange coins in either the Amsterdam or Munich train stations (if you forget).

Traveler's Checks

Everyone knows that it's foolish to travel abroad carrying only cash. If you carry traveler's checks, there are only two possible problems: you can't get them accepted, or you lose them. Fortunately, there are solutions to both problems.

Getting traveler's checks accepted

You'll sometimes run into a place that won't take your traveler's check. If this happens, you can try two things.

- Ask the person in charge to call the nearest bank. Try not to create a scene, but be polite and firm in your suggestion that he or she verify the authenticity of such checks.

- Volunteer to go over to the bank and cash your check there.

Lost traveler's checks

Keep a record of your checks — both cashed and uncashed — separate from the checks themselves. For example, don't carry them both in your wallet. If you should lose your checks, do the following.

- Go to the branch office of the company that issued the checks and report the loss there.

- Be sure to bring your passport as identification.

- Note that Avis will refund up to $100 in lost American Express checks on weekends and holidays if American Express offices are closed.

Credit Cards and Money

Many travelers enjoy the convenience of credit cards while they're in Europe. If you use yours, be careful to protect them.

Protecting credit cards

- Take along only the credit cards you'll need; leave all others at home in a safe-deposit box. Protect credit cards as you would cash or your passport.

- Photocopy all of your credit cards at one time. Give one copy to a friend and take another with you. This will be very useful if you lose a card while traveling.

- Note how many cards you're carrying and count them periodically. Many thieves are smart enough to take only one or two cards from a wallet, making the theft less noticeable.

- When you charge something, be sure to verify the total amount charged to you, sign the charge slip, and keep the customer copy. Unfortunately, a growing number of establishments alter charge slips in an effort to defraud customers. An extra digit on the charge slip can cause the bill to soar by $100 or more. Never throw your slips away until the charges have been billed and paid!

- Ask shops, restaurants, and hotels to convert total amounts into dollars and cents and then write the amount on the charge slip. This way you know exactly what you'll owe your credit card company despite currency fluctuations!

- If you buy a ticket with a credit card and then have to cancel or change your travel plans, ask for a **refund receipt** when you return the ticket for credit. Note the ticket number and the date and place you bought it, so that you can contact the credit card company if the credit does not show up on your bill.

Using credit cards to get cash

- With most credit cards you can easily get cash abroad. You'll need both your card and your passport for these transactions.

- Check with credit card companies for current policies and cash limits.

When the money runs out

- You can wire home and ask someone to send you an international money order.

- The American consulate can help in emergencies, but you'll have to repay money lent to you before you will be allowed to travel abroad again.

- If you haven't got enough money to pay duty on your return to the U.S., customs will take a personal check with two forms of identification.

- As ghoulish as it may sound, the easiest way to pick up a small amount of cash when you're **really** in a tight pinch is to sell a pint of your blood.

Tipping

About the only western European country where tips are generally frowned upon is Iceland, so traveling is simple there. Tipping policies are very complex in all other countries. The smartest thing you can do is to ask travel agents, airline personnel, and those who give you service about the tipping policy in each area.

Confusion about tipping can add 10 to 20 percent to the total cost of a trip. Here are some basics for you to follow so that your tipping will be proper but not extravagant.

When tips are included

- Although tour packages generally include all gratuities for services included in the tour contract, ask about the policy on tipping before signing a contract.

- Ocean liner ticket prices may or may not cover tips, so you should check into the tipping policy upon boarding. Airline personnel do not expect tips.

- At most European restaurants and hotels, a tip will automatically be added to your bill in the form of a service charge of 10 to 20 percent of the total bill. If you pay this charge, you're not expected to add an additional tip.

Separate tips

- You should always tip a maitre d', waiter, wine steward, porter, doorman, bellman, chambermaid, bartender, concierge, or service person for any unusual or extraordinarily fine service.

- You should tip cabdrivers, provided that a service charge has not been included in the fare on the meter. Service charges are often included on meters in Belgium, Denmark, and the Netherlands. Ask if you're not sure.

- You should tip washroom attendants if you use their services. Give them as little as you can get away with.

- You should tip theater and movie ushers who guide you to your seat — again, a very small amount will do.

Handling beggars

Beggars are most common in France, Italy, Portugal, and Spain, although you'll run into a few panhandlers in the central and northern countries as well.

- Sometimes begging borders on extortion. For instance, if you leave your car to do some sightseeing, you'd do well to give a few small coins to the leader of the group crowding around you. He then becomes the car's protector. Surprisingly, you rarely get ripped off if you pay this small fee. (Not surprisingly, if you don't pay, you may find that minor "accidents" occur in your absence.)

- Say "no" to most other requests and keep moving.

- If you are approached by a woman with a baby over her shoulder and an outstretched palm, or by a young woman asking you for money because she hasn't eaten in a week, offer her something to eat. She'll usually turn it down.

Protecting Yourself and Your Belongings

Suspicion and wariness require energy and are not very pleasant sensations, but they do prevent trouble, which would be even more unpleasant.

Protecting your belongings

- Leave all expensive jewelry at home. You can pick up all sorts of gold and silver imitations for a song — that's what the Europeans do! Follow their lead.

- Never carry all of your valuables in one place. Split up your documents and money. If you put your passport, tickets, money, traveler's checks, and credit cards in one place, they're all gone in one shot. **This is basic street sense.**

- Keep anything valuable out of sight and in inconspicuous containers. If you have to leave something valuable in a car (not a good idea), put it in the trunk. Stow your cameras in an inexpensive carrying bag — one that looks as if it could just as easily be carrying groceries.

- Don't set anything valuable near an open window or on a curbside table (as when dining **al fresco**).

- Never take public transportation, especially buses or trams, after cashing a large amount of money at the bank. Get the money back to your hotel safe and take just what you need for the day.

- **Just what you need for the day** is the key phrase. You don't need to carry a passport, three credit cards, all your traveler's checks, most of your money, and your airline tickets — leave them in the hotel safe. Take just enough to get you by — one credit card will often do the trick.

How to carry valuables when you must — pickpocket-proofing

There are times when everything you own is either on your body or in your bags. Violent crime is not common in Europe, but rip-offs of bags and pickpocketing are. Here are some tips:

- A small, durable traveler's pouch that can be attached to a belt and worn under your pants or skirt is the **best** place to carry valuable documents and money. Anyone with a basic knowledge of sewing can make one of these bags and equip it with a good zipper. These hidden pouches are sold in the market as well. Get one!

- Second best but good is the inside pocket of a coat or jacket that has been modified with a zipper. You can alter these pockets so that they're twice as deep and twice as hard to pick. The zipper is crucial. No zipper? Use a safety pin as a deterrent to nimble fingers.

- Never carry your wallet in a rear pocket! A pickpocket can rip it off in a second. A side pants pocket is only a little better. If that's all you've got, buy a nappy-surfaced wallet or put a rubber band around it — this can give pickpockets a fit.

- If you're carrying a purse, put it in front of you with your arms crossed over it. Your wallet should be at the bottom. If your purse is at your side or behind you, a thief will slash it open with a razor blade and be gone in seconds.

- Don't carry cameras hanging from your neck. Thieves just pull them off — hurting your neck in the process!

Situations pickpockets like

- Pickpocketing is most common in crowded areas such as markets, buses in rush hour, subways, and beaches.

- Pickpockets prey on careless and drunk tourists — in that order. If you want to tie one on, carry only what you can afford to lose.

- Be wary of minor accidents: being bumped, having your foot stepped upon, being shoved. If your mind is not on your money, you will be vulnerable to pickpockets.

- Avoid commotions of all kinds. Pickpockets love to create them. Move away from any commotion as quickly and unobtrusively as possible.

- Pickpockets often pose as drunks. If someone wraps his arms around you, watch your wallet — he's probably feeling for it.

- If you're being pushed around in a crowd, drop your arms and turn around to face the person bumping you. A thief will tend to turn his head and move away quickly.

Protecting valuables in airports and train and bus stations

- Safety lockers, if available, provide a good way to store excess baggage or valuables. Ask at information booths for the location of storage facilities.

- Stay with your bags — assume that if they're left unattended for a second, they'll be ripped off. Chances are good that they will be.

- Try to travel light so you can carry your bags with you onto planes, trains, and buses. The minute your bags are out of sight, you have no way to keep track of them.

Protecting valuables in cars

- Try not to leave anything valuable in a car. A good thief can get into a car or trunk in a few seconds.

- Sometimes you have to leave things in a car. If you do, open the glove compartment to show a potential thief that it's empty. Put your gear in the trunk. Don't leave it too long, and absolutely never leave baggage in a car overnight.

- If you travel in your own car or RV, consider a built-in safe — somewhere underneath the car — it doesn't have to be large. Many experienced travelers use this "hidden compartment" for valuables and documents — it's unlikely that someone will find it.

- Note that thieves are attracted to cars with plates from other countries. So if you're in Germany with French license plates, you're tipping your hand.

Protecting valuables in a hotel

- Many hotels have safe-deposit boxes at the front desk. Take advantage of them. There's usually no charge, unless you lose the key — the charge for a replacement will be stiff.

- When getting valuables out of a safe, be attentive. This is one time when thieves will try to distract you.

- If you're in a budget hotel, don't leave valuables unattended. Carry them into the shower or bathroom if you have to.

- Note that almost all hotel rooms have doors with locks and bolt locks. Use them. If the door doesn't close tightly or if the locks seem flimsy, jam a chair underneath the knob to make the door difficult to open.

Protecting valuables at the beach

- Leave as much as you can at your hotel, preferably in a safe-deposit box.

- Pin your money to a beach robe or piece of clothing that no one would suspect as a hiding place. Leave nothing of great value in your purse or bag, which will be the first thing stolen. The purse becomes a decoy.

Preventing muggings

- During the day, walk close to walls. Do the opposite at night, walking far away from the walls.

- Never completely turn your back to the sidewalk when looking for a house number or unlocking a door.

- If you've just been to the bank and are carrying quite a bit of cash, walk against the flow of traffic. This makes it easy to spot anyone following you.

- Be wary of approaching motorbikes.

- Finally, if you do get robbed, don't resist. Thieves are usually scared to death; they just want to get the money and run. Give it to them. Say absolutely nothing. If you don't move, resist, or talk, your chance of bodily injury is minimal — that's what the experts say!

Losing things

It is very easy to lose things while traveling because you're constantly disoriented, frequently tired and fuzzy, and often moving at such a quick pace that it's hard to keep track of where you are or what you've got.

- Consider a special bag for things that are really important to you. Carry everything in that one bag except money and valuables. You'll be less likely to forget the bag than an individual item, like a pair of sunglasses or a small camera or a favorite pen or a lighter.

- The quickest way to lose something is to set it down. You may put a camera on the seat next to you, and the next minute, you're four blocks away and realize that the camera didn't come with you. What a sinking feeling and a mad dash to claim it — if it's still there!

- Try to establish a place for everything. This routine helps you know where things are at all times. This has a calming effect and helps cut down on the loss of items through carelessness, fatigue, or simple oversight.

Hotel fires

Here are a few basic tips to follow in case of a hotel fire:

- Note fire exits. Use these, not elevators, in an emergency.

- Fire alarm? Check your door to see whether it's hot before going into the hall. Take your key with you.

- Escape down if possible. If not, go to the roof.

- If you can't leave your room, call the front desk or fire department. Soak towels and place them under the door. Cover vents. Saturate everything with cold water, especially the doorway.

- Smoke is more often a threat than fire. Stay low to the floor. Breathe through a damp towel. Open windows only to clear **your** room of smoke. Otherwise, keep them closed.

Earthquakes

Earthquakes are the most common in southern Europe. Here are tips just in case:

- Many larger buildings have been constructed to sway (but not give way) during major quakes. Do not be alarmed by this motion.
- Get away from walls and windows and take cover, preferably under a table, desk, or bed.
- Standing in a doorway is a good option in smaller buildings or structures that may collapse.
- Never use elevators during a quake and avoid stairways as well. You're better off staying put in a room!
- If you're out on the street, go to the center of the road if possible — watch out for panicky drivers. The facades of buildings tend to crack and fall away in earthquakes, so try to keep clear of them.
- If you're driving, slowly come to a stop and simply sit out the quake in your car.

Safety for Women

Attitudes toward women vary from country to country. Women who travel in Europe — especially those who go alone — should take note of the following precautions.

Personal safety for women

- Do not hitchhike. Although many women encounter few, if any, problems hitchhiking in Europe, the police files are filled with exceptions to prove the rule: hitchhiking is more dangerous for women than for men, especially for women traveling alone.
- Make use of inexpensive public transportation instead of hitchhiking. Second-class train travel won't break the bank and can be combined with travel on buses, trams, subways, and trolleys to get you just about anywhere. You'll meet many fascinating people traveling on public transportation — the low-risk, low-cost way to travel.
- When using any form of private transportation, never travel alone — not even in taxis. Robbery — and rape — in taxis is common enough to be frightening.
- Schedule most of your long-distance travel for the day. Try to avoid travel at night when you're more vulnerable.

- Travel light. Remember that the weight of your luggage will affect both your attitude and your vulnerability.

- Try to get by with a single piece of luggage, one no larger than a carry-on bag for a plane. This gives you freedom and mobility in every situation, from boarding public transportation to checking into a hotel.

- Two women traveling together are much better off than a single woman, but they should still be wary and avoid provocative situations.

- In a hotel, have your key in your hand as you make your way to the room. You'll avoid fumbling through your purse outside the door.

- If it's possible, always let someone know where you're going and when you intend to be back. This could be a friend or just someone at the front desk of a hotel.

Problems for women in southern Europe

Women do not go out at night alone in southern Europe — with the exception of prostitutes and foreigners who don't know better. Find an escort for evening entertainment or go with a tour. If you travel alone in Italy and Spain, you must cope with the aggressive behavior of men. In these countries, men will pinch women's fannies — extremely hard. This sounds funny to everyone except to the woman who finds herself black-and-blue. Three suggestions:

- Have someone you trust walk directly behind you in a crowd. And place your back against a wall when riding in an elevator.

- Walk against, not with, the main flow of pedestrian traffic when you can.

- If you know who's doing the pinching (it can be hard as hell to figure out!), turn and face him. Say **"Basta!"** in a firm, no-nonsense tone of voice. This means "Enough!" — and that's usually enough.

Up-to-date information on personal safety

- Updates regarding travel safety are available from the U.S. Department of State, Citizens' Emergency Center at (202) 647-5225.

- Updates are available in Canada from the Department of External Affairs in Ottawa at (613) 992-3705.

14 Eating and Drinking

Crusty and warm French bread fresh from the **four** . . . moist filets of herring smothered in bits of onion on a piece of rich rye bread . . . succulent snails simmering in sizzling garlic butter . . . Spanish **paella** — chunks of chicken, meat, and seafood served on a hot bed of saffron-soaked rice . . . fettucine, lasagne, rigatoni — pasta in every imaginable form . . . pastries from tarts to petits fours: just a few of the taste treats that are in store for you.

There are two basic ways to order such food in European restaurants: **à la carte** or **table d'hôte. À la carte** means that you order and pay for each item separately. **Table d'hôte** means that you order an entire meal, from soup to nuts, for a set price.

- A set-price meal is usually a better deal than an **à la carte** meal. Most set-price meals include the cover and service charge, as well as the cost of either a beer or a carafe of wine.

- Synonyms for **table d'hôte** are **tourist menu, menu, set-price meal, menu touristique, prix fixe, menu turistico, prezzo fisso.** If you want to order a set-price meal, ask the waiter to point them out to you on the menu.

Fashionable Restaurants

In Great Britain, better restaurants have been given star ratings by Egon Ronay (a travel writer) and the automobile clubs. These ratings are usually posted at the front entrance. On the Continent, the most reliable ratings have been done by Michelin. Once again, restaurants are proud of these ratings and display them for all to see.

Reservations

- If you absolutely must eat at a certain fine restaurant, you can make reservations from the States by writing the management and including a deposit. Better restaurants usually require reservations, although this is not a universal law.

- Or, if you are staying at a nearby hotel, ask the management there to contact the restaurant on your behalf, particularly if there's a language barrier. (This is a service that you should reward with a tip.)

- Or you can call the restaurant yourself as soon as you arrive in Europe.

Best times for best meals

Better restaurants tend to be more crowded in the evening than at lunch, so be flexible if you really want to eat in a certain place.

Dress requirements

- Ask whether there are any dress requirements when making reservations, to avoid being turned away at the door. Very few restaurants have stringent dress codes these days.

- A dark sports coat with tie for a man and comparable dress for a woman are suitable in almost all restaurants at noon and night. However, some places insist on more formal evening attire on certain nights.

Drinking with meals

In Europe, it's considered gauche to have an American-style cocktail before dinner. Alcohol dulls taste buds and makes it more difficult to appreciate good food.

- Replace cocktails with a glass of sherry, white port, or similar light apéritif.

- Order water after ordering wine or skip water altogether, if it's not important to you. In more sophisticated restaurants, it's considered gauche to order water with your meal.

- Don't feel that you have to splurge on a high-priced wine, which will double the price of your meal. Do what most sensible and experienced gourmets advise: settle for a good, medium-priced wine that goes well with the meal.

• Order wine by the glass if you prefer, just as you would in less fancy places. This is highly recommended for people who drink lightly.

Ordering wine

• If you know which wine you want, order it.

• If the wine list does not give enough information to let you make an intelligent choice, ask the waiter or wine steward to bring several possible choices to the table. Don't hesitate to ask a wine steward or waiter for advice.

• You should be shown the bottle before it's opened. If a bottle arrives already opened, send it back. No European would allow such a thing to pass.

• If the waiter tells you that he doesn't have the bottle of wine you ordered, but does have one just like it, ask the price. This will avoid angry confrontations at bill time.

Wine etiquette

• If you choose a red wine, ask the waiter to open it immediately, to let it breathe. If it's the only wine you'll be having with your meal, you can ask him to pour it right away.

• If you choose a white wine or some Portuguese wines, note that they should be chilled. The long-necked bottles of German and Alsatian white wines make this difficult, unless they're turned upside down in an ice bucket. A good waiter will do this without being told. Don't let the wine get too cold or it will lose some of its taste and bouquet.

• After the waiter opens a bottle, he should hand you the cork. Squeeze the cork to make sure it's solid, then give it a quick sniff to check for any rancid odor. Set it on the table. The waiter will then pour some of the wine into your glass.

• Watch out for two things as you taste wine: a foul taste from the cork or an acid (vinegar) bite. You will eventually get a bad bottle of wine, and it is not bad manners to send it back. However, bad bottles are very rare.

• If you think the wine is borderline, let someone else taste it for a final decision — even the waiter. This may not be perfect etiquette, but your enjoyment should come first.

• Large wine glasses and water goblets are best for drinking wine. If you think the glasses are too small, ask for larger ones.

Wines for a Splurge

Country	Region	Best labels
Red Wines		
France	Bordeaux (five-year-old)	Lafite Latour Haut-Brion
	Burgundy (three-year-old)	Romanée-Conti Le Musigny Le Chambertin Clos de Fèves Le Corton
	Beaujolais (one- to three-year-old)	Brouilly Chénas Chiroubles Côte de Brouilly Fleurie Juliénas Morgon Moulin-à-Vent Saint-Amour
	Rhône	Châteauneuf-du-Pape Côte Rôtie Hermitage
Italy	Chianti (Classico) Bardolino Barolo Valpolicella Barbaresco Gattinara (Monsecco)	
Spain	Rioja	
White Wines		
France	Bordeaux	Sauternes Graves
	Burgundy	Chablis Pouilly-Fuissé Saint-Véran Pinot-Chardonnay Mâcon
Germany	Mosels* Rheins	
Italy	Soave Verdicchio Orvieto	

*Look at label: **Qualitätswein** is good; **Qualitätswein mit Prädikat,** better.

European Table Manners

- It's not unusual for lunch or dinner to last two or three hours.

- You can put your forearms (not your elbows) on the table and fit right in.

- When you eat with a European, always wish him "good appetite." If you can't say it in the native language, say it in English.

- In many countries, foods will not be served simultaneously or on the same plate, but as a succession of dishes.

- Europeans eat with their forks in their left hands so that they don't have to shift them back and forth when they use their knives. (It makes sense.)

- Many restaurants use the same knife and fork for all courses. You're expected to wipe them off with a piece of your bread.

- You can also use bread to wipe the plate clean. Or put bread on a fork to mop up sauces.

- Europeans often skin fruit with a knife and fork.

- An American will spit seeds and pits into an open hand before placing them on a plate. A European will spit them into a hand cupped as if it were holding the bottom of a glass, then he will put the pits on the plate.

- An American places his knife and fork side-by-side on the plate to signal that he is done with his meal, while a European often crosses them.

- When toasting someone in Europe, don't clink the glasses together. Do look the other person squarely in the eye.

- Note that most Europeans do not order coffee with the meal, but drink it afterwards. Coffee tends to be very strong.

Good (but Less Fashionable) Restaurants

You really don't have to splurge to eat well in Europe. After all, most Europeans don't eat in the fancier places, but they still demand quality for their money. And they get it.

Signs of a good restaurant

- Look for a menu (in the native language) posted outside near the entrance. This will make it easy for you to judge both the food and the price range before going in. Places with good food and charm often have menus written out in longhand. Specialties change daily, and this is the easiest way for the restaurant to keep up with them.

• Look for a series of set-price meals on the menu. In Europe, it's common to see four or five set-price meals on a menu. A set-price meal will include an hors d'oeuvre, a main dish (or two), vegetable, salad, dessert, bread, and so on. You won't pay for these items separately or **à la carte.**

• Look for a well-dressed clientele with a sprinkling of businessmen.

• A well-lit interior — cozy and cheerful.

• Lots of people during the main meal hours.

• Only one or two waitresses working, because the restaurant's small and intimate.

• Good, moderately priced wines.

• Cloth napkins.

• Flowers simply arranged in inexpensive vases.

Saving on tips

In most European restaurants, a service charge is added to the bill, so check to see if it's there before leaving an additional tip.

• If you see something like **service compris** or **servizio compreso** written on the menu itself, the tip is included in the prices listed, and the waiter should not add any further charges to the bill. Check it, however, since many waiters make conscious efforts to dupe American tourists.

• If you see **service non compris, service en sus,** or **service net** on the menus, service is not included.

• If you're not sure whether the service charge is included in the listed prices, just ask.

Cover charges

In many restaurants, you pay what is known as a cover charge. Sometimes it's included in the listed prices, sometimes it's not.

• Look for **couvert, coperto,** or **cubeirto** noted somewhere on the menu.

• Even if you don't find these words, ask the waiter whether there is any cover charge.

Cutting the cost of meals

- Eat your main meal at lunch. You'll enjoy the same food at a fraction of the price you'd pay in the evening.

- When a menu lists several separate but similar dishes, order the least expensive dish. The more expensive dishes are usually a snare for tourists and snobs.

- Share a meal with a friend if you're really strapped. Just ask for another plate. You'll be charged a small extra fee for this service.

- Ask the waiter whether the restaurant serves half portions. If it does, you'll cut the cost of the meal considerably.

- Don't order the same dish as someone else at your table if you're both hearty eaters. If you both order crab, they'll often split the crab in two. If only one of you orders crab, they'll give that person the whole thing.

- Follow the drinking habits of the area in which you're traveling. Replace cocktails with a local drink.

- In modest restaurants, ask for a house, ordinary, open, local, table, or regional wine. These terms refer to wine served in carafes (pitchers). Carafes come in one-quarter, one-half, and one-liter sizes. You may have to use sign language to indicate what you want.

- Avoid ordering a rosé for "split parties." Order a bottle of red and a bottle of white. For those who want rosé, blend the two in a glass — that's how it's done. Note too that most sparkling wines **(Schaumwein, spumant, spumante)** are inferior and overpriced.

- Skip soft drinks, butter, and ice. Most Europeans go without these "luxury" items. When you see the prices, so will you!

- Skip coffee at the end of a meal, if you can, because it's very expensive.

Watching out for con games

Most restaurants are reputable businesses. But a lot of money can be made by fleecing unsuspecting tourists — so beware.

- Avoid places with tour buses waiting outside, or any establishment that hires a food pimp to stand in the doorway and usher you in! Good places don't have to be sold.

- If a waiter tells you that there are no set-price meals today, despite what the menu out front says, get up and leave the restaurant. That menu is a trap for tourists, since **à la carte** prices will be higher.

- Bait-and-switch techniques are common worldwide. One of the most common: "We don't have the dish you ordered, but we do have one just like it." Ask for the cost of the new dish!

- If a waiter places unsolicited gifts on the table, such as butter or unordered hors d'oeuvres, ask him how much they cost. If the cost seems unreasonable, send them back.

- Some waiters write the bill on the tablecloth (really made of paper) or blurt out a figure after mental gyrations lasting a minute or more. To avoid being overcharged, add the bill up yourself. You might make a mental note of the approximate cost while ordering.

- If you think someone has overcharged you, say, "The last time I was here the wine (or whatever item) was less expensive." If they've made an error, they'll excuse themselves and change the price.

Picnics

A long-time favorite form of entertainment, the picnic is one of the best ways to keep food costs down in Europe. Europeans avoid the high cost of dining-car food by doing this on trains — so why not give it a try? Naturally, if you picnic on the roadside, be sure to get well off the shoulder, to avoid possible accidents and a fine.

Shopping for supplies

You'll find most kinds of food in supermarkets, although in smaller towns you may have to go to several shops to get what you need. Each shop will specialize in one product: baked goods, meats, cheeses, produce, wine, and so on. Foods will be sold in metric measures: a kilo, made up of 1,000 grams, is equivalent to 2.2 pounds; a liter is about a quart.

- Never buy picnic food in train stations. Go to a nearby market where prices will be much lower.

- Carry a fishnet or plastic bag with you, since many smaller stores won't provide bags.

Buying bread

- Try to buy bread early in the morning when it is warm and fresh. Since these breads go stale quickly, buy only the amount you'll need.

- Ask to have a larger loaf cut in two if you won't need it all. You'll pay for the half loaf only!

- To prevent bread from going stale, wrap it loosely in a moist towel.

Buying meat and cheese

- Meat will often be sliced to your specification. You can specify either a certain number of slices or an exact total weight.

- Whenever you buy meat in a shop, ask for a little less than you think you'll need. Butchers **always** cut extra, knowing that no one will refuse meat that's already been cut!

- As with fresh bread, you may have trouble with cheese drying out. Wrap it loosely in a towel lightly moistened with vinegar.

- Some cheeses, like Camembert and Brie, taste best **au point,** a French expression meaning creamy in the center. However, these cheeses should be stored in a plastic bag, or the aroma will overpower you as they ripen.

Buying produce

- Don't be intimidated into buying poor produce just because the owner decides to stuff bruised apples in your bag — but don't offend the owner by fingering too much of his stock.

Buying wine

In some shops, you'll find huge casks from which you can buy wine in varying degrees (**degrés**) of quality. The better the wine, the more expensive it is. Although the French can distinguish them, you won't be able to tell the difference yourself, except between the worst and the best wine.

- Choose the middle-priced wine.

- Always ask to taste these wines. Some of them may have gone bad. Do the same when buying large flasks of wine (as in Italy).

- Supply your own bottle if you can. If you don't have one, they'll give you one at a small charge.

- Never discard bottles, since you'll get a refund for turning them back in. And never cross a border without returning bottles, since they may not be accepted in another country.

• If you forget to bring a bottle opener, don't despair or use your teeth. Just twist a key or small coin under the metal folds of the cap until they start to bend out. Keep moving the key around the base of the cap until it pops off. It takes a little time, but it works.

• If you forget to bring a corkscrew, push two nails or sharp objects into the cork. Place any long metal object between them and twist. This device will work, though not as well as a corkscrew.

National Specialties and Customs

Every country has its characteristic way with food. During your travels, don't miss opportunities to taste special dishes! The following list is by no means exhaustive, but **"Bon appétit,"** anyway.

Austria

Austrians are world famous for their pastries and desserts.

• Savor the local custom of **Jause,** a midafternoon snack, at a coffeehouse. Coffeehouses have become an Austrian institution, a kind of social and intellectual meeting place, where you can sample a dozen varieties of coffee, including Turkish, which is "hot as hell, sweet as love, and twice as black as night."

Belgium

Over a hundred Michelin rating stars have gone to Belgian restaurants, including one of the rare three-star places outside France (the Villa Lorraine in Brussels).

• Try **moules,** steamed mussels prepared in a variety of ways. Use one of the shells as a pincer to pull the meat out from the other shells — a European custom that works perfectly.

• Try some of the Ardennes ham, if you get a chance!

• Eat at a country inn. Many rural inns boast kitchens that would do France justice. Some of them are in the **relais de campagne** chain. Write to the French National Tourist Office (see p. 228) for a pamphlet that includes simple maps and up-to-date prices.

• Try French fries and Belgian mayonnaise.

Denmark

Don't leave Denmark without trying a smorgasbord. The Danish smorgasbord, a cold table of Danish specialties with such delicacies as fresh herring and local cheese, is well worth a splurge. They are generally served at lunch and follow a specific pattern, which you should observe. A smorgasbord can fill an afternoon and even the largest empty stomach.

- When your waiter comes to your table, give him your order for **schnapps** for the first course and beer thereafter. You can substitute apple juice or soft drinks for both, if you prefer nonalcoholic drinks. Etiquette demands that you have something to drink with the meal, even though it jacks up the bill.

- Take your plate to the buffet and serve yourself any amount of herring and fish you want — but only these, nothing else. Then return to your table and enjoy them. When you're done with the fish, leave your plate on the table and get a new one from the buffet table. You can return as often as you like within any course, but you can't circle back to a previous one.

- Now serve yourself salads and cold meats — as little or as much as you'd like. When you've eaten them, leave your plate behind once again and try the hot dishes on a new, clean plate.

- Follow the same procedure for the finale, the cheese and fruit. When you've finished this dessert, the waiter will appear to take your order for coffee. (Note that the fellow has been around all along, removing dirty plates from the table.)

- Other treats: **smørrebrød** (open-faced sandwiches), **fadøl** (draft beer), and **wienerbrød** (pastry). Milk's a steal, too.

- Don't confuse **kr** ("kroner" — Danish money) for **kl** ("hour") when you read Danish menus.

- In the countryside, stop in at one of the rural inns known as **kroer** (**kro** is singular). You'll sample typical Danish fare, from freshly sliced smoked salmon to just-caught shrimp.

France

- Sunday lunch in France is similar in popularity to our Saturday night dinners out. Without a reservation you'll have a tough time getting into a restaurant. The French dress up for this special occasion. You should too.

- When driving into the countryside, carry a list of the **relais de campagne.** These little inns are noted for superb food and service. Get the brochure by writing the French National Tourist Office (see p. 228). It gives full information, including simple maps.

- Few French drink cocktails, considered much too hard a drink to begin a meal. If you order a martini, you'll be served vermouth with a Martini label. Don't make a scene. It's delicious!

- Bread and **croissants** (crescent rolls) are equally delicious when newly baked. You'll get them with your continental breakfast.

- In France you'll discover over 500 varieties of cheese. Note that when you're served cheese on a platter, you should always leave the cheese in the same shape as when it came to you (triangles should still be triangles). It is considered very poor manners to do otherwise!

- Always feel free to sample a number of varieties of cheese when in a restaurant. Ask for a small piece **(un petit morceau)** of three or four. There's no extra charge.

- Soup, omelets, **steak frites** (steak with French fries), **yaourt** (yogurt) — these cost **very** little in most French restaurants and are excellent!

- In small French restaurants, you mix your own dressing from ingredients provided on the table. Pour several spoonfuls of oil on a dish, mix in a little vinegar and a bit of mustard. Sprinkle with salt and pepper. Now mix thoroughly and pour over the salad.

- When eating fondue in France, the custom is to kiss the person next to you if you drop bread or meat into the pot. (Men and women sit alternately around the table.) You also buy a bottle of wine for the group.

- The famous fish soup **bouillabaisse** is made only for two or more people. You'll find that it's fantastic in Marseilles.

- French fries are rarely served with catsup. You'll be offered mustard, vinegar, or fresh mayonnaise in most instances. Again, **vive la différence!**

- Popcorn, only recently popular, comes sugared unless you ask for salt **(du sel).**

- An exception to the rule that lunch is a bargain: meals are more expensive at noon in Nice.

- Many French foods are seasoned with garlic. To cut the aftertaste and reduce bad breath, eat cheese and a couple of sugar cubes drenched in crème de menthe at the end of the meal.

Germany

- Expect excellent cooking in any of the Romantik hotels and restaurants. These charming inns offer regional cooking at its best (see p. 74). The same is true for the castle hotels, combining old-world atmosphere with outstanding local cuisine (see p. 72).

- You'll find typical restaurants in most towns offering peasant fare: rough bread (just baked), sausages, sauerkraut, schnitzel, and home brew. Very reasonably priced.

- You'll find that the food in most German railroad stations is surprisingly good.

- Remember when it comes to food, the **Wurst** is best in Germany.

- When you're offered a large radish in a beer hall, try it. You pay for the radish, cover it with salt, and when the water pours out, you eat it.

Great Britain

- English breakfasts are usually outstanding, with everything from porridge to eggs and bacon. The bacon is usually served on the undercooked side. If you want it crisp, ask for burnt bacon or bacon American style.

- Otherwise, avoid "traditional English" fare — it's still not very good. Instead, sample foreign cooking! The exceptions are noted below.

- Don't think that pubs only offer good beer. Many of them serve snacks and full meals as well — at reasonable prices. Steak-and-kidney pie is a staple, usually filling and nicely prepared at the right price.

- If you want something milder than straight beer in a pub, ask for a shandy. You'll get beer and something similar to 7-Up mixed together.

- Splurge in London by trying one of the East Indian spots that offer spicy cooking — a real change of pace that'll curl your hair.

- Join the British for tea from 3:45 to 5:45 p.m. daily. Dress up and do it right at the following London hotels: Brown's, the Connaught, the Dorchester, the Hyde Park, the Ritz, the Royal Lancaster, or the Savoy.

- Ask for a serviette when you want a napkin; otherwise, you will have ordered a diaper.

- The term **rare** for meat translates to mean slightly pink or well done. Ask for your meat **bloody,** a term that will pale many an intrepid waiter's face.

Greece

Everyone admits that there is a language barrier, so don't be surprised when you're asked to go into the kitchen to pick out your lunch or dinner. Without putting your finger in the pot, point out the dish you'd like to eat.

- Meal hours are late by American standards. Lunch begins at 1 p.m. and goes to 4 p.m. Dinner begins about 10 p.m. and stretches to midnight (more or less).

- Take an afternoon snack, as many Greeks do, at cafés, since dinner is late. You don't have to eat and run at these places; you can dawdle all you want. Try some of the sweets.

- Don't expect to leave large tips in Greece, but do leave token tips. The tip for the waiter goes directly on the plate, while the busboy's gratuity should be left on the table.

- In Athens, you can get something close to an American coffee by asking for **Nescafé.**

Ireland

No one goes to Ireland for its cuisine. The food's just as good and just as bad as English food, so the same advice applies.

- Eat a big breakfast in the morning — porridge, eggs, bacon, sausage, soda bread, tea. It may be the best meal you'll get all day.

- Head for the nearest pub and have a sandwich or some oxtail soup for lunch. If you want a big meal, have it at noon, since Irish restaurants serve only light dinners in the evening. If you do go to a fancy restaurant for dinner, be sure to try the salmon.

- Guinness stout, is, of course, the national drink. It's rich, dark, foamy, and somewhat bitter, and in Ireland it's served at room temperature. Give it a chance.

- You'll never drink alone in an Irish pub. Someone will soon join you and buy you a drink. In fact, it's an Irish custom to buy drinks for everyone in the group, and you'll be expected to do likewise. By the end of the evening (pubs close at 11:30 p.m.), you're likely to have a line of drinks waiting for your attention.

Italy

- In most restaurants, pick the table that suits you and sit down. Then look at the closest waiter for a nonverbal sign of approval. If the table is reserved (which is rare), he'll point you to another one nearby.

- You are not expected to order a full meal right from the start, although you can if you prefer. Italians frequently order only one dish at a time, **à la carte.**

- You'll often find displays of food at the entrance to a restaurant. If you don't understand the menu, you can always point to things you'd like.

- You can expect a surcharge for the music of a local band or symphony at a restaurant or café.

- Make a meal of spaghetti, which Italians consider to be no more than an antipasto or warm-up dish. Italians eat less sauce on their spaghetti than Americans do. If you want more, ask for some (**"Più di salsa, per favore"**). Meatballs aren't served with spaghetti in Italy.

- **Al pomodoro** means "with tomato"; **alla Bolognese,** "with meat"; **al vongole,** "with clams." **Scallopine** refers to slices of veal, **salsa** or **sugo** is "sauce," and **al dente** pasta is "slightly chewy."

- Italian pizza disappoints many Americans, because it's crusty and served cool (almost cold). In many pizza spots, you can buy it by the slice. You pay by weight.

- Italy is one place in Europe where you can get excellent ice cream — and enough of it!

Netherlands

- If you're trying to keep costs down, look for an emblem with a fork on it in restaurant windows. This is a symbol for a restaurant serving tourist menus. About 600 such restaurants are found in Holland.

- Don't leave the Netherlands without trying the Indonesian **rijst-tafel** (rice table), consisting of a dozen or more dishes laid out for one of the world's greatest culinary adventures. It's a symphony of food, very expensive but worth every florin.

- Seafood tends to be vastly overpriced. Herring's the exception. When the herring comes in, the Dutch go wild, chomping it down right in the streets together with bits of onion spread on rough bread.

Norway

- Simple continental breakfasts are often included in room prices. Some hotels serve larger, more typical Norwegian fare that may include a morning **smorgåsbord** with everything from sliced tomatoes and cucumbers to pickled herring and sardines.

Rømmeggrøt, a filling, fattening porridge, may be difficult to enjoy, though it's authentic.

- Breakfast may include many varieties of milk, some of which are similar to sour cream or buttermilk. For "normal" milk ask simply for **melk.** When in doubt, sample a small amount first. But remember that many Norwegians prefer buttermilk on their cereal!

- Norwegians tend to eat a light snack for lunch. A heavier, more satisfying meal is served in the late afternoon or early evening from 4 to 6 p.m. It's a better buy than lunch in most restaurants.

- For a coffee break try **vaffler,** traditional waffles that are served cold.

- You'll find excellent peasant food in **caffestova,** coffee rooms featuring hearty cuts of meat, fresh potatoes and vegetables — all served in simple surroundings at reasonable prices. Such places are not oriented to tourists; that's the reason they're such an exceptional value. They're often tucked away on second floors with only a simple sign on a first floor door or side of a building. Ask for the nearest **caffestova** if you're having trouble locating one.

- Open-faced sandwiches, **smørrebrød,** are served in simple cafés and fancier restaurants as well. Extremely popular and very tasty — don't leave without trying them.

- Beer can be quite expensive, but often is the only practical choice.

- Some other specialties most Americans enjoy: fresh trout or salmon (expensive but excellent); shrimp and crayfish, popular along the coast and in southern Norway; any of the preserves that taste almost like fresh fruit; goat cheese; and multer berries, beige mountain berries, as expensive as they are distinctive in taste.

Portugal

- The government supports a network of country inns **(pousadas)** throughout the country. Rooms in these inns are a great value, and so are meals. Country inns offer regional specialties and drinks at bargain prices. You do not have to stay in a **pousada** to eat there, but you should call ahead for a reservation.

- In Lisbon and tourist resorts nearby, you'll be pushed into hearing **fado,** wailing love songs sung by black-shawled women in nightclubs. Wherever you hear **fado,** you'll pay a social security tax on the total amount of the bill. Keep it small.

- Chicken and seafood are the staples, along with potatoes and rice. The latter are served with everything, so ask for green vegetables or salad to break up the monotony.

- Try the chicken **piri-piri**, spicy and delicious.

- Also sample the seafood and beer combination offered in **cervejarias**. Noisy, informal, jammed — but great.

- Try the **cataplana** if you get to the Algarve — an excellent stew.

- Savor the almond sweets, too. This area is one of the main almond-producing regions in the world.

Spain

- Throughout Spain, you'll find **paradores,** inns that offer both rooms and meals at reasonable prices. You can get a list of these inns from the National Tourist Office of Spain (see p. 229) or Iberia Airlines.

- Meal hours in Spain are late. Lunch from 2 to 3 p.m., dinner from 10 p.m. to midnight (an hour or so earlier in the winter). If you want to rub elbows with the Spanish, you must change your eating habits.

- If you want to try typical or regional cooking, ask for a nearby **tasca** or **restaurante típico.** You may have a language barrier once inside, but the food will be worth the effort — both interesting and reasonably priced.

- Join the locals in sampling **tapas,** snacks found on the counters of bars and small restaurants. Order a glass of wine, which is generally delivered with something to nibble on. If you're with a group of hungry people and want a larger order of any particular item, ask for **una racion.** Don't be afraid to use sign language; just point to whatever food you want!

- Fish is one of the most reliable dishes throughout most of Spain, particularly along the coast. Obviously, it's best if **pescada fresco** or fresh fish. Ask if in doubt!

- Don't bother ordering beef. It won't measure up to your expectations.

- Sweets, liqueurs, and cheese will cut through the odor and aftertaste of garlic.

- The safest choice for dessert: fresh fruit, usually ripe and juicy. Peel it. **Flan,** a custard with caramel sauce, can be a good choice in more expensive restaurants but something to avoid in lesser places. Note that pastries in Spain are not as sweet as you're used to, but they're something you'll want to try anyway.

• For an inexpensive breakfast or late afternoon snack from 6 to 7 p.m., try **churros,** thin, round doughnuts or **porra,** thick, straight doughnuts. Neither are as sweet as our version. You dunk them in **café con leche** (coffee and milk) or hot chocolate (**chocolate**), the latter very thick and creamy. You find these in bars and small cafés.

• **Paella,** bits of fish and meat smothered in saffron rice, should be on your must-try list. It takes 40 thousand blossoms of an autumn crocus to make one pound of saffron — which explains why saffron is so expensive.

• **Arroz,** rice, is a staple.

• Stick to red wines throughout much of Spain, but give the white ones a chance in Barcelona.

• **Sangria,** a fruit-filled punch made of different wines, is sweetened with sugar or honey and served in an ice-filled pitcher.

• In the northwestern region around Oviedo, try the local apple cider **cidra,** somewhat similar to champagne and poured with a flourish from a bottle held high above the glass — a real show.

• In Galicia, north of Portugal, don't miss the **ribeiro** wine, sour with lots of body.

• If you prefer drinks with a mild alcoholic content, ask for wine or beer **con gaseosa.** The drink will come mixed with charged water similar to 7-Up in taste.

• A special treat: if you're in Madrid during the summer, try a **leche merengada,** frozen milk and egg whites sprinkled with cinnamon. If you would like it flavored with coffee, ask for a **blanco e negro.**

• Also cold and a summer drink, but more unusual with a flavor similar to that of coconut: **horchata.** It originates in the area around Valencia but can be found in other areas as well.

Wales

• At pubs, order food at the bar and carry it self-service style to your table.

• Our beer is called "lager" in Wales.

• Lamb and mutton dishes are a treat.

Drinking Guide

Europe is filled with special drinks, from **schnapps** and **slivovitz** to **genever** and **grappa.** Start off with a few drinks of **aquavit,** chilled in the snow until it's so cold it slides down your throat like a chip of ice; or sip the licorice-tasting **pastis,** which turns cloudy with a splash of water or piece of ice; or try chugging **aguardente,** favorite of Portuguese fishermen, while you watch it burn holes in the deck where you spilled it.

Cutting costs on drinks

- Always bring a bottle of booze into Scandinavia, where costs are astronomical! And stick to local specialties wherever else you go — imports are always expensive.

- Eschew minuscule drinks served between acts at London theaters, and pop around the corner to a local pub for a real drink instead.

- Avoid ordering individual drinks if you're in a group at nightclubs. Ask for the price of the least expensive bottle of wine, to be shared by all at the table.

Local peculiarities

- Order a double (for which you'll pay double) in England to end up with something similar to a shot of booze.

- When sampling a smorgasbord (see p. 148), you're expected to gulp, not sip, the **aquavit:** if you let it warm up, you'll be able to taste it (and you don't want to).

- **Genever,** a Dutch liquor, comes in two strong forms: **oud** (old) and **jong** (young). Both of them could peel varnish off a table.

- Port wine is always passed to the left (port vs. starboard?) — even if the person who wants it is sitting to your immediate right.

For wine lovers

- Head immediately for France, Germany, Italy, Portugal, Austria, and Spain. Great Britain, Greece, Hungary, Switzerland, and Yugoslavia have limited wine production, too.

- White wines are the best buy in Germany; reds are the best buy in France and Italy.

- Try the young Austrian wines **(Heurige)** in early May. Places serving these wines hang a sprig of evergreen from the eaves.

- You may not care for the resin in the wine in Greece. If that's the case, ask for **aretsinoto krasi,** unresinated wine.

- In Sicily, drink only bottled wines (Segesta, Marsala, Corvo Malvasia).

- Try a very interesting Portuguese wine, **vinho verde,** which is consumed young and cool. It comes from the northern part of the country and is often overlooked by travelers.

Sampling drinks and wines for free

Wherever liquor and liqueurs are made, you can take a tour of the distillery and sample the results for free. One of the most popular tours is in Cognac, where the authentic brandy known as "the heart of wine" is made.

- A well-marked, 62-mile trail winds its way through Scotland from one distillery to another, for those who would like to sample some of the world's great Scotches.

- In northern Portugal, you'll find the **entrepôts** for port wine at Vila Nova de Gaia, the town across the river from Oporto. You'll be able to sample everything from newly fashionable white ports to 30-year-old tawnies.

- Not quite free, but very inexpensive, are the port wines served at the Vinho do Porto do Solar, Rua São Pedro Alcantara 42, Lisbon. Ask the concierge for a map showing its exact location in the center of town.

- Throughout France, you can sample free wines wherever you see the sign **"Dégustation gratuite."** It would be hard to drive anywhere without seeing several of these.

- To sample champagne, try the **caves** of Épernay and Reims.

- For Italian wines, head to the Bolla Vineyards near Verona.

- And for Spanish sherries, try the **bodegas** (Gonzales, Byass and Company, Ltd.) near Cadiz.

For beer lovers

Most breweries offer tours and free beer to participants. Very popular are the Tuborg (Copenhagen) and Heineken (Amsterdam) tours. Don't be prejudiced by what you've heard and read about German beers being the best. They're fabulous, but so are Belgian and British brews.

- Order tap instead of bottled beer whenever you can. It comes out in a frosty, froth-covered mug containing a quarter-, a half-, or a full liter of brew. To show the amount of beer you want, just point to the size glass (mug) you'd like.

- **Tap beer** in five languages: **bière à pression** (French), **Bier vom Fass** (German), **birra del barril** (Italian), **cerveza de (en) barril** (Spanish), **cerveja a late (a giraffa)** (Portuguese).

- Always ask for **export öl** in Scandinavia, to get beer with more than a smidgeon of alcohol.

- Look for beer halls **(cervejarias)** in Spain and Portugal where you can wash down many types of shellfish with ice cold beer.

- Don't worry about brand names in Germany, where every hamlet produces exquisite beer. Stick with the local brew!

- Try pub crawling, one of the most popular forms of entertainment in Great Britain. It consists of sampling many beers in many pubs during the evening. Pubs (locals) offer fabulous people watching and suddenly become "private" — for whoever's still left inside — at closing time. Note that pubs close from about 2:30 p.m. to 6 p.m. daily.

Basics on water

- The water in the WC (toilet) of a train is not drinkable. Bring your own in a flask. That's what Europeans do, since the cost for bottled water on trains is unbelievably high.

- You'll find faucets for drinking water in train stations and nearby parks. If you've forgotten to bring a flask, buy water or juice by the bottle in stores near the station. It will be very reasonable.

- In some restaurants you'll find carafes of tap water on the table, for which there is no charge. Do what the locals do and drink it — unless you espy unusual forms of aquatic life in the bottle.

- If there is no water on the table, you'll have to ask for it. Ask for tap water to avoid the charges for bottled mineral water. Here's **tap water** in five languages: **l'eau du robinet** (French), **Leitungswasser** (German), **l'acqua du rubinetto** (Italian), **a agua a torneira** (Portuguese), **la aqua del grifo** (Spanish).

- If you order mineral water, waiters will ask you whether you want mineral water with or without **gaz,** or carbonation. If you don't want fizzy water, shake your head and say **no gaz.** This pidgin talk will get the message across.

- If a waiter brings an open bottle of mineral water to your table, send it back. European custom demands that the bottle be opened at the table.

Soft and cold drinks

- Cold milk is a common drink in Holland, Scandinavia, northern Germany, and Great Britain. Skip it in other areas (or buy it in grocery stores). Beer could really be considered a soft drink in parts of Scandinavia, since the alcohol content is minimal.

- The inflated price of soft drinks in restaurants eventually discourages most Americans from drinking them abroad. However, bottled soft drinks, sold by the liter in grocery stores, are quite reasonable.

15 Getting Around

Inter-European travel can be quite complex. It would be a good idea to read about the modes of transportation you've chosen for traveling around Europe before you go abroad. Then refresh your memory by reading it one more time at the beginning of your trip.

Flying

Most of the ideas that will help you enjoy plane travel to the fullest have been covered in earlier sections. However, here are some hints that are most pertinent to flying around Europe.

Departure taxes

In some countries, you'll have to pay a departure tax at the airport when you check in. This is one good way of using spare change. However, it can be extremely frustrating if you have to cash a traveler's check (and lose on the exchange) just to pay this tax.

- Ask the airline ahead of time whether you'll be subject to such a tax on departure.

Arranging for Cars

Having your own car will offer you great flexibility; however, you'll need to know a few details to prevent trouble when arranging to pick one up in Europe.

Picking up a new car at the factory

- In addition to the basic documents, get the **Green Card** for insurance, the **registration card** as proof of ownership, a nationality sticker (needed to cross borders), and the **list of service stations** that provide maintenance repairs.

- Tell the clerk that you have a first-aid kit and a triangular "Danger" sign, even if you don't, since prices are inflated for these items at the factory.

- Check the car from top to bottom. Make sure everything works: the horn, wipers, lights, seats, seat belts, etc.

- Ask the clerk to show you how to work the jack. (This is a good way to make sure there is one and that it works.) Check on the spare tire: take it out and look at it carefully.

- Give the car a quick check to make sure all fluids are up to the "Full" mark. Don't assume anything is right.

- Get a good road map, if you haven't already done so.

- Have the car filled up. (The factory will give you just enough gas to let you get to the pump outside, and sometimes less than that.)

- Ask for directions to the road leading to your first destination. This one step can save you an hour or more of aggravation!

Car insurance

- Insure your car through the factory for the shortest time permissible. For longer trips abroad, extend the coverage through a private European insurance company. If you're on a short trip, accept the fact that insurance will be a rip-off: you have no choice, anyway.

- You'll need a permanent address abroad if you want to extend coverage through a private company. The permanent address can be that of a friend or relative.

- Check your insurance company's Green Card, which is a kind of folder consisting of many sheets of green paper. At the bottom of each sheet, you'll see abbreviations for European countries. If any of these have been crossed out, your insurance will not be valid there.

- If you'll be traveling in any of the Scandinavian countries (Denmark, Finland, Norway, Sweden), make sure that none of their names has been crossed out. If any one name has been crossed out, your insurance will not be valid in the other countries because of a reciprocal insurance agreement.

Buying a used car

You'll find long lines of car owners carrying placards advertising their cars in front of American Express offices, especially in the fall.

- Don't look for recent models. They cost the same (or nearly the same) as brand-new cars when sold on an export basis.

- Make sure that all local taxes have been paid. If you buy a model slated for export, you won't have to pay them at all.

- If you're buying the car from a private party, make sure that you can legally have the insurance transferred to your name.

- Buy a car that can be serviced in the area where you'll be traveling.

- Assume that everything's going to fall apart 10 minutes after you buy it, and make an offer accordingly.

Questions about Rental Cars

- What is the full car-rental price for the length of time you plan to travel?
- Are there any additional taxes or service charges to pay?
- Is there an extra charge for leaving the car in another city? (Tell them where you intend to leave the car.)

- Is there an extra charge for full collision coverage? If so, what is it? Pay it. If full collision coverage isn't available in an area (as in the Azores), do not drive a rental car there. An accident and the ensuing legal hassles could keep you a prisoner in a foreign country for a long time.
- If the car breaks down, who pays for repairs?
- Do repairs have to be done in specific garages, or can they be done anywhere? If specific places are established, get a list.

- Who pays for oil, gas, and lubrication?

- Is there a documents charge?

- How much is the deposit?

- Can you pay the bill in dollars? (Great if you can.)

- What will the charge be if you should arrive later than agreed upon to return the car?

- If you cut the trip short, what will the charge be?

- If time and mileage come out to be less than the amount of your unlimited mileage agreement, will you be allowed to pay that smaller amount?

- How much is the charge per gallon for filling the car on return? You may save by filling it yourself?

- Are all the documents (Green Card and registration) in the car?

- Is there a map in the car? Is there a booklet on service stations for this make of car?

- Is the tank full of gas?

- Where's the jack? (Have them show you how it works.)

- Is there a spare tire in the car? (Check to see.)

- Are the tires in good condition? (Check by sticking a small coin into the tread to judge its depth.)

Renting a car in advance

- Make sure that you have the exact address where you are to pick up the car.
- Get a written confirmation of the arrangement in advance.

Renting a car once you arrive

Why not rent a car where it will be most economical to do so? If you will be traveling extensively by car, plan to start your trip in the country where the costs are lowest (p. 65).

- Rates are often lower in small towns outside the main tourist destinations.

- During the off-season, you can get substantial price reductions on car rental from agencies abroad. Call, or have the concierge call, several agencies to get a few comparative prices. Savings at smaller agencies can range from 25 to 50 percent off the large companies' prices. (Be sure to tip the concierge for his efforts!)

- Rent small cars, which are better in every way. They slurp less gas, are roomy if you're traveling reasonably light, can go anywhere, can weasel into tiny parking spots, and cost less on fees for ferries and toll roads.

- Unlimited mileage agreements at a set cost per week are usually your best bet.

- In some areas, there are age limitations on applications for car rental. These vary from age 23 on the low end to age 70 on the high end.

Shipping a car to the U.S.

There's only one word to describe this whole process — painful.

- Note that shipping rates vary, but northern ports are generally less expensive.

- Ask the manufacturer about reduced rates from specific ports.

- Make sure that the shipping cost estimate includes such services as draining the gas tank, steam cleaning the car, and waxing it (for protection against salt).

- Buy marine insurance.

- Arrive at the pier with as little gas as possible, since the gas tank will be drained.

- In the U.S., you'll have to clear the car through customs or pay an agent to do it. Either way, you'll pay duty and a handling charge.

- If you leave the car in storage for more than three days, you'll pay a daily storage charge.

- Brace yourself for a dock strike, which may delay the unloading of your car.

Driving

A car gives you much better access to the undeveloped areas of Europe than you have with other means of travel. But driving does have its drawbacks. You will have a lot to adjust to, and a lot to remember about driving laws and customs. For the adventurous, though, nothing beats it!

Gas

On the Continent, gas is usually sold by the liter (a little more than a quart). In Great Britain, it's usually sold by the imperial gallon (about five quarts). Prices may be double the pump total in some areas.

- Since gas station hours and days of business are unpredictable, play it safe and try not to get too low on gas.

- Note that European gas stations often charge for services like inflating tires, cleaning windshields, and checking the oil. Ask for such services — or do them yourself.

- In warm weather, buy gas in the early morning or late in the evening. You'll get more gas when it's cool.

- Fill up especially frequently when you're in Spain, Portugal, Yugoslavia, Greece, Norway, Sweden, or any of the islands. Open gas stations are long distances apart in these areas.

- Supergrade gas (95-octane) is generally worth the extra cost.

- Always ask for a specific amount of gas in the foreign currency, or the attendant may try to squeeze every last cent out of you.

- Fill up before crossing a border into a country where gas costs more. The following countries are listed in order of **increasing** gas prices: Spain, West Germany, the Netherlands, Austria, Switzerland, Norway, Ireland, Great Britain, Denmark, Luxembourg, Belgium, Finland, Portugal, Italy, France, Sweden.

Italian gas coupons

In Italy, you can cut gas costs by getting a **Carta Carburante Turistica,** which allows you to buy special coupons. This card is sporadically available to motorists driving a car with non-Italian plates. At present, you have to own the car to get these.

• Get the card as you cross the border into Italy.

• Use the card to buy coupons for a set number of gallons, allotted on a per-diem basis. These coupons (when available) are sold at local branches of the Automobile Club of Italy.

• To get coupons you'll need the registration number of your car.

• Check with the Italian Government Tourist Office to see whether coupons are or will soon be available (p. 228).

When the gas tank is empty

• When the gas tank is empty, use the mileage marathon technique: accelerate as slowly as possible to 20 miles per hour, then immediately turn off the ignition while moving into neutral gear. Let the car slow down to five miles per hour. Start the engine again and repeat the same steps. This technique can double and even triple gas mileage in an emergency!

• If your steering wheel locks when the ignition is off, this technique will not work. It's also not recommended for steep downhill grades — but you may have to take a gamble. Finally, it's illegal in some areas — but, late at night on a deserted road, you won't really care!

• If you have to stop, don't race the engine

• If the car won't stop running when you turn off the ignition, pop it dead in gear (not very good for the car, but you'll save gas).

• Don't allow the car to sway from side to side: this will save you one to two miles per gallon.

Road travel

The only fast roads in Europe are the superhighways. Other roads can be tied up by traffic, trucks (belching diesel smoke), repairs, mopeds, and even herds of goats.

Coastal and mountain roads must follow the natural contours of the hills, meaning hundreds of curves per mile. Passing is virtually impossible on many of these highways. You move as slowly as the slowest link in the chain.

• Start trips early and end them early.

• Try to average no more than 150 miles per day; even that's quite a bit.

- Do just the opposite of what most Europeans do. Instead of taking a break for lunch, drive between noon and 2 p.m. in order to take advantage of better traffic conditions.

- Avoid driving in cities. City traffic is almost always impossible, except on Sundays. On weekdays, if you must drive in cities at all, avoid morning and evening rush hours.

Maps

Good maps can make a trip an enjoyable, rather than a frustrating, experience. Chapter 3 has tips on where to obtain them before you reach Europe, but some prefer to buy them abroad.

- Select maps to conform with the kind of travel you are planning. Why buy expensive, detailed maps if you'll only be traveling between major cities? On the other hand, you'll appreciate such detail when you are exploring some rural areas.

- Many of the foreign automobile and touring clubs offer very good maps; those of the Touring Club of Italy are excellent.

- The Michelin maps, available in most bookstores abroad, are reliable. Make sure they're up-to-date (dates are printed on the cover of the map).

- In Great Britain, you can buy ordnance maps, extremely detailed for off-the-beaten-path trips. In Ireland, look for Geodetic Survey maps.

Driving Customs in Europe	
This chart outlines some of the regional peculiarities that you'll run into abroad. Note that you must wear a seat belt in most European countries and that children under 12 should be placed in the back seat, according to local ordinances.	
Austria	Don't drink and drive — not even one drink! Have chains for winter driving. In the mountains, cars going uphill have priority. Driving is slow in most areas.
Belgium	You must wear a seat belt. Watch for cyclists — thousands of them. Exceedingly slow driving.
Denmark	Stiff penalties for drinking and driving. Many ferries. Parking on the right side of the road only. Slow driving.

Finland	Stiff penalties for drinking and driving. Fill up frequently — don't get caught without gas. Have low beams on during the day from September 1 to April 30. Good, if long, driving.
France	**Always** give priority to cars on the right. Watch for mopeds and cyclists. Have chains for mountain driving in winter. Keep lights on in fog, mist, or poor light. Good driving overall.
Germany	Gas stations open all day on Autobahns. Very high speeds on Autobahns. Blink lights if you want to pass someone. Slower traffic must stay on the right! Excellent driving overall.
Great Britain	Drive on the left. Slow driving overall. Leave turn signal on while passing.
Greece	Ignore horns. Watch for flocks of goats and sheep. Back roads quite steep. Dangerous dirt roads through the mountains.
Ireland	Drive on the left. Tight, winding roads. Watch for flocks of animals. Fill up frequently. Slow driving.
Italy	Gas coupons occasionally available. See p. 165. Don't park in green zones, or the car may be towed. Charges on **autostrade** are steep; you pay when you exit. Cars are very helpful on Isola d'Elba. No cars can go to Capri. Off-season and round-trip reductions on ferries to Sicily. Chains are required in mountains in winter. Good driving on main roads, very slow on secondary routes (bad along the coast).

Luxembourg	Tight, winding roads. Watch for cyclists. Wear a seat belt. Good driving overall.
Netherlands	Wear a seat belt. Watch for cyclists. Use major roads when in a hurry. Leave car parked in Amsterdam. Good driving overall.
Norway	Don't drink and drive. Don't speed excessively (you will lose your license). Fill up frequently. Good, if long, driving overall. A "mile" is six American miles.
Portugal	Narrow roads in many areas. Cobblestone dangerous when wet. Frequent road repairs. Fill up often when off the beaten path. Watch for flocks of animals. Slow driving.
Spain	Stick to major highways for fast driving. Roads skirting the coast are slow. Trucks are a real problem. Flash lights or sound horn to pass. Righthand blinker on trucks is the signal to pass (all clear). Very slow driving overall.
Sweden	Don't drink and drive. Fill up frequently when off the beaten path. Good driving overall. A "mile" is six American miles.
Switzerland	Cars going up the mountain have priority. Yellow postal buses have priority (you must get over on the shoulder, in some cases). Chains are needed to cross passes in winter. Most driving is not in the mountains. Very good driving overall.

Yugoslavia	Have any dents or scratches noted in your passport, next to your visa, on entry into the country. You may be charged with an accident otherwise.
	Fill up frequently.
	The coastal route is packed during the summer.
	Slow driving overall.

Superhighways

Using superhighways is the fastest and most efficient way to get around in Europe. **Superhighway(s)** are called **autoroute(s)** (French), **Autobahn(en)** (Germany), **autostrada (autostrade)** (Italian), **auto estrada(s)** (Portuguese), and **autopista(s)** (Spanish).

- You'll have to pay tolls on many of them, but if you're in a hurry, they'll be worth the price.

Speed limits

Maximum speeds are posted in kilometers per hour (kph) except in Great Britain, which is not on the metric system. The main difference you'll find is the high (in some cases unlimited) speeds allowed on the major freeways.

- To convert into miles speed limits or mileage signs given in kilometers, divide the figure by 10 and multiply by 6. For example: 80 kph ÷ 10 = 8; 8 × 6 = 48 mph.

- In areas designated for high speed, slower traffic must stay to the right. If someone approaches you from behind, you must move over to make way. Often, cars coming from the rear will blink their lights as a warning signal for you to move over. Since speeds in the left lane can reach 120 to 140 miles per hour, if you do not move over, you can cause a serious accident.

Parking

One of the biggest headaches for the motorist in Europe is finding a place to park the car. You can almost always find space in a garage, but the daily charge of several dollars adds up quickly. Most people prefer to park on the street and take their chances with vandalism. If you've got an aerial, push it down. "Bend-the-Aerial" is a favorite European game, "Break-off-the-Aerial" is a popular variation.

- If you do find a parking place, take it and leave the car parked for good.

- If the place you find has a meter, take it until an unmetered parking place opens up.

- Don't put money into the meter. Accept the fact that you're going to get a ticket.

- Some people think parking tickets make good souvenirs — you'll have to decide about that for yourself.

Parking tickets

"No Parking" signs may be placed on the walls of buildings or painted on the walls, and are sometimes very difficult to see. Make sure you're not blocking someone's driveway, which may be closed with an iron gate. However, keep in mind that police in Europe rarely tow cars with foreign license plates unless they're blocking traffic or the commissioner's driveway. But don't expect immunity from the law just because you're a foreigner.

- Do not park in green zones in Italy, especially if you're driving a car with Italian plates. If you park in these areas, your car will be towed away at your expense.

- Do pay the little men in Italy who stick tags on your car: it costs about 16 cents to park.

- Do pay the boys in Naples who hover over you like a swarm of gnats. Give the oldest boy in the group about 50 cents, to be divided up as he sees fit. Make a motion with your hand indicating that it's to be shared (try to give him lots of small change).

- You are supposed to use time discs in blue zones of Europe. These discs can be obtained free of charge in many banks, gas stations, and police stations. They may be nuisances to get, but if you **don't** want a parking ticket collection, you'll need them.

Moving violations

- **Don't drink and drive** — particularly in Austria, Denmark, Finland, Norway, and Sweden, where penalties are stiff for having had even one drink. This charge can put you in the clink for three weeks, foreigner or not.

- If you're stopped on any charge, stay cool and show your international driver's license. Generally, except for drunken-driving tags, fines can be paid on the spot, and your license can sometimes get you out of a fine altogether. You'll be given a receipt if you must pay.

- If you are driving someone else's car, you cannot cross borders without written permission from the car's owner.

- If you are traveling with a minor, you cannot cross borders without written permission from the minor's parents.

- Follow local customs concerning headlights. Use parking lights in cities (flashing on your low beams as you approach intersections) if others do so.

- Don't get annoyed at the French for flashing their high beams at you when you're on low. Since they're used to yellow fog lights, white low beams appear too bright to them.

- Watch for a trucker's signals to pass — usually a wave or a turn signal. Say thanks with two bips of your horn; otherwise, leave the horn alone.

- To find city centers, look for signs saying **"centre ville"** (French) or **"centro città"** (Italian), or head for the highest visible church spire.

- Be prepared for an occasional trek into the scrub, in preference to foul (or nonexistent) bathrooms. But never choose the outside edge of a mountain trail. Those innocent-looking low bushes might really be the tops of tall trees clinging to the side of the mountain! This is not a joke; it's a warning from mountain police who have to fetch out the bodies of unwary tourists each year.

- Always yield to traffic on the right (including pedestrians and cows), especially in France.

- Never cross white or yellow center lines.

Motorcycling strategies

- When passing long lines of cars, watch for the occasional irate motorist, who (in a fit of jealousy) will swing his door open to knock you off the road.

- Since a motorcycle can't stop as quickly as a car, leave plenty of space between you and the car in front of you.

- Stay in the center of your lane: this will discourage motorists from squeezing by you as if you were on a bicycle.

Car repairs

Repairs are generally less expensive in smaller towns. In southern European countries, repairs often cost a fraction of what they'd cost in the North.

- Always drop your car off at night for repair the next day. This allows the engine to cool off.

- Get an estimate in writing.

- Agree on a pickup time. Have the mechanic note it on your estimate.

European Road Service

Austria	Use emergency phones placed at one-mile intervals on main roads.
Belgium	Local number for **Touring Secours VAB-VTB (Wacht op de Weg)** or **RACB.**
Denmark	Local number for **Forenede Danske Motorejere.**
Finland	Nearest filling station.
France	Local number for **Police Secours-assistance.**
Germany	Local number for **Strassenwacht.**
Great Britain	01-262-2638. Use phones placed at one-mile intervals on main highways.
Greece	107.
Ireland	Nearest filling station.
Italy	Use phones placed at one-mile intervals on **autostrade.** Ask for **Soccorso autostradale.** In other areas, dial 113 and ask for **Soccorso autostradale.**
Luxembourg	311031. Ask for **Secours automobile.**
Netherlands	Local number for **Wegenwacht** (patrols from 7 a.m. to 11 p.m.).
Norway	Local number for **Norges Automobile Forbund** (patrols from June 20 to September 1 only).
Portugal	Nearest filling station. If you break down on Ponte Abril leading into Lisbon, put a white handkerchief on the car door to signal for help.
Spain	Nearest filling station.
Sweden	Local number for **Larmtjonst AB.**
Switzerland	Use emergency phones placed at one-mile intervals on main highways.
Yugoslavia	Nearest filling station.

Breakdowns on the road

- Members of American automobile clubs can be covered for emergency road service abroad by paying small extra fees for temporary membership in foreign clubs. Contact the AAA or other automobile clubs for full information.

- If you have a breakdown on a superhighway, lift your hood and wait — and wait, and wait. Mobile road service or police will eventually come your way.

- If you're out in the boondocks, wave down a car for help. Or an oxcart, or a moped, or a . . . .

- If you rent a car, ask for a list of numbers to call in case of a breakdown. Get numbers for all the areas you'll be visiting (see below).

- If you buy a new car, check the glove compartment to make sure that there is a pamphlet listing service stations.

Car ferries

- You can get information on ferries at the American Express office in most cities.

- Watch for off-season discounts.

- Ask about round-trip discounts.

- In the peak season, try to reserve space in order to avoid delays. If you don't have a reservation, you'll be placed on a ferry on a first-come, first-served basis.

- You can make reservations ahead of time through some railroads. Inquire at the train station.

- The smaller your car, the less you pay.

Taking Trains

Whether or not you use a Eurailpass, taking trains can be a great way to get where you want to go. A few pieces of information can really help make travel go smoothly.

Validating a Eurailpass

You will have to validate your Eurailpass at the station where you start your first rail trip. Small slip-ups can cause big trouble at this point, but you can prevent them.

- Before your turn comes, write down the dates your pass will be valid. Before the clerk writes the dates on the pass, compare your dates with his. This simple double-checking procedure may save you considerable grief, since any erasures on the pass may cause it to be challenged by conductors.

- If a mistake should still occur somehow, ask the clerk to fill out a paper showing the correct validity dates. If a conductor causes problems later on, show him the slip.

- If you board a train without getting your pass validated, the conductor will do so for a five-dollar charge, which must be paid in the proper foreign currency.

Cutting costs without Eurailpasses

- Travel second class — it's 33 percent cheaper as a rule. Go first class in Greece, Italy, Portugal, and Spain if you find second class trying.

- Make a point of asking for the least expensive fare. Check into reductions for group travel, round-trip fares, excursion fares, youth fares, one-day fares, one-week fares, one-month fares. Look into circular tours; midweek fares; weekend fares; regional, family, gross-kilometer fares; seasonal and holiday fares; senior citizens' discounts . . . . Got the picture?

- Avoid taking trains that require you to pay supplemental charges. Their speed or comfort comes at a price.

Insuring the best train ride

- Get reservations for popular trains, to avoid waiting in lines (see p. 62). If you didn't make them in the U.S., make them as soon as you arrive in a city. Lines are shortest in midmornings, Monday through Thursday.

- Get a nonsmoker seat if you don't smoke.

- Ask for a window seat, which gives you the window and also a fold-out table for writing, playing cards, or picnicking.

- When traveling to a city where you don't have a room reservation, plan to arrive on the earliest train.

Getting to train stations

In a number of cities, you'll find that there are several train stations, so that making connections can become a headache. Of course, you will have to know which train station to go to for which destination. During rush hours, use the underground (subway) whenever possible to get from one station to another. It's both expensive and painfully slow to cross cities by taxi.

Provisions for train travel

- If you want to cut costs, bring your own food and drink. You may want to bring your own water: the water in WCs on trains is not drinkable.

- Bring local currency for each country you'll travel through, if you plan to buy food or drink or to rent a **couchette** (bunk bed) on board. Buy currency at banks to get the best exchange rate.

In train stations

- Note that European train schedules use the military (24 hour) system of time so that 12.00 means noon, and 24.00 means midnight. The system is designed to keep you from confusing 5 a.m. (5.00) with 5 p.m. (17.00).

- Ask a native speaker to pronounce the name of your destination in the appropriate foreign language, so that you will be able to recognize it over the public address system when it is announced.

- If you have lots of luggage, look for pushcarts, which are free — but usually scarce. If your cart won't budge, squeeze or press on the handle to release the brake. (Traveling by train with lots of luggage can only be compared to making frequent and unsuccessful attempts at suicide.)

- Don't be fooled by European train designations. "Direct" may only mean "direct to the next station." Ask the clerk for the fastest train to your destination that doesn't require a supplemental charge. On the board listing trains, **Dep** is an international abbreviation for **Departure; Arr** is an abbreviation for **Arrival.**

The Super Trains

The nostalgic will be sad to learn that the famous Trans Europ Express trains (TEE) no longer operate.

• The TEEs have been replaced by a network known as EuroCity. The network consists of fifty-six day and eight night trains connecting more than two hundred cities. Although Finland, Greece, Ireland, and Portugal do honor the Eurailpass, they are not a part of the EuroCity system.

• EuroCity trains offer both first and second class tickets. The latter cost about one-third less.

• The TGVs (trains á grande vitesse) of France are part of the EuroCity network. Reaching speeds of just under 170 mph, they are among the world's fastest trains.

• A Eurailpass is valid on all EuroCity trains.

• The TGVs require reservations, even with a Eurailpass. These reservations may be made either in the U.S. or abroad.

• In the U.S. you can make reservations through travel agents or directly with the French National Railway. The latter has offices in Beverly Hills, Chicago, Coral Gables, Montreal, New York, San Francisco, and Vancouver.

• Reservations may be made up to two months ahead of any scheduled train departure.

Aboard trains

• Check to make sure the specific car you get on is going to your destination. Trains are often split up en route!

• If you have to get up for any reason, leave something on the seat — a newspaper, magazine, inexpensive hat, or handmade sign that says "occupied."

• If you stretch out, be sure to take your shoes off. This will prevent encounters with the conductor.

• Think twice before renting a **couchette** (a bunk bed in a compartment). If you do rent one, the conductor will give you a sheet (something between a hospital gown and a shroud), a blanket, and (if you beg) a pillow. The compartment will be noisy; and it will be either too hot or too cold. Whether your luggage remains outside or goes with you in the compartment, it will be vulnerable to thieves while you sleep.

Getting off trains

- Never get off a train until you've reached your final destination, unless you're sure the train will be in the station for a specific time.

- Never throw away a ticket until you've passed through the exit gates in the train station at your destination.

- Get information on the next train you'll be taking before you leave the station. If you find out this information right away, you won't have to return to or call the train station later.

- To save on washroom fees, always find a nearby restaurant if you need a toilet. Get a light snack and go to the bathroom there.

Hitchhiking

Hitchhiking in Europe is far safer than the alarmists would have us believe, and many dangers can be avoided by traveling in pairs. Hitchhiking's illegal on superhighways — but that's where you get the long rides — so be prepared for occasional exchanges with the police. Keep them friendly by being polite and not arguing with them.

Prearranged rides

- Try to arrange rides before you even hit the road. Look for notices at the American Express office to see whether anyone is heading in the right direction. Check the bulletin boards at student halls and other youth-oriented places.

- Post your own notice, telling where you want to go. Make it easy to read and eye-catching — if it's funny, all the better. Use color to make it stand out. Be sure to tell people reading the notice how to contact you.

- Be willing to share gas costs with the drivers. It will still be less expensive than a train fare.

Where to hitch

- Use public transportation to reach the outskirts of a town and stand by a stoplight or stop sign. Don't bother trying to get rides from a city center to the outskirts, since Europeans rarely pick up short-haulers — except for women hitching alone.

- Try standing near gas stations, rest stops, restaurants, and ferries.

- Don't hitch where there are truly inexpensive alternatives (as in Spain) or where it's generally disliked (as in southern France).

Before you hitch

- Make sure you have a map with you so you will be familiar with towns en route to your final destination.

- Make big, easy-to-read signs. Write down your destination and the name of the next major town from where you are waiting, in order to pick up either long or short rides.

- Write the name of your destination in the appropriate European spelling: Athens (Athinia), Belgrade (Beograd), Brussels (Bruxelles), Copenhagen (København), Florence (Firenze), Geneva (Genève), Lisbon (Lisboa), Munich (München), Naples (Napoli), Rome (Roma), Venice (Venezia), Vienna (Wien), and so on.

- If there is room on the sign, include the word **please: s.v.p.** (French), **bitte** (German), **per favore** (Italian), **faz favor** (Portuguese), **por favor** (Spanish).

- Stay as clean as possible. If your clothes are not fresh, splash on some cologne.

How to hitch

- Try to be either the first or the last person in a line of hitchhikers.

- Carry as little gear as possible, and place what you've got behind you. Motorists don't like to pick up people who are carrying a lot of baggage.

- Take off your glasses (or your sunglasses) and hold your sign in front of you. Face the traffic. Extend your arm, your open palm toward the oncoming cars, your thumb up.

- If you can get someone to stop and talk to you, you've got a ride. Be polite but assertive.

- When you arrive in any large city, ask the driver to let you off near a tourist office or central train station (for easy access to information and room-finding services).

Hitchhikers' Success Rates

In hitchhiking, it's not who you are, but who is along with you that determines how quickly you will get a ride.

Combination	Results
One woman	Immediate success.
Two women	Quick success.
One woman, one man	Short wait.
Three women	Slightly longer wait.
One man	Long wait.
Two men	Long, long wait.
Three men	Join the army.

Cautions for hitchhikers

- Stay away from curves. Place yourself on a straight stretch of road.

- Stop only in areas with good shoulders.

- If you are hitching after dark, wear something light colored. Stand under a reflecting sign.

- Get well off the road to sleep or eat.

- If you notice that someone is a poor driver, ask to get out right away. No ride is worth a collision.

- Travel with a companion: the ideal team is a man and a woman. You'll avoid robbery and rape this way. Do not allow yourselves to be split up (the woman in the front seat, the man in the rear of a truck).

When to hit the road

- Sunrise is great, sunset is almost as good, and nighttime is good but dangerous.

- Midday, particularly in the South, is awful, as are weekends, particularly Sundays in religious areas. Holidays are a bust.

Etiquette for hitchhikers

- The people already waiting at a hitchhiking area have the priority in choosing a spot, such as the front or back of a line of hitchhikers.

- If a car stops at the middle of a line of hitchers, it's every person for himself or herself. Generally, the person closest to the car will get the ride.

- You should entertain the driver, not go to sleep or sit silent. But don't demand attention — be sensitive to the driver's interest in conversation.

Vagabond lodging

Wily vagabonds on a budget soon learn that there are soft-water showers in many beach areas where you can wash off a week's grime for nothing. In cities, the favorite spots to sleep out are parks, church grounds (including cemeteries), and train stations. Youth hostels have been created with hitchhikers and bikers in mind (see p. 122); campgrounds offer showers, food, and safety for very little money (see p. 124).

- If you try sacking out on a beach, be as inconspicuous as possible. They're often patrolled.

- If you don't mind noise, ask permission from gas station attendants to sleep on any available grass. Most stations sell snacks, and you can use the washroom.

- If you sleep out, put all your valuables down in the bottom of your sleeping bag, not in your knapsack.

Taking Public Transportation and Taxis

The easiest way to learn about the ins and outs of public transportation is to ask the concierge or someone who speaks English at the hotel to explain it to you.

You can also easily ask the help of many people on the street in Austria (with some problems), Denmark, Finland, Germany (with some problems), Gibraltar, Great Britain, Iceland, Ireland, Malta, Netherlands, Norway, Sweden, and Switzerland (with some problems). In other countries, you may have frequent problems communicating. When you do, go to the nearest large hotel and ask the person at the front desk for help. Just remember that people usually like to help other people.

Public transit questions

- What is the best way to get from A to B?
- What is the least expensive way?
- Where do I get tickets or tokens? How much are they?
- Can I get a reduction for buying a pass or a set number of tickets?
- How do I get onto the bus or tram? (You must board some vehicles from the back.)

Public transit bargains

- **Amsterdam:** packets of tram tickets at discount prices, available at cigarette shops displaying Amsterdam Transportation Company emblems.
- **London:** "Go As You Please" tickets, at the Travel Enquiry Office at Piccadilly Circus.
- **Munich:** One-day **Turistenkarten,** at the Central Railway Station.
- **Paris:** booklet or **carnet** of 10 tickets, at subway **(métro)** ticket windows.
- **Rome:** one-week pass at Central Station.
- **Stockholm:** three-day pass, at the tourist office.

Public transit tours

By using public transportation, you can often make tours at a fraction of the cost of organized tours.

- **Amsterdam:** pay for circular tours from and back to the Central Railway Station.

- **Helsinki:** public tourist tours cost a pittance.
- **London:** take bus No. 15 from Selfridges or on Oxford Street with panel marked "Aldgate"; or take No. 11 east from Victoria with panel marked "Liverpool Street."
- **Rome:** take bus No. 30 from Central Railway Station.
- **Paris:** the **bâteaux-mouches** on the Seine cost less in the morning.

The subway in Paris

In Paris, the best way to get around is to take the subway **(métro).** It will take you quickly and inexpensively to all major attractions.

- Get a pocket métro map from an information office on arrival or ask for one at the hotel. Have someone explain the system to you.
- Basically, you buy tickets for each trip from a booth in front of the station. These are cheaper in packets **(carnets)** of 10 tickets.
- You enter the system finding the platform of the train heading in the right direction. Always carry the pocket map with you since it can be difficult to read the maps in the cars.
- If you get lost on the **métro,** go to the nearest mechanical map and press the button for your destination. The whole route will light up. The name of the route is in bold print. You might have to move from one subway line to another to go all the way.
- Be careful not to go through the wrong gate when you get off a subway. There are two kinds of doors: one for connections **(correspondance)** and one for street exits **(sortie).** If you take the wrong gate, you will have to pay another fare.

Taxis

In all but a few countries, such as Spain, Greece, and Portugal, taxis are extremely expensive. Try to avoid them by taking advantage of inexpensive, very good public transportation, including subways, buses, and trams.

- If you have to take a taxi, find out the approximate cost of the trip ahead of time by asking at the information desk or the front desk in a hotel, or by asking the cabdriver himself. Find out also if there are minimum charges — perhaps the walk will be worth it.
- Be wary of asking a hotel to call you a cab, especially if you're staying in a more expensive hotel. Many of these establishments

are served by special cabs — ones that offer extra comfort at an extra price. The less expensive cabs have already been warned to stay clear of such hotels, unless they are called by the hotel itself (a problem in Vienna). Insist on an ordinary metered cab!

- Always try to share the cost of a taxi with other people. This can be easily done on rides to major cities from outlying airports.

- Accept the fact that taxi rates go up late at night when public transportation is not available.

- If you think a cabdriver has swindled you, tell him that you're taking down the number of the cab and will report him to the central transportation authority or the police. If the driver has in fact duped you, he'll probably lower the fare on the spot.

Taxis in Paris

No system is more complicated than the taxi system of Paris. Here are the basics to help you out.

- The cab must have a meter. No meter? Skip the cab.

- There are three basic rates listed as fares *A, B, C* on the meter. *A* covers central Paris on weekdays. It's the cheapest (still expensive) fare. *B* covers suburbs at any time and central Paris from 8:00 PM to 6:30 AM weekdays, and on Saturdays, Sundays, and holidays. *C* applies only to suburbs in the evening.

16 Communicating

The one consideration that most often discourages Americans from going to Europe in the first place is the "language barrier." Naturally, you can become better acquainted with Europeans if you can really speak their languages, but you can still have a great time in Europe with practically no foreign vocabulary. For one thing, you have sign-language fluency that you won't believe until you've tried it!

Another thing that concerns travelers is losing touch with the folks back home. In this age, though, you're as close as a phone to your family and friends, and mail delivery is quite reliable.

So relax — read this chapter — and enjoy!

Speaking

You'll have little trouble communicating in areas where there's heavy tourist traffic. You'll usually find someone who can help you out in most hotels, restaurants, banks, shops, and travel terminals. Only off the beaten path will you run into a language barrier, but even if you can't speak a word of a foreign language, you'll still get by.

Basic expressions

Since it takes years to learn a foreign language, most people don't even try. However, you should take the time to learn a few basic expressions and how to count to 10, not only because it will prove helpful but also because it's the right thing to do.

No book can show you how to pronounce foreign words correctly! Have a native speaker pronounce them for you (and don't be afraid to ask).

Asking directions

If you get lost, you may have a problem getting directions to your destination. In asking directions, the most important word is **to.**

- Open your mouth and say "ahh," as if you were in a dentist's chair. Follow "ahh" by the name of the place you're going: "ahh Paris," "ahh Trendelburg," and so on.

- If you'll point to a map as you do this, most Europeans will understand. Go ahead and use English in the rest of the sentence: for example, "I would like to go **ahh** Madrid."

Basic Expressions

English	French	Italian	Spanish	German	Portuguese
hello	bonjour	buon giorno	buenos dias	Guten Tag	bom dia
good-by	au revoir	arrivederci	adios	Auf Wiedersehn	adeus
slowly	lentement	lentamente	lentamente	langsam	lentamente
please	s'il vous plaît	per piacere	por favor	bitte	faz (faça) favor
thank you	merci	grazie	gracias	danke	obrigado (obrigada)
how much	combien	quanto	cuanto	wieviel	quanto
yes	oui	si	si	ja	sim
no	non	no	no	nein	não
I don't understand	Je ne comprends pas	non capisco	no entiendo	ich verstehe nicht	não entendo
how are you	comment allez-vous	come sta	como esta	wie geht es ihnen	como esta
how do you say	comment dit-on	come si dice	como se dice	wie sagt man	como se diz
_____ " in	_____ " en	_____ " in	_____ " en	_____ " auf	_____ " em
English	français	italiano	español	Deutsch	português

Numbers

one	un	uno	uno	eins	um
two	deux	due	dos	zwei	dois
three	trois	tre	tres	drei	tres
four	quatre	quattro	cuatro	vier	quatro
five	cinq	cinque	cinco	fünf	cinco
six	six	sei	seis	sechs	seis
seven	sept	sette	siete	sieben	sete
eight	huit	otto	ocho	acht	oito
nine	neuf	nove	nueve	neun	nove
ten	dix	dieci	diez	zehn	dez

• Remember that many cities are spelled differently in foreign languages. If someone doesn't understand you, maybe it's because you're not speaking his or her language! What good does it do to ask for Venice in Italy, when Italians call the city Venezia? Here are the major cities and their correct foreign spellings.

Foreign City Names			
Athens .... Athinai		**Lisbon** .... Lisboa	
Belgrade .... Beograd		**Munich** .... München	
Brussels .... Bruxelles		**Naples** .... Napoli	
Copenhagen . København		**Rome** .... Roma	
Florence .... Firenze		**Venice** .... Venezia	
Geneva .... Genève		**Vienna** .... Wien	

Tricks for communicating

• Don't be complicated. Say "Menu," not "I would like a menu, please."

• Repeat statements only once — slowly and without raising your voice. No go? Smile and say "Thank you" in the foreign language.

• If your vocabulary is limited, try to communicate in writing. Carry paper and a pen, and get waiters and clerks to write down prices for you.

• Drop your inhibitions and give sign language a try!

• In short, don't be intimidated by the language barrier. Don't let it stop you from venturing into remote areas that have been barely touched by modern tourism.

Writing

Letters from home, and the postcards you send, can be especially important while you're traveling. No news may be good news, but news is still fun when you're far from home.

Staying in touch

• Duplicate your itinerary to give to friends and relatives you'd like to keep in touch with. Airlines sometimes can reach travelers for urgent messages if they have information on flight plans. But don't count on it!

- Ask correspondents to write "Hold for arrival," followed by the approximate date you'll be arriving, on all mail they send to hotels.

- Ask friends to **type,** not write, the address on the envelope. A typed address increases the odds that you'll get your mail!

- Ask them to address each envelope to an individual person, not to a couple. Otherwise, the couple may have to show up to collect it.

- Tell people to send all letters airmail and to allow a week for delivery. Surface mail reaches Europe in six to eight weeks.

Alternative mail drops

If you have an exact itinerary but don't know where you'll find lodging, you can choose either of the following methods of receiving your mail abroad.

- Have the mail sent in care of American Express in the cities you'll be visiting. With either a credit card or some of their traveler's checks, this service is free. Expect long mail lines in the peak season at these offices. Your mail will be returned to sender after 30 days. Note that for a charge you can have mail forwarded from any American Express office.

- Have mail sent to General Delivery: **Poste restante** (French), **postlagernde Sendungen** (German), **Posta restante** (Italian), **Fermo posta** (Spanish), **posta-restante** (Portuguese). There's usually a small charge at General Delivery, and letters will be sent back after 10 days. But the lines are usually short in comparison with those at the American Express office.

Sending mail home

- Stamps are sold at tobacco and stationery shops and in most hotels.

- Aerograms are the least expensive way to write letters to the U.S. You can buy these at the post office.

- Postcards are nearly as expensive to mail as letters, but are fun to receive.

- You'll often find inexpensive postcards in department stores and at street stands. They are cheaper than the ones found in hotels and are just as nice.

- Note that most hotels provide free envelopes and stationery. If you find none in your room, just ask.

- See page 224 for advice on sending packages home.

Phoning and Cabling

The telephone can do so much for you as you travel — help you book rooms and seats, hunt bargains and compare prices, and, of course, let you talk to people long distances away. European phone systems are sometimes idiosyncratic, but you can make good use of them with a few hints.

Local calls

The simplest places to make local calls are the hotel and the post office, where operators can help handle your calls.

- If you make local calls in a hotel, check on possible surcharges ahead of time. You can also use public pay phones, as in the U.S.

- There are no such surcharges at central post offices. You pay only for the call. Payment is often based on time alone.

- Note that many public phones require tokens, which you can buy in tobacco shops, post offices, bars, newsstands, and wherever public telephones exist.

- Note that in some areas you deposit coins or tokens **after** your party answers — and in some cases, you keep dropping them in throughout the call!

- If you have trouble locating a name in a foreign telephone book, ask for help. Note that some alphabets have extra letters, such as å, aa, ö, ø, and ô, which come at the end of Scandinavian alphabets.

Long-distance calls from hotels

Many hotels add their own charges to long-distance calls made from their rooms. In recent years, these charges have sometimes been three times the cost of the call — and the practice has sent warning ripples through the tourist industry.

Ireland, Israel, Portugal, and the Trust Houses Forte hotel chain in Great Britain belong to Teleplan, a system organized to reduce hotel surcharges. Perhaps other countries will join their efforts with similar programs.

- Never, never make a long-distance call from a hotel room without checking on the hotel surcharge first.

Avoiding hotel surcharges on calls

- If you can dial directly to the U.S. from your hotel room, play the "call back" game. Dial your friend, give him the number of your hotel and your room number, and ask him or her to call you back immediately. Since you pay only for the actual length of a call in Europe, your charge should be for a minute or less. Even if the hotel adds a surcharge of 100 percent or more, the total shouldn't break your bank.

- Note that U.S. telephone credit cards are accepted in many European countries and cut the cost of surcharges.

- If you don't have a telephone credit card, call collect. The overall rate for a collect call is quite high, but surcharges are lower. **Collect** in five languages: **P.C.V.** (French), **R-Gespräch** (German), **pagamento a carico del destinatario** (Italian), **à cobrar** (Portuguese), **pago revertido** (Spanish).

- Note that some hotels are raising surcharges on collect calls — ask ahead of time.

- Avoid surcharges of any kind by making long-distance phone calls from the main telephone terminals in central post offices and in some railway stations and airports. The operator will tell you how long you should expect to wait to get a connection: times vary from a minute to several hours.

- Since these main telephone terminals can be packed in peak hours, avoid the crowds by going at unusual hours. Remember that it's many hours earlier in the day in the U.S.

- You'll be asked to write down your name, address, and telephone number; then the number, full name, and address of the person you're calling.

- You can call person to person, as in the States, but it's more expensive. **Person to person** in five languages: **préavis** (French), **Foranmeldung** (German), **personale** (Italian), **persona a persona** (Spanish and Portuguese).

Cables

A cable often costs as much or more than a telephone call. It's paid for on a total word basis, which includes the name and address of the person to whom you're sending it. You can send a cable from central post offices in most major cities.

- Compare costs before you cable someone. A phone call may turn out to be more economical than you had expected.

Little black book

- Carry a small book to keep addresses and contact information. It's surprising how often you'll use it.

- Business cards are often useful.

- Better are postcards from your hometown with your address already on them (use the gummed labels). Foreigners appreciate these cards, and you'll often receive them in the mail at the most unexpected times!

17 Doing Things

This section is devoted to special-interest activities. You'll find information on shopping; sightseeing, the arts and nightlife; sex; photography; skiing and other outdoor sports — including tennis, golf, bird-watching, hunting, fishing, cycling, gliding, and nude sunbathing; and foreign study and work.

Shopping

You may be one of those people who enjoys shopping, who loves every minute spent in fashionable stores, street markets, and typical boutiques. If so, you will find Europe a delight.

Bargain hunting abroad

- Since most articles you can buy in Europe are also for sale in the U.S., study American prices before going abroad. Unless you do this, you will not know whether you're really getting a bargain.

- Unless a European item is much lower in price or of much higher quality than you can get in the U.S., don't buy it. You'll lose on the currency exchange, you'll have to lug or mail it home, and you may even have to pay duty on it. If you can't make a saving of 40 to 50 percent off the U.S. price, don't buy!

- Shop around before you decide to buy something in Europe. By checking out several stores, you'll save many dollars.

- Ask what each shop's exchange rate is right away. If the rate is better in a bank, pay in local currency.

- Never buy American items abroad (this applies to everything!). Domestic brands are just as good.

- Never buy items in shops catering to crowds of tourists. Such items will always be sold at inflated prices.

- Ask about airline discounts. Air France offers discounts at Le Printemps in Paris. All you have to do is show your ticket.

- You can find superb bargains by settling for goods that have barely visible flaws, particularly in the case of porcelain and glass products.

- Always say "hello" and "good-by" to shopkeepers, even if you don't purchase anything in the store. This is basic courtesy in Europe.

Good-Buy Guide to the Best in European Goods

The following chart will help you come up with some good buys in Europe, including articles typical of the area in which you're traveling. Most of the good buys included in this chart will be less expensive in Europe than in the U.S.

When in this country	Buy these items
Andorra	Excellent buys in cameras, crystal, dolls, leather, porcelain, stamps, watches, and wood products.
Austria	Antiques, art, Austrian jade, ceramics, costume jewelry, crèches, enamelware, fashions, figurines, guns, handbags (petit point), handmade blouses, knitwear, lace, leather, lingerie, porcelain **(Wiener Augarten)**, skiwear, wood carvings, wrought iron.
Azores	Local handicrafts.
Belgium	Antiques, ceramics, chocolate, copperware, crystal, diamonds, glass, handmade shotguns, lace, leather, linen, paintings, pewter, silverware, wrought iron.
Canaries	Local handicrafts, liquor.
Denmark	Ceramics, china, food products, furniture, furs, Georg Jensen silver, glass, linen, pewter, Royal Copenhagen porcelain, teakwood, toys, watches.
Finland	Brass, ceramics, crystal, glass, jewelry, leather, pewter, wood products.
France	Alençon lace, antiques, Daum crystal, fashions, gloves, Lalique glass, leather, lingerie, paintings, perfume, scarves.
Germany	Beer steins, binoculars, cameras, comforters (down filled), cuckoo clocks, cutlery, leather, music boxes, pewter, Rosenthal porcelain, toys, watches, wool products, wood carvings.
Gibraltar	Cameras, crystal, luxury items, perfume, tobacco.
Great Britain	Antique jewelry, antiques, books, cashmere, china, fabrics, glass, mod clothes, pewter, pipes, shoes, silk, suits, tobacco, tweeds, Wedgwood china, woolens.

Greece	Antiques, crocks, embroidered blouses, furs, leather, olivewood candlesticks, patterned coats, pottery, rugs, tote bags, silver jewelry, skins, wood carvings.
Iceland	Ceramics, pony skins, sheepskins, silver filigree, whalebone items, wool sweaters.
Ireland	Antiques, china, crystal, knitwear, lace, linen, rugs, silver, tweeds, whiskey.
Italy	Glass, gloves, gold jewelry, high fashion, leather (Florence), prints, shoes, silk, silver jewelry, straw goods.
Luxembourg	Ceramics, crystal, jewelry, lace, linen.
Madeira	Lace, local handicrafts, Madeira wine.
Malta	Baskets, brass, ceramics, copper, dolls, embroidery, filigree, lace, perfume, pipes, pottery, wrought iron.
Majorca	Leather goods, Majorcan pearls.
Monaco	Dolls, jewelry, perfume.
Netherlands	Antiques, blankets, books, cheese, china, crystal (Leerdam), Delft porcelain, diamonds, figurines, gin **(genever)** in stone bottles, oriental rugs, pewter, pipes, posters, prints, silver, tobacco.
Norway	Ceramics, glassware, pewter, sealskin boots, silver, skiwear, sweaters, Swiss watches, wooden salad bowls.
Portugal	Azulejo tiles, book covers, china, clay roosters, copper, cork, embroidery, filigree, furniture reproductions, guitars, handicrafts, lace, pewter, port wine, pottery, rugs, Vista Alegre porcelain, wrought iron.
Scotland	Cutlery, Scotch, silver jewelry, sweaters, tweeds.
Spain	Gloves, high-fashion clothes, jewelry, lace, leather (Barcelona), mantillas, pottery, saffron, Talevera porcelain.
Sweden	Cutlery, handicrafts, Hasselblad cameras, modern furniture, Orrefors glass, pottery, silver jewelry, suede, steel products.
Switzerland	Cameras, cheese, chocolate, cuckoo clocks, embroidery, fondue sets, lace, music boxes, ski gear, steel products, toys, watches.
Yugoslavia	Copper, embroidery, filigree, lace, leather, rugs, wood carvings, wrought iron.

Value Added Tax (VAT)

- In most European countries you pay a luxury tax on many goods. Tourists are allowed refunds of this tax.

- Always ask if you can get a refund and what the procedure is.

- Many shoppers use credit cards as a way to get an immediate refund. You ask the clerk to make out one slip for the purchase, another for the VAT refund — the simplest method of avoiding this stiff tax.

Duty-free shops

- Avoid most duty-free shops in airports and train stations, as they are now classic rip-off establishments. Prices there are often higher than comparable prices in quality stores.

- You can pick up truly duty-free goods on all international ships and ferries. Everyone else knows this also, which means that the lines will be long.

Bargaining

It's actually improper for you to pay the asking price for goods in Spain, Portugal, Greece, and on most islands. It's equally improper in almost every European country when you shop at open markets, small owner-operated shops, antique shops, art galleries, and flea markets.

Bargaining is not only accepted in these settings, but it is also expected. If you're not used to bargaining, here's a chance to learn how.

Basic bargaining

Bargaining is an attitude, a position, a style. The attitude is wariness; the position is "I won't buy unless it's a fair price." The style is tough but breezy, with a good sense of humor.

- Take your time and comparison shop first. When you've decided on what you really want, begin the bargaining game. Frivolous bargaining is unfair and a waste of the merchant's time.

- Ask for the price. Propose your own, undercutting the stated price by whatever you think you can get away with.

- State the U.S. cost in fair and accurate terms. Tell the merchant that you have no intention of buying unless you can make a substantial saving — of at least 40 to 50 percent. Shopkeepers respect this simple, honest approach to buying.

- State that you'll have to shop around because you want to come up with the best price in town and are willing to spend the time to do it. Prices will often slide down on the spot!

- Let a missing person play the bad guy. "Oh, I think it's beautiful. But my husband (or wife) would be very upset if I spent that much."

- Be complimentary but shrewd, saying, "It's one of the finest pieces I've seen, but I really think it's overpriced."

- Evoke the expert. "I've got someone who really knows about these things. I'd better ask his advice before I spend all that much."

- Find a flaw. Almost everything has one, especially high-quality, handmade articles. I don't like this approach myself, but it does work. Try it only as a desperation ploy.

Advanced bargaining

- Play the add-on game: "I'll pay your price if you'll throw this extra item in." That so-called extra item may be exactly what you were after in the first place!

- Play the lump-sum game: "I'll pay you this much for this, that, and that." You play the lump-sum game after finding out the prices for the individual items. Naturally, you shave off a fair percentage for buying them as a group.

- If the price doesn't come down to what you're willing to pay, thank the merchant and be on your way. You'll be surprised how quickly this brings on a new round of negotiating. You'll sometimes be a block down the street before it starts!

Luxury-shop bargaining

Polite bargaining is very effective in places where you don't want to be too aggressive. Don't let anybody tell you that it doesn't work! It does work, even in so-called luxury shops where you'd least expect it to. The following questions are all polite ways of asking, "How far will the price come down?"

- "Will the item soon be on sale?"

- "Is there a reduction for foreigners?"

- "Is there a discount for paying in traveler's checks?" This discount is quite common.

- "Are there professional discounts for writers (priests, teachers, doctors, lawyers, etc.)?" Become a professional for a moment if you think you can get away with it.

- "Is there a discount for cash purchases?" This is an implied threat to use a credit card.

Popular flea markets

- In Amsterdam head for Waterloopein on Saturday by taking the No. 9 tram or the No. 5, 11, or 55 bus.

- In London, go to Bermondsey early Friday morning (catch the bus by dawn) on the No. 1 bus from Trafalgar Square. Also popular but not as good is the Portobello Market on Saturday, reached by bus No. 15 on Oxford Street (panel marked "Ladbroke Grove").

- In Madrid, try El Rastro, south of the Plaza Mayor along Ribera de Curtidores, on Sunday. Get there by taking a taxi to Plaza del Cascorro.

- In Paris, go to the Porte de Clignancourt on the subway line of the same name, or take the No. 85 bus to rue des Rosiers, on Saturday, Sunday (best), and Monday.

Sightseeing, the Arts, and Nightlife

Europe offers a fascinating blend of sightseeing, the arts, and nightlife. Since these are often oriented to the tourist, you'll make substantial savings by being somewhat wary.

Local tours

- Tours of any city's famous sights are organized by local and large European tour companies. Such tours are well organized but usually expensive.

- Tourist offices often organize and promote local tours. These also tend to be overpriced.

- Student organizations create similar but less expensive tours — a good option for all.

- Generally, you can put together an equivalent tour for yourself using local buses or trams, for a fraction of the cost of more organized tours.

- For free information on suggested sights and routes, pick up brochures, maps, and detailed commentary from local tourist offices and from your hotel. Good sightseeing suggestions are often listed in the yellow pages of local phone books.

- If you're a romantic and want to try a buggy or gondola ride, expect to pay in spades, not hearts.

- Whenever you're agreeing to pay for a "special" ride, have the price put down in writing. Make sure that this is not a per-person price. One way to avoid hassles is to pay ahead of time!

Walking tours

- You can easily walk around the most interesting parts of these major cities: Amsterdam, Antwerp, Athens, Berlin, Bruges, Brussels (the center), Dublin, Edinburgh, Florence, Hamburg, Helsinki (with the tourist tram), Innsbruck, Lisbon, London (the center), Luxembourg City, Madrid (the center), Munich (with the tram), Oslo (with the tram), Salzburg, Stockholm, Toledo, Venice, and Vienna.

- You can walk much of Rome and Paris, although in these cities you'll need to use buses and subways to see all the major sights comfortably.

- Look for booklets, brochures, and special maps geared for walkers in the places you visit.

Zoos

The **Berlin** zoo, the game parks of **Great Britain,** and the deer park at Klampenborg six miles north of **Copenhagen,** will be of interest to many tourists, particularly families traveling with children.

- For information on any of these, contact the appropriate national tourist office (see pp. 227-229).

Museums and galleries

Check ahead before making a special trip, since museums and galleries often close at odd times. For example, the Louvre is closed on Tuesdays.

Admission to most museums is free on certain days. The Louvre is free on Sunday and Wednesday.

- Look for special flat-rate cards, good for admission to many places. Ask at national tourist offices (listed in the Appendix) about special flat-rate cards.

- Note that students with student I.D.s (see p. 15) can often get reduced prices.

- Don't wear high heels to visit galleries and museums. Many forbid them because of the damage they do to floors. This is particularly true in France.

Theaters, movies, concerts, casinos

- You can often get into a London theater if you show up in person just before show time. This approach works best for singles.

- When an event or festival is solidly booked, try bribery. Go to the gate and slip the controller the equivalent of several dollars in foreign currency. "Well, maybe we could find a place for you."

- Arrive at foreign movies on time, because ticket takers may not let you in if you're late.

- To get into a casino, you may be asked to show your passport, and you may not be allowed in unless properly attired (i.e., sports coat and tie, or comparable dress for a woman).

Sex

Hardly a person goes to Europe without taking advantage of some of the most provocative aspects of the culture. After all, that's part of the fun, even on stodgy tours.

Whether it's for a pleasant dinner companion or for a traveling partner, you will find it easy to meet members of the opposite sex while traveling.

- If you have a choice, consider taking a ship to Europe. Ocean voyages are wonderful settings for meeting excellent travelers. I can absolutely guarantee that you'll meet at least half-a-dozen attractive people if you take a ship to Europe.

- Tours are also a good source of companions. Your mutual destinations will highlight mutual interests.

- Train travel creates situations that encourage meeting new people. If you're game, make a point of being friendly to your fellow travelers — Europeans will wait for signals that you're interested in them.

- Younger travelers will find youth hostels, student tours, and similar youth-oriented places natural meeting spots. Each summer the American Express offices all over Europe become social headquarters for virtually six million Americans. They're an excellent source of impromptu traveling companions.

- Older travelers (as well as younger ones) will find that the lobbies, bars, and dining rooms of the finer hotels are good places to meet attractive, interesting people. Gigolos (men who may or may not be paid specifically for their company) collect in these areas. They can be delightful, but unscrupulous.

- **For women only:** don't expect to meet local men as easily in northern Europe as you will in southern countries. Greece has perhaps the best prospects for meeting men. Italy is legendary.

- **For men only:** it is easiest for men to meet women in central and northern European countries.

Sexy but classy shows

The Raymond Revue Bar in **London** and the Crazy Horse, Lido, and Folies Bergères in **Paris** are stylish, sexy shows. See a show at the Lido from the bar: get there by 9:30 p.m., order one drink, and make it last for the whole show — and it will still be expensive.

Photography

Europe offers a visual feast to photographers. Be sure you bring enough film to record it! (I'm assuming that you have a 35-millimeter camera; if you have some other type, some of these tips won't apply.)

Equipment

- Be familiar with the workings of your equipment before you go abroad.

- Change all batteries and carry a few spares.

- A broad camera strap makes taking pictures easier and carrying cameras more comfortable.

- Equip each lens with a Polaroid filter. Leave the filter on at all times, not only to improve photos but also to protect the lens).

- Bring photographic lens tissue or liquid lens cleaner.

- Don't forget your instruction book if you're not completely familiar with your camera or haven't used it frequently in recent months.

Register your equipment

- Don't forget to register equipment to avoid problems coming back through customs (see p. 98).

Film

- Avoid any film with "Professional" printed on the label. These require refrigeration!

- Specify either slide or print film. Slide film allows you to see each picture before ordering prints — a real savings.

- Figure on a 36-exposure roll for each day of travel abroad — at the minimum.

- Get films with different ASAs, (a measurement of light sensitivity). You can then use the appropriate film for specific light conditions.

- Since processing costs vary considerably, comparison shop in area stores.

- For information about processing abroad, Kodak provides this pamphlet: International Photographic Headquarters (No. XAC-16).

- Try to keep your film cool.

Security inspections

- Don't have film in cameras when you go through security inspections at the airport. They may be opened. If you forget or can't avoid having film in the camera, ask the inspector not to open the back.

- The X-ray machines at airports can damage unexposed or undeveloped film, particularly those with ASAs over 400. Moreover, the effect is cumulative, so don't let the film go through these machines.

- Politely ask the inspector at all check points for a visual inspection. If you carry film in a separate case, this takes only seconds. In general, inspectors cooperate fully with this request and with a minimum of hassle. In a few places, they won't.

- Don't put film in checked luggage, which can be subjected to high-level radiation. Even lead pouches are no guarantee that the film will not be harmed. Carry all film on board with you.

Protecting camera gear

- Dust can be a problem — bring a plastic bag for each lens and camera to protect them, even if they're already enclosed in a leather carrying case.

- If you carry cameras in plain bags, potential thieves will be less likely to suspect that you're carrying them.

- Always zip up the bag — even if you're nearby. Leave nothing exposed to chance and sticky fingers.

- Hand carry all camera equipment onto a plane or bus. This way you won't lose it if your luggage is lost or crushed.

- Never, never, **never** leave anything valuable on a plane during a stopover, no matter what the stewardess may say.

- Wear a camera around your shoulder, rather than around your neck in public places. A thief snatching at your camera can easily hurt your neck in his eagerness.

- Do not leave cameras in car trunks or glove compartments. Not only are they vulnerable to theft, but the heat of the closed compartment can damage the camera.

Photo-taking etiquette

- Wherever you see the symbol of a camera with a line drawn through it (as in Yugoslavia), photography is forbidden. Unless you want to spend three days answering questions in the local police station, don't take photos in these areas. You'll encounter similar restrictions in certain towns in Holland and at various historic and religious sites as well. Observe them.

- In Moslem areas you must be especially sensitive, since the Moslem religion discourages photography.

- Don't sneak photos, particularly of people. If you want to take someone's picture, be forthright and friendly — it will work wonders.

- Take along someone who speaks the language, if possible. If not, a smile rates second-best, but it's still good. Just lift the camera slowly, nod your head, and smile. If the person turns away or tosses his hand at you, don't take the photo. Or just say "please" (see p. 186) as you lift the camera, to get a reaction.

- Don't be afraid to pay for pictures. You can carry some small change for this purpose or plan to pay in a different way. Cigarettes will often cut the ice. Carry American brands, since the bland tobacco appeals to many foreigners as a change of pace and costs a carload abroad.

- Other thank-you gifts: American coins (like Kennedy half-dollars); knickknacks, like pins or U.S. flags, medals, badges, and stamps (some people go gaga over the brightly colored ones.)

- If you work with a Polaroid or other instant camera, you can count on instant rapport with your subject.

- Don't gush or dawdle once you've taken a picture. Smile, shake hands, offer a gift — then go on about your business.

Skiing

Skiing is excellent in France, Germany, Italy, and Switzerland. If you intend to stay in a fashionable ski hotel, you must make reservations months in advance.

Ski packages

Many package deals combine airfare, beds, meals, and lift tickets in one price. These are available from ski clubs, airlines, and specific tour operators specializing in skiing. Most tour packages are couple oriented, with stiff charges for single supplements.

- If possible, go on a 14-day, rather than an eight-day tour. You should allow yourself several days just to get used to altitude.

- To cut costs, try some of the lesser-known resorts in France and Italy, ski before February or after mid-March, and avoid the Christmas and Easter holidays.

Sources of information

- Always check snow conditions before going skiing. For information, call (212) 757-6336 (Switzerland) or (212) 944-6917 (Austria) between December 15 and March 15.

- Get in touch with the U.S. Ski Association, 1750 East Boulder Street, Colorado Springs, CO 80909, for information on ski clubs that might be going to Europe.

- Many airlines offer ski packages. Compare these with British packages offered in the travel sections of the **London Sunday Times** or **London Sunday Telegraph.** You might come up with an interesting trip by combining travel to London with a British ski package.

- Also contact Steve Lohr's Ski World, 770 Lexington Avenue, New York, NY 10021, (800) 223-1306 or (212) 751-4200.

- Consult the appropriate national tourist office (see pp. 227-229) as well, though their information is generally less specific than you might want.

Lift tickets

- If the price of your lift ticket has not been included in the ski package, buy weekly passes only if you're an excellent and hardy skier. Otherwise, buy coupons or point-card tickets, which allow for several runs.

- If you do buy weekly passes, you'll need photomat photos to attach to the pass. Bring some from the U.S.

Clothes and boots

- Check on dress requirements with the tour operator or airline. Most ski resorts are quite informal, but a few are not.

- Lugging heavy boots is a chore, but it's worth it. Nothing is worse than the blisters caused by ill-fitting rental equipment.

Other Outdoor Activities

Skiing may well be the sport with the broadest appeal to most travelers. However, in this section you'll find helpful hints on other sports as well, even though some have limited followings.

Birdwatching

Birdwatching can be delightful throughout Europe. Here are some of the prime spots you won't want to miss.

- Slimbridge, 12 miles west of Stroud in the Cotswolds of **Great Britain.** One of the finest wildfowl preserves in the world.

- Gannets at Eldey Rock, ducks on Lake Myvatn, pink-footed geese at Thjorsarver, and puffins on the Westmann Islands — birds by the thousands in **Iceland.** Remote and difficult trips for ardent bird lovers.

- The Camargue in southern **France,** west of Marseilles, famed for its flamingos. Go in May.

- The Neusiedlersee lake, east of Eisenstadt in **Austria,** best in late spring.

- The Las Marismas area of the Guadalquivir River in southern **Spain,** accessible by horseback and filled with ducks (mostly widgeon) in the fall.

- The flat coastal area of Zuidilijk Flevoland in the **Netherlands.**

Cycling

The tremendous popularity of the Tour de France gives you some idea of the reverence for cycling in **France.** Cycling is also highly recommended in **Belgium, Denmark, Germany** (the North), parts of **Italy, Luxembourg,** and the **Netherlands.**.

- Read **Bicycle Touring in Europe,** by Karen and Gary Hawkins.

- Buy or rent a 10-speed bike (damage in transport and difficulties with repairs argue against bringing one from the U.S.). Rental is quite easy in Amsterdam and Copenhagen. Occasionally, a city such as Florence encourages the use of bikes and has a fleet available at low prices. Always contact the local tourist information offices abroad for advice.

- Remove the tire pump from the frame whenever you stop to eat, rest, or sleep. Many cyclists carry the pump in their gear to avoid being ripped off. Routinely lock the bike.

- Carry a tool kit and material for tire repairs. Reflective striping on you and the bike can help avoid accidents. Bring a flashlight since flats have a way of taking place at dusk.

- Don't overextend yourself. Until you're in shape, you should keep long-distance riding to a minimum.

- Read the section on motorcycles for hints on recommended gear, including the best rain gear money can buy!

Fishing

Some of the best deep-sea fishing anywhere can be found off the **Canaries** near the coast of the Sahara. A limited number of charters is available in Gran Canaria. Excellent trout and salmon fishing can be found in **Iceland**, but the entire trip must be worked out in minute de-in advance. Be prepared to camp out or stay in modest hotels. The big advantage: many hours of daylight in the summer.

During mid-May, the mayflies hatch in **Ireland,** a country famed for its brown trout fishing.

Some of the finest trout and salmon rivers in the world are found in **Scotland.** Most stretches are privately owned, which means that a trip should be extremely well planned and well financed. Many hotels have their own fishing privileges. While it's generally very expensive, careful research can uncover reasonably priced daily licenses on some streams.

- Be sure to consult local guides or tackle shop clerks about local conditions and techniques.

- Pack only your own most essential tackle, since local customs will probably dictate what you'll use. Rent or buy what's needed when you arrive.

Gliding

Gliders should head to **Great Britain** and **Germany,** both of which have centers for the sport.

- Both the British and German National Tourist Offices offer free pamphlets on gliding (see pp. 227-228).

Golf

During the summer, you'll want to try the famous courses in **Scotland.** Enjoy golf in southern **Spain** and **Portugal** during the winter. Many courses are open at this time and are often associated with comfortable luxury hotels.

- If you belong to a private club in the U.S., bring a letter of introduction from the secretary as a way of breaking the ice at private Scottish clubs.

- If you stay in certain hotels, you'll have access to other private clubs as well.

Hiking

Hiking is possible almost anywhere in the world, but it's a national pastime in Germany, Great Britain, and Switzerland.

- For information on hiking and available trails, contact the appropriate national tourist office (see pp. 227-229) for free pamphlets and maps.

Hunting

Some of the best duck hunting in the world takes place near Valencia in southeastern **Spain.** Only a certain number of days are set aside for hunts, and blinds must be paid for and reserved months in advance. Very expensive and aristocratic!

Many Americans go to **Scotland** each fall to hunt grouse. Once again, this is an aristocratic pastime with arbitrary stays in ultraexpensive luxury hotels.

• You will hunt with double-barreled guns; no pumps are allowed.

• Bring formal evening attire.

Nude sunbathing

Europeans view this as a sport.

The Island of Sylt off **Denmark** turns into a nudists' mecca during the warmer months, as does St. Tropez in southern **France.** Also highly recommended are the islands off the coast of **Yugoslavia.**

• Bring sunscreening lotion if you're not ordinarily a nudist — for obvious applications.

Studying and Working

What better ways are there of getting to know a country (and not incidentally, its language) than to live and learn with its people?

Foreign study

To enter a university abroad on equal footing with the rest of the students, you must already have completed two years of college in the U.S. However, you can take many courses (but none for credit) with only a high school diploma.

Courses abroad are considerably less expensive than in the U.S., because education has been subsidized by the government. But summer study, geared mainly to foreigners, is very expensive in comparison with the regular courses.

• Arrange for a student visa if you're planning long-term study. Contact the appropriate national tourist office (see pp. 227-229) for help with visas and other information.

- Explore low-cost housing and meals for which students are eligible.
- Arrange to have your **school transcripts** (with imprinted seals); a **health certificate** signed by your doctor, which attests to your good health; and your **birth certificate** (or a notarized copy) translated.
- Get several extra passport photos.

Language courses

- Note that the finest French is spoken around Tours in central France, while the best Italian is heard in Tuscany, the region surrounding Florence.
- You can learn French cheaply in superb, graduated French courses for foreigners in major university towns in France.
- You can learn German at the Goethe Institute, also set up for foreigners, in schools throughout Germany. But it's expensive.
- You can learn Italian and Spanish cheaply in less expensive courses for foreigners at universities in Italy and Spain, respectively.

Working abroad

All in all, it's not a bright picture for Americans seeking work in Europe. It's much easier to earn money in the U.S. Jobs abroad are scarce, and for long-term jobs abroad you'll need work permits, which are a hassle to get. However, lots of menial work is available illegally, for which you won't need a work permit!

- Women can readily get **au pair** jobs — a combination of light housework and babysitting. They pay practically nothing, but often include room and board.
- English teachers and tutors are often needed — at low wages.
- Athletes can sometimes get jobs for city teams if they're highly skilled and willing to work for a small wage and/or room and board.

18 Staying Healthy

Certain health problems come up frequently when people travel, so frequently that they become standard jokes. However, for the person suffering the indignities of diarrhea, nothing seems amusing. These hints can prevent and cure some of the most common ailments that may appear in Europe.

Health Care Abroad

Health care abroad can be excellent, but you have to know the ropes to take advantage of the good and to avoid the bad.

Doctors and drugs

- If you need a doctor for a minor illness, you can trust the concierge of any hotel to come up with the name of a doctor. If you feel that language will be a problem, you can get the names of English-speaking doctors from American consulates, motor clubs, Intermedic, and IAMAT (see p. 25).

- If you can't find an American consulate, try a British one. Or, call a representative of an American shipping company or airline. They can usually help.

- To find a pharmacy that's open all night, go to the nearest one. If it's closed, look on the door and you'll see the name and address of the pharmacy open that night.

Hospitals and clinics

- Avoid public hospitals if you are seriously ill. I've found European public hospitals to be inspired by Dante, going so far as to put a cast on a leg that didn't need one. And even that was done badly. Go to a **private clinic.**

General Health Problems

Many discomforts or minor ailments that come with travel are easily prevented or cured.

Altitude sickness

In higher altitudes you may experience loss of appetite, nausea, mental confusion, fatigue, and shortness of breath — that's altitude sickness.

- The simple, but somewhat drastic solution is to move to a lower altitude.
- **Diamox,** a medication, can relieve its symptoms.
- Slow down the pace. Relax and let your body get used to the lack of oxygen.
- Avoid alcohol, its effect being tripled at high altitudes.
- Drink lots of liquids — fruit juices, water, colas.
- Eat less and eat your main meal in the middle of the day.
- Sleep more. Here's the perfect excuse for a nap after a tiring trip.

Amoebic dysentery

You can't do much to prevent getting this disease. If you do get it, it's just bad luck. There are a number of drugs that will kill amoeba, and they're available abroad and in the United States.

- You may have to submit a stool sample to know for sure that you've got amoeba. However, a negative stool sample does not mean that you don't have amoeba. Some doctors say that stool samples are negative so frequently that they may be a waste of money. They treat for amoeba without them.

Anxiety

It's very common for travelers to experience anxiety in Europe.

- Try to get plenty of rest, have a good meal with a beer or glass of wine, and take a tranquilizer, if absolutely necessary.
- Get physical. Exercise relieves stress. It's hard to be uptight after two hours of snorkeling in the Mediterranean.
- Don't feel compulsive about sightseeing and schedules!

Bee stings

The normal reaction to a bee sting is pain, swelling, and itching. A not-so-normal reaction to a sting produces hives, rash, swelling in the throat area, spasms, and even breathing problems. A severe reaction results in shock and falling blood pressure, which can lead to death (see p. 221).

- Reduce pain with aspirin, reduce swelling with ice, and relieve itching with calamine lotion.

- No calamine lotion? Use toothpaste, not as good but passable.

- If you or someone else has a severe reaction, seek medical help immediately!

- If you plan extensive hiking, cycling, or bike riding through Europe, seriously plan for the possibility of bee stings by carrying Epipen made by Center Laboratories.

Blisters

Nothing can ruin sightseeing or hiking faster than a blister.

- Wear comfortable walking shoes that you've used at home before your trip. Don't worry about how they look. No one else gives a damn. Comfort and convenience should always come ahead of fashion while traveling.

- The minute you feel a blister forming — stop! Try to cover the tender spot with a Band-Aid or some moleskin. If you don't stop, a blister will form.

- If you do get a blister, clean it with soap and pure water. Rub your foot with alcohol if possible. Keep the blister covered with a Band-Aid until it heals.

Constipation

- Try to follow a routine and get plenty of exercise during the day. Walk whenever possible. Not only does it help the body, but it also proves one of the most enjoyable ways of getting to know a town or city.

- Drink mineral water or mix bran into fruit juice as a laxative if this is a chronic problem. You can get bran at health-food stores and carry a small packet with you.

Diarrhea

This is the number-one problem for travelers. It is not funny, because it can ruin a vacation.

How to prevent diarrhea

- Do not premedicate for diarrhea. This will kill helpful bacteria in your system. However, you might want to take freeze-dried **acidophilus** tablets, made up of the same kind of bacteria found in kefir and yogurt. Many travelers swear by them.

- They are sold at pharmacies but are quite expensive. These tablets should be kept cool. For a short trip, they make sense, but for longer trips, forget it!

- Pepto-Bismol both prevents and cures diarrhea in many instances, according to recent independent studies. The product comes in both liquid (most effective) and tablet (most convenient) form, with dosage indicated on the container.

- Drink only tea, beer, wine, distilled liquor, bottled soft drinks, and **carbonated** bottled water (be sure the water is opened at your table). Noncarbonated bottled water may or may not be safe.

- Coffee often causes diarrhea. If you're a coffee drinker, switch to tea.

- Avoid tap water that hasn't been purified, even for brushing teeth. Ice for drinks is often made from tap water. Most problems with water occur in Italy, Portugal, and Spain.

- If you drink from a can or bottle, wipe off any moisture around the area from which you'll be drinking. Use straws if possible.

- You can purify water by adding Halazone tablets (fine if fresh, but they break down in time), by boiling it for 10 minutes, or by adding five drops of 2 percent tincture of iodine to one quart of water and letting it stand for thirty minutes. If the water is cloudy, add 10 drops. Alcohol will **not** purify water!

- You can also use liquid chlorine bleach. If it's a 1 percent solution, add 10 drops per quart and let stand 30 minutes. If it's a 4 to 6 percent solution, add only two to four drops per quart. The water should have a slight odor of chlorine. If it doesn't, add a few more drops.

- If you want to play the odds, let the hot water run from the tap until it's scalding — then fill up a container and let it cool off.

- Stay away from foods sold by street vendors, never eat raw meat or fish (including shellfish), and avoid salads. Stick to fruits and vegetables that can be peeled.

- Stay away from milk or milk products unless you're sure they've been pasteurized. This includes local cheeses in rural areas!

- Avoid precooked foods that have been allowed to stand for awhile.

Diarrhea: treatment

Diarrhea generally lasts three to four days. If it goes on for more than five days, or if you notice blood in your stool, see a doctor. Following are tips for **temporary** treatment.

- If you have to travel, resort to **Lomotil.** It locks in infections, but you don't have much choice.

- As soon as you can, lay off the Lomotil (don't take it for more than three days). Switch over to something milder. Your doctor will suggest a a prescription. We found **Imodium** effective.

- Note: do not buy drugs for diarrhea abroad. Never buy **Entero-vioform.** This preparation, which cannot even be sold in the U.S., is said to cause blindness and other complications.

- The main danger of diarrhea is **dehydration.** So here's a diarrhea potion: In one glass put 8 ounces of fruit juice, 1/2 teaspoon of sugar, and a pinch of salt. Fill another glass with 8 ounces of purified water and 1/4 teaspoon of soda. Alternate swallows from each glass until both glasses are empty. Yum!

- Or, pour salt and soda into a bottle of cola and swill that.

- Drink clear broth, hot, with lots of salt.

- Avoid fatty, spicy foods and stick to bland foods until you've recovered.

Ear problems

- If your ears begin to hurt during the landing of a plane, try to yawn. This should release some of the pressure.

- If you'll be flying on your trip and have a stuffy head, use a decongestant before landing. This will make it easier to relieve the pressure.

- Babies should be given a bottle to suck on during a landing.

- Sometimes your ears get plugged with water after a swim. If you've tried everything from dancing on one foot to shaking your head like a madman and nothing works, have someone poor warm (not hot) water into the ear. Let it sit there for a minute and then roll over. This often works.

- Bug in your ear? Use a flashlight to draw it out.

Exhaustion

Travel, more tiring and stressful than everyday living, may catch you off balance. Exhaustion can lead to more serious health problems as your resistance is lowered. Listen to your body, which speaks in sign language. It will always tell you what pace to keep.

• If you're traveling with people who want to move at a faster pace, split up and plan to meet them at a later date.

• If you're caught on a whirlwind tour, skip part of it. Don't worry about missing something you've paid for — a trip is for fun.

• Match your style of travel to your energy level. If you don't feel well, pamper yourself with a nicer hotel or a more comfortable mode of transportation. Consider making your trip short but sweet.

Exposure to cold

• Eat more food; drink hot liquids.

• Exercise moderately to increase body temperature, and cover all exposed areas, especially the head, hands, and feet.

• If your hands get cold, shove them inside your clothing against your body.

• Remember never to rub cold and exposed skin and to thaw overly cold hands or feet in water only slightly warmer than skin temperature.

Exposure to heat

• Wear loose clothing, light in color and weight.

• Wear a hat and stay in the shade as much as possible.

• Try following the local custom of napping from noon to four in southern countries during the July and August heat.

• Drink lots of water with fresh lemon and lime juice, and make sure there's salt in your diet.

• Avoid alcohol and smoking — if it's humanly possible.

• Travel in desert areas at dawn or dusk.

Eye (something in it)

Nothing is more frustrating than getting something in your eye and being unable to get it out. Here's the secret:

• Pull your upper eyelid out and down as far as you can. Let go. The irritant will often come out on the first try.

- If that doesn't work, have someone else look for the spot. Have them touch it gently with the end of a tissue. The piece of grit will usually adhere to the tissue and be out of your eye in an instant.

Feminine hygiene

- **Sanitary napkins** in five languages: **bandes hygiéniques** (French), **Damenbinden** (German), **compresa hygiénica** (Italian), **absorviente feminina** (Spanish), **absorvente feminina** (Portuguese).

- Tampons may only be available at pharmacies in some areas.

Fever

For mild fever take aspirin, drink lots of liquids, and keep cool. A high fever signals a trip to the doctor.

Food poisoning

Headache, nausea, vomiting, and diarrhea (often all at once) — these are the signs of food poisoning, which can only be described as the next worst thing to death.

- See a doctor. Some food poisoning can be fatal. Note that there is little that can be done for most cases except to ride it out.

Giardia

Giardia is spreading and causing problems in water worldwide. The only thing that knocks it dead is boiling.

- Diarrhea and pain are two symptoms. Doctors can prescribe antibiotics to knock it out.

Hemorrhoids

- Bring medicine and **Tucks,** which contain witch hazel to relieve itching.

- Carry your own toilet paper. American brands are much softer than most paper available in Europe.

Hepatitis

Hepatitis is spread by food and drink as well as sexual contact with an infected person. You can prevent most forms of hepatitis with hepatitis B serum and gamma globulin. See p. 23.

- If you get hepatitis, a good diet and rest are the only cure. No booze or cigarettes will be allowed.

Infections

All infections should be taken seriously, even if they seem minor.

- Clean them frequently, preferably with alcohol, and treat them with an antibiotic ointment.

Insomnia

- Exercise, lots of liquids, and a good diet high in protein will help you avoid insomnia.

- Certain foods contain sleep-inducing substances. Drink a little beer to take advantage of its lupulin (a product of hops). Eat a light snack with milk. It contains both L-tryptophan and calcium — both cause drowsiness. L-tryptophan tablets are now sold in pharmacies and health-food stores.

- Take a warm bath just before going to bed. This helps relax muscle tension.

- If noise bothers you, carry earplugs. Try **Flents,** which can be molded to your ear and block out most noise. They're found in pharmacies throughout the United States.

- Keep the room dark by pulling down the shades. If that's not enough, use a mask.

- At home and during travel follow a routine that sets up or triggers sleep. For many people this is reading a book or magazine.

- Certain things cause insomnia: heavy drinking, late meals (the norm in southern Europe); spicy foods (also very common); chocolate and colas, which contain caffeine; and afternoon naps.

- Sleep-inducing drugs work, but they can cause sleep disturbances and other side effects that may do more harm than good. No one ever died of insomnia.

Jet lag

- See p. 103.

Motion Sickness

You're either susceptible to this, or you're not. And you know very quickly whether or not you are. If you don't want to take the chance, there are many medications available, such as Benadryl, Bonine, Dramamine, Marezine, Phenergan, and Scopolamine (Transderm-V). The last consists of a little pad placed behind your ear.

- These drugs may have side effects, and some of them must be prescribed by a doctor.

- If you forget to take the pills, eat frequent, but light snacks during the voyage. Skip alcohol altogether.

- Lie down away from annoying smells or noise. The diesel smell of a motor is enough to make you sick even if you're not prone to seasickness. The smell of food or tobacco can also be nauseating.

- If you're in a car, ask to drive. Drivers rarely get motion sickness.

Sunburn

Sun damage is believed to be cumulative. More and more skin specialists are warning people to stay out of the sun.

- The sun in southern Europe is extremely intense from 11 a.m. to 3 p.m., one reason why natives are eating lunch or taking a siesta at this time. Consider following their lead.

- The sun is very dangerous at high altitudes. Watch yourself in the mountains.

- If you use a sunscreen, you can stay out in the sun longer. You may want to begin with maximum protection products. Following are companies that sell these: Clinique, Eclipse Total, Elizabeth Arden, Estée Lauder, Lancôme, Orlane, Pabanol, Piz Buin Exclusive, Pre-Sun, Solbar Plus, and Supershade.

- Sunscreens contain PABA. The higher the percentage of this, the more protection. The number on the container will indicate the power of the sunscreen and runs from a low protection of 1 up to 15 for best protection.

- Do not use products containing 5-methoxypsoralerv (5-MOP). These are believed to be dangerous, although many Europeans use them.

- Put on all sunscreens at least 45 minutes before going out in the sun. Although some sunscreens claim to be good after swimming, apply them again anyway.

- Wear a hat and good sunglasses to protect your head and eyes.

- Drink lots of water when you're out in the sun.

- Remember that certain drugs, including tetracyclene, diabetic medications, sulfa drugs, and tranquilizers, can make you sunsensitive. If you're taking medications, ask the doctor about sun sensitivity.

19 Troubleshooting

Even in the best-planned trips, something is bound to go awry. Here's hoping that you never have to refer to this section!

Terrorism

In 1986 there were several million visitors to Europe from the U.S. Twelve were killed in terrorist incidents. That same year over 40,000 Americans were killed on U.S. highways, and 15 died in elevator accidents. If you're still concerned, here are a few tips from experts.

- Choose neutral air carriers in Europe such as KLM (Dutch), SAS (Scandinavian), or Swissair (Swiss).

- Use smaller airports near major cities, such as Gatwick near London, instead of Heathrow.

- Go through security checks and wait in secured areas, not in public areas.

- Don't flaunt the fact that you're an American or wear flashy jewelry. The latter is an invitation to trouble anywhere in the world.

- Incidents of terrorism sometimes affect visa requirements, as happened in France in 1986. For information on obtaining visas, see p. 12.

Losses

No one wants to think about losing something while planning an enjoyable trip, but losses occur with such regularity that you should be forewarned with the following tips.

If you lose your passport in the United States or Canada

- If your passport is lost or stolen in the United States, contact the Passport Office, Department of State, Washington, DC 20524 **immediately.** You'll need the information that you've recorded on a photocopy of the original passport.

- Canadian citizens should report lost or stolen passports to the closest Canadian passport office. You'll find one in each province.

If you lose your passport in Europe

- If you lose your passport in Europe, contact the nearest American or Canadian consulate.

- Report the loss to the local police. They will give you a receipt, which you can use as a temporary I.D. You must carry it with you at all times.

- Carry two spare passport photos, a notarized copy of your birth certificate, a photocopy of the information on pp. 2 and 3 of your passport, and a note listing your passport number to speed up the process of getting a new passport.

Lost traveler's checks and credit cards

- If you should lose your traveler's checks or credit cards, immediately report the loss to the company. You're liable for $50 at most for unauthorized use of any credit card, but if you report the loss before any unauthorized use takes place, you're not liable at all. Paying nothing is better than paying $50!

- Make a list of the numbers of your unused traveler's checks. Avis will refund up to $100 in American Express traveler's checks on weekends, holidays, and late nights if local American Express offices are closed (see p. 129).

Robberies

- If you are robbed, report it to the hotel or restaurant management. Also report it to the police. If you follow this procedure, you can get reimbursed by your insurance company. Ask for a copy of the report as proof of your good will.

- Prevent a robbery in the first place by following the hints on p. 132.

Accidents

Yes, accidents do happen. Even minor ones can cause serious disruption of your trip. Here's advice to smooth over the bumps.

Immediate actions

- If another car is involved, or if you cause serious damage to property, or if you hurt someone, you should stick to the spot like glue. Take photos if you can.

Summoning help

- Naturally, if someone is hurt, try to get an ambulance or the police immediately. In rural areas, flag down an oncoming car and ask the driver to get help for you. Administer basic first aid when necessary by stopping bleeding, getting the person breathing, and keeping the person warm to prevent shock. But don't move anyone who is hurt. Let the police or medics do that!

- If someone you know has been seriously hurt, try to have him admitted to a private clinic. You may want an English-speaking doctor (see p. 209). If the situation is critical, the nearest hospital will have to do, but public hospitals in some areas can offer cures that are worse than the original complaint.

After an accident

- Be prepared for lengthy questions and a detailed report. Note that these reports can be used in court. If you're at fault in a serious accident, you may be liable for a prison sentence.

- Expect trouble if you don't have your passport with you. You may spend some time behind bars — even if the accident wasn't your fault.

- Contact your car insurance company. The insurance company will tell you what to do regarding repairs.

- If you own the car and intend to ship it back to the U.S., have all repairs done in the U.S. The reason: not only can you collect for the damage done to the car, but you can also claim a much lower value and pay a proportionately lower tax coming through customs.

Emergency Phone Numbers

This list of numbers might prove helpful in an emergency. Note that emergency numbers are often listed in the front of telephone books abroad, as they are in the U.S.

These numbers are to be used only in an emergency situation — not for such things as a flat tire or breakdown! They will not work everywhere — as in some rural areas — but they're better than no numbers at all.

Austria	133 (police), 144 (ambulance)
Belgium	900 or 901
Denmark	000
Finland	000
France	Local number of **Brigade de Gendarmerie**
Germany	110
Great Britain	999
Greece	100 or 109 (police), 525555 (ambulance)
Ireland	Local number of **Garda**
Italy	113
Luxembourg	012
Netherlands	222222 (in Amsterdam or The Hague), 94 (in Rotterdam), (03438) 4321 (anywhere else)
Norway	331290 (police), 201090 (ambulance)
Portugal	115
Spain	091 (in Madrid or Barcelona)
Sweden	90000
Switzerland	17, 117, 11, 12, 111, 112 (no money needed for call)
Yugoslavia	92 (police), 94 (ambulance)

Arrests

If you're in doubt about your legal rights, ask to speak to someone from the nearest American consulate. Note that your rights are defined by local law, not American law!

Drunken driving

If you get arrested for drunken driving, you may be in real trouble. In many countries, it will mean an automatic jail sentence of a month or more, for locals and foreigners alike.

- Note that the legal definition of drunkenness may apply after no more than a drink or two in Scandinavia and Austria. If your drunkenness causes an accident, you're open to criminal charges.

- Take a taxi if you've had too much to drink!

Minor traffic violations

If you're arrested for minor traffic violations, you will be asked to pay a fine (see pp. 171-172).

Drug violations

If you're arrested for smuggling drugs, you may well spend many years in a foreign jail. It may be tempting to bring hash from Morocco into Spain, but a six-year jail term is hardly worth the risk.

- Never carry illegal drugs, even small amounts, across a border!

Political violations

Some countries impose stiff fines and jail terms for any activity directed against the state or its political system. This would include insulting behavior and denigration of a national flag.

- Mind your manners — you are a guest.

Duties and U.S. Customs

The brochure *Know Before You Go* gives detailed information on customs procedures. You can get it from the U.S. Customs Service, P.O. Box 7407, Washington, DC 20044, (202) 566-8195, or from any local customs office.

Duty regulations

- Products made in some developing countries can be imported free of any duty. For a list of the countries and exempt products, ask for *GSP and the Traveler,* available free from the U.S. Customs Service, P.O. Box 7407, Washington, DC 20044.

• You are now allowed to bring back free-of-duty goods with a total retail value of $400. You pay only 10 percent duty on the next $1,000. After that, you pay varying duties, depending upon the nature of the imported article.

Customs inspections

• Be sure to have ready your registration slip for valuable articles that you took from the U.S. to Europe, or you'll have to pay duty on them if you're over the $400 limit (see p. 98).

• Have all sales receipts at hand, to prove the actual cost of things purchased in Europe. Note that customs officials know relative retail values almost to the cent. You're not going to get by with a doctored sales receipt. Furthermore, the new allowances seem liberal and appropriate.

• Note that a customs official may ask you to empty your pockets, and very rarely will he (or she) check your body. If it makes you feel better, you're expected to be slightly nervous. But don't make jokes, jabber, or volunteer information. Answer all questions as politely and briefly as possible.

• Note also that U.S. Customs inspectors carefully check baggage for porno, plants, drugs, perfume, excess alcohol (you can bring back one quart), and excess cigarettes (you can bring back 200) and cigars (you can bring back 100).

Possible snags in customs

• If an official catches you bringing in something that you haven't declared, admit the mistake immediately. Just say that you forgot about it. Avoid confrontations and arguments.

• If an official breaks an item while searching bags, file a U.S. government form SF9-5 with the regional customs office in the state where the damage takes place. You'll be reimbursed.

U.S. Customs regulations on packages shipped separately

• You can send any personal article home without paying duty, as long as it was purchased in the U.S. Mark the package "American goods returned."

• You can send a friend one duty-free gift every day just as long as its retail value is less than $50. Mark the package "Unsolicited gift (value less than $50)." Clearly state what the gift is on the package.

• You can also send many separate gifts in one large package, as long as each gift is individually wrapped and marked with the name of the recipient. The nature of every gift within the large package must be marked on the outside.

• You must pay duty on all items you send to your home, but not on those gifts sent to friends. Many travelers arrange to send items to friends who will hold them for their return.

Shipping Goods Home

The safest and surest way of getting any article to your home is to carry it with you. The second-best way is to ship it home; the least sure way is to have a shop ship it.

In the nine Common Market countries and Austria, you'll pay 8 to 18 percent VAT (Value Added Tax) on all purchases unless they are sent out of the country. In short, you don't pay local taxes for packages shipped to the U.S.

Shipping goods through shops

You may want to oversee the wrapping of your purchase to make sure that the right item is packed and that it is properly protected (which it generally is).

• If you have a store ship your package for you, have the shipping date clearly marked on your bill of sale.

• Ask the clerk to note the cost of any insurance, the value of the insurance, any shipping charges, and the mode of delivery.

• Specify airmail or surface mail. Airmail costs more, but is safer and faster. Surface mail may take months to arrive and increases the odds of damage.

Using brokers

Goods may come into the U.S. through a broker, who may or may not inform you of their arrival. Unless it's clearly understood that packages are to be delivered to your home address, they may simply sit in storage in some remote warehouse. Try to avoid using brokers whenever possible.

• Get the name and address of any middlemen.

• Be prepared to pay storage fees for any package that sits in the warehouse. If you want your goods, you will pay the charge.

Shipping goods on your own

- Check with the post office if you'll be mailing large or heavy packages. Size and weight limitations apply.

- If you find you have to send a package through a freight office, call several and compare costs and service before signing on the dotted line.

- Use twine instead of tape. Twine can be sealed with wax if you want to insure the package. In some countries, you will not be able to insure international mail.

- If you're sending books back, be sure to get the special book rate.

- Don't plan to send fragile items, since they will usually be broken in the mail — not because the package was poorly wrapped or mishandled, but because it was unwrapped in customs, only to be poorly rewrapped! Carry fragile items with you or skip buying them altogether. (If you do buy something fragile, try to arrange to pick it up at the end of the trip.)

Appendix

National Tourist Offices

Always write the tourist office that's closest to you, or your letter may be returned telling you to do just that.

Note that addresses change constantly, with offices bobbing up and down New York's Fifth Avenue like corks. To verify an address, simply call the business section of a local library and ask the person there to look the address up in the appropriate phone book.

An alternative: call an international airline and ask them what the current address is. For example, call Air France for the French National Tourist Office, Lufthansa for the German National Tourist Office, etc. All airlines have toll-free numbers listed in the telephone book.

Austrian National Tourist Office

Austrian National Tourist Office
500 Fifth Avenue, Suite 2009
New York, NY 10110
(212) 944-6880

Austrian National Tourist Office
500 North Michigan Avenue, Suite 544
Chicago, IL 60611
(312) 644-5556

Austrian National Tourist Office
4800 San Felipe Street, Suite 500
Houston, TX 77056
(713) 850-9999

Austrian National Tourist Office
11601 Wilshire Boulevard, Suite 2480
Los Angeles, CA 90025
(213) 477-3332

Austrian National Tourist Office
2 Bloor Street East, Suite 3330
Toronto, ON M4W 1A8
(416) 967-3381

Austrian National Tourist Office
1010 Ouest rue Sherbrooke,
Room 1410
Montreal, PQ H3A 2R7
(514) 849-3709

Austrian National Tourist Office
736 Granville Street, Suite 1220
Vancouver, BC V6Z 1J2
(604) 683-5808

Belgian National Tourist Office

Belgian National Tourist Office
745 Fifth Avenue, Suite 714
New York, NY 10151
(212) 758-8130

British Tourist Authority

British Tourist Authority
40 West 57th Street
New York, NY 10019
(212) 581-4700

British Tourist Authority
John Hancock Center, Suite 3320
875 North Michigan Avenue
Chicago, IL 60611
(312) 787-0490

British Tourist Authority
Cedar Maple Plaza, Suite 210
2305 Cedar Springs Road
Dallas, TX 75201
(214) 720-4040

British Tourist Authority
World Trade Center
350 South Figueroa Street, Suite 450
Los Angeles, CA 90017
(213) 623-8196

British Tourist Authority
2580 Cumberland Parkway, Suite 470
Atlanta, GA 30339
(404) 432-9635

British Tourist Authority
94 Cumberland Street, Suite 600
Toronto, ON M5R 3N3
(416) 925-6326

Danish Tourist Board

Danish Tourist Board
655 Third Avenue
New York, NY 10017
(212) 949-2333

Danish Tourist Board
P.O. Box 115, Station N
Toronto, ON M8V 3S4
(416) 823-9620

Finnish Tourist Board

Finnish Tourist Board
655 Third Avenue
New York, NY 10017
(212) 949-2333

French Government Tourist Office

French Government Tourist Office
610 Fifth Avenue, Room 222
New York, NY 10020
(212) 757-1125

French Government Tourist Office
9401 Wilshire Boulevard, Suite 314
Beverly Hills, CA 90212
(213) 272-2661

French Government Tourist Office
645 North Michigan Avenue, Suite 630
Chicago, IL 60611
(312) 337-6301

French Government Tourist Office
1 Hallidie Plaza, Suite 250
San Francisco, CA 94102
(415) 986-4174

French Government Tourist Office
1981 McGill College Avenue, Suite 490
Montreal, PQ H3A 2W9
(514) 288-4264

French Government Tourist Office
1 Dundas Street West, Suite 2405
Toronto, ON M5G 1Z3
(416) 593-4723

German National Tourist Office

German National Tourist Office
747 Third Avenue
New York, NY 10017
(212) 308-3300

German National Tourist Office
444 South Flower Street, Suite 2230
Los Angeles, CA 90071
(213) 688-7332

German National Tourist Office
2 Fundy, P.O. Box 417
Place Bonaventure
Montreal, PQ H5A 1B8
(514) 878-9885

Greek National Tourist Organization

Greek National Tourist Organization
645 Fifth Avenue
New York, NY 10022
(212) 421-5777

Greek National Tourist Organization
168 North Michigan Avenue
Chicago, IL 60601
(312) 782-1084

Greek National Tourist Organization
611 West 6th Street, Room 1998
Los Angeles, CA 90017
(213) 626-6696

Greek National Tourist Organization
1233 rue de la Montagne, Suite 101
Montreal, PQ H3G 1Z2
(514) 871-1535

Greek National Tourist Organization
68 Scollard Street
Lower Level, Unit E
Toronto, ON M5R 1G2
(416) 968-2220

Iceland Tourist Board

Iceland Tourist Board
655 Third Avenue
New York, NY 10017
(212) 949-2333

Irish Tourist Board

Irish Tourist Board
757 Third Avenue
New York, NY 10017
(212) 418-0800

Irish Tourist Board
10 King Street East
Toronto, ON M5C 1C3
(416) 364-1301

Italian Government Travel Office

Italian Government Travel Office
630 Fifth Avenue
New York, NY 10111
(212) 245-4822

Italian Government Travel Office
500 North Michigan Avenue,
Suite 1046
Chicago, IL 60611
(312) 644-0990

Italian Government Travel Office
360 Post Street, Suite 801
San Francisco, CA 94108
(415) 392-6206

Italian Government Tourist Office
1 Place Ville Marie, Suite 2414
Montreal, PQ H3B 3M9
(514) 866-7667

Luxembourg National Tourist Office

Luxembourg National Tourist Office
801 Second Avenue
New York, NY 10017
(212) 370-9850

Netherlands Board of Tourism

Netherlands Board of Tourism
355 Lexington Avenue
New York, NY 10017
(212) 370-7367

Netherlands Board of Tourism
225 North Michigan Avenue, Suite 326
Chicago, IL 60601
(312) 819-0300

Netherlands Board of Tourism
605 Market Street, Suite 401
San Francisco, CA 94105
(415) 543-6772

Netherlands Board of Tourism
25 Adelaide Street East, Suite 710
Toronto, ON M5C 1Y2
(416) 363-1577

Norwegian Tourist Board

Norwegian Tourist Board
655 Third Avenue
New York, NY 10017
(212) 949-2333

Portuguese National Tourist Office

Portuguese National Tourist Office
548 Fifth Avenue
New York, NY 10036
(212) 354-4403

Portuguese National Tourist Office
500 Sherbrook Street West, Suite 930
Montreal, PQ H3A 3C6
(514) 843-4623

Portuguese National Tourist Office
2180 Yonge Street (Concourse Level)
Toronto, ON M4S 2B9
(416) 487-3300

Spain, National Tourist Office of

National Tourist Office of Spain
665 Fifth Avenue
New York, NY 10022
(212) 759-8822

National Tourist Office of Spain
8383 Wilshire Boulevard, Suite 960
Beverly Hills, CA 90211
(213) 658-7188

National Tourist Office of Spain
Water Tower Place
845 North Michigan Avenue,
Suite 915 East
Chicago, IL 60611
(312) 944-0215

National Tourist Office of Spain
5085 Westheimer, 4800 Galleria
Houston, TX 77056
(713) 840-7411

National Tourist Office of Spain
Casa del Hidalgo
Hypolita and St. George Street
St. Augustine, FL 32084
(904) 829-6460

National Tourist Office of Spain
60 Bloor Street West, Suite 201
Toronto, ON M4W 3B8
(416) 961-3131

Swedish Tourist Board

Swedish Tourist Board
655 Third Avenue
New York, NY 10017
(212) 949-2333

Swiss National Tourist Office

Swiss National Tourist Office
608 Fifth Avenue
New York, NY 10020
(212) 757-5944

Swiss National Tourist Office
250 Stockton Street
San Francisco, CA 94108
(415) 362-2260

Swiss National Tourist Office
P.O. Box 215
Commerce Court Postal Station
Toronto, ON M5L 1E8
(416) 868-0584

Yugoslav National Tourist Office

Yugoslav National Tourist Office
630 Fifth Avenue, Room 280
New York, NY 10111
(212) 757-2801

Climate Chart

This chart gives you a capsule picture of each country's weather, followed by a breakdown of its average temperature (in degrees Fahrenheit) and rainfall (in inches) on a month-to-month basis. Naturally, temperatures drop by 10 degrees or so in the evening to rise again by 10 degrees or so over the average at midday — so take these overall averages with a grain of salt.

Nevertheless, the chart does provide a good, accurate idea of what to expect in the way of weather at any time — and might influence your decision on when to make a trip to Europe.

Country		J	F	M	A	M	J	J	A	S	O	N	D
Andorra: Almost all people go to Andorra in the summer, although late spring and early fall can be quite mild.	rain	1.5	1.5	1.5	1.5	3	2	2	2	1.5	1.5	2	1.5
	temp.	27	31	37	49	57	63	67	67	60	49	35	31
Austria: Most mountain resorts are open in summer and winter only. Major cities tend to be shrouded in a gray mist during the winter, while both spring and fall can be pleasant in the valleys. Bring a raincoat.	rain	1.5	1.5	1.5	2	3	2.5	3.5	3	1.5	1.5	2	1.5
	temp.	29	33	40	51	58	64	68	66	60	50	40	34
Azores: Very bleak in the off-season. Try to go in the summer.	rain	5	4	4	2.5	2.5	1.5	1	1	3	4	5	4
	temp.	57	57	58	59	61	65	69	71	70	66	62	59
Belgium: Off-season weather is poor in Belgium. Occasionally, you'll find mild weather in November, known as "St. Martin's Summer." March is one of the worst months. From April to mid-October you'll find the nicest weather, but it's unpredictable, so bring a raincoat!	rain	2.5	2	2	2.5	2	2	3	3	2	3	3	1.5
	temp.	36	38	43	47	55	61	63	63	59	50	44	39
Canaries: For these isolated islands off the North African coast, good weather is the main attraction. Temperature and rainfall vary from island to island. Lanzarote and Fuerteventura may go for months, sometimes years, without rain, whereas La Palma and Tenerife tend to be lush along the coast. Very mild even in midwinter.	rain	1.5	1.5	1	.5	0	0	0	0	0	0	2	2
	temp.	63	63	64	65	67	70	75	76	73	72	69	64

Corsica: Go in the summer. Too bleak in the off-season.
- rain: 3, 2.5, 2, 2, 2, 1, .5, 1, 1, 2, 3.5, 4
- temp.: 45, 47, 51, 54, 61, 67, 71, 71, 71, 61, 52, 47

Crete: Warm and dry much of the year. Mild but not swimming weather in winter. Torrid summers.
- rain: 4, 2, 2, 1, .5, 0, 0, 0, .5, 2, 2.5, 4
- temp.: 53, 54, 56, 62, 69, 75, 79, 79, 75, 69, 62, 56

Denmark: Best visited from mid-May to mid-September, but bring a raincoat.
- rain: 2, 1.5, 1.5, 1.5, 1.5, 2, 3, 5, 2.5, 2.5, 2, 2
- temp.: 32, 32, 35, 43, 53, 60, 63, 62, 57, 48, 42, 36

Finland: Best visited late May to early September.
- rain: 2, 1.5, 1, 1.5, 1.5, 2, 3, 3, 3, 2.5, 2.5, 2
- temp.: 20, 19, 24, 35, 48, 57, 62, 60, 51, 40, 33, 27

France: Whole country lovely from April to late October. North (including Paris) cold and damp during the winter season. Riviera mild in the off-season, but not warm enough for swimming.
- rain: 2, 2, 1.5, 1.5, 2, 2, 2, 3, 2, 2, 2, 2
- temp.: 36, 38, 44, 50, 57, 62, 66, 65, 61, 52, 44, 39

Germany: Whole country lovely from April to late October. Munich very cold during the winter. Heavy snowfalls in the South and mountain areas, including the Black Forest.
- rain: 1.5, 1.5, 1, 1.5, 2, 2.5, 2.5, 2.5, 2, 2, 2, 1.5
- temp.: 29, 32, 39, 48, 57, 63, 66, 65, 59, 47, 40, 34

Gibraltar: Very hot during the summer, quite mild in winter.
- rain: 6, 4, 5, 2.5, 1, 1, 0, 0, 0, .5, 2.5, 5
- temp.: 52, 55, 57, 61, 66, 70, 75, 75, 72, 67, 61, 57

Great Britain: Nicest weather in June. Good weather much of the time from April to late October, although you'll need a good umbrella. Cold with occasional snows during the winter.
- rain: 3.5, 3, 3, 2.5, 2, 1.5, 1.5, 1, 1, 2, 3, 4.5
- temp.: 38, 40, 43, 47, 51, 53, 61, 60, 53, 51, 43, 43

Greece: Scorching hot weather from late May to early September. Mild in spring and fall, so-so in winter — OK for sightseeing but not for swimming. Very cold in the North at that time.
- rain: 2.5, 1.5, 1.5, 1, 1, .5, .5, .5, .5, 2, 2, 3
- temp.: 48, 50, 54, 59, 68, 76, 81, 80, 74, 66, 58, 52

Iceland: Basically a summer-only island as far as tourism goes, because that's when the weather is best. Bring rain gear nevertheless.
- rain: 3.5, 2.5, 2.5, 2, 1.5, 1.5, 2, 2.5, 3, 4, 3.5, 3.5
- temp.: 32, 32, 34, 37, 44, 49, 52, 49, 47, 41, 36, 34

Ireland: Wet much of the time, even in the summer. Wet, penetrating cold in the winter.

rain	3	2	2	2	2.5	2	3	3	3	3	3	3
temp.	40	41	43	46	51	56	59	59	55	50	44	42

Italy: Excellent weather in most areas from April to late October. Very mild in the South during the winter, but not mild enough for enjoyable swimming — except in heated pools. Rome, Florence, and Venice can be stifling in the summer heat, and most Italians take a break from noon to 4 p.m.

rain	3.5	3	2	2	.5	.5	.5	3	3	4.5	4.5	4
temp.	46	48	52	56	63	70	76	75	70	62	54	49

Liechtenstein: Same sort of weather as Austria.

rain	1.5	1.5	1.5	1.5	3	2.5	3.5	3	3	2	2	1.5
temp.	29	33	40	51	58	64	68	66	60	50	40	34

Luxembourg: Often damp and misty, even during the summer. Cold and drizzly in the off-season.

rain	3	2	2	2	2.5	2.5	2.5	3	3	2	2.5	2.5
temp.	32	34	41	47	55	60	62	62	57	48	40	34

Madeira: Noted for its mild off-season weather. A favorite of the British at Christmas. At its best in spring (lush flowers) and fall (wine harvest).

rain	3.5	3.5	3	2	1	0	0	1	1	3	4	4
temp.	60	60	61	61	63	66	70	71	70	69	65	61

Majorca: Hot and bright sun during the summer, very mild even in winter — but not mild enough for ocean swimming.

rain	1.5	1.5	1.5	1	.5	.5	0	0	1	2.5	3	2
temp.	50	51	53	58	62	70	75	76	72	64	57	52

Malta: Dry, hot summers with mild winters — again, "mild" in the Mediterranean does not mean ideal for swimming.

rain	3.5	2	2	1.5	.5	0	0	0	1.5	6	4.5	3
temp.	53	53	56	60	65	73	78	79	75	70	62	57

Menorca: See Majorca.

rain	2.5	2	2	2	1	1	0	1	3	5.5	4	3
temp.	50	51	53	57	59	70	75	75	71	64	57	53

Netherlands: Best weather from mid-April to late October, with frequent showers. Cold in the off-season: you'll need a warm coat.

rain	2.5	2	2	2	2	2	3	3.5	3	3	3	2.5
temp.	34	35	41	47	53	60	62	62	57	50	43	37

Norway: Almost all tourists visit Norway from mid-May to mid-September, to take advantage of the mild summer weather and long days of light. Dark and cold in the off-season!

rain	2.5	1.5	1	1.5	1.5	3	3.5	4	3.5	3.5	2.5	2.5
temp.	23	25	31	41	51	58	62	61	50	40	34	28

Portugal: Very hot summers from late May to late August, ideal spring and fall weather (bright, dry, mild, breezy). Cool, windy, wet winters, with February the worst month.

rain	4.5	3	4	2	1.5	.5	0	0	1.5	2.5	3.5	4
temp.	51	52	56	60	62	68	71	72	70	64	58	52

Sardinia: Basically a summer-oriented vacation spot, although pleasant in late spring and early fall as well.

rain	2	1.5	1.5	1	1.5	.5	0	.5	1	3	2	2
temp.	48	49	53	57	62	70	75	75	71	64	57	51

Sicily: Noted for excellent off-season weather. Many clear, warm winter days — not hot, however! Very hot in the summer. Nicest in spring and fall.

rain	4	2	2.5	1.5	1	0	0	.5	1.5	5.5	4	3
temp.	50	51	53	57	64	71	77	78	73	66	58	52

Spain: Madrid is "nine months winter," according to a Spanish saying. And so it can be cold and snowy in the highest capital of Europe. Best visited in late April, May, late September, and October. The Costa del Sol offers mild winter weather, torrid summers — very popular with Scandinavians!

rain	1.5	1.5	2	2	2	1	.5	.5	1.5	2	2	2
temp.	41	43	50	54	60	69	75	74	67	57	48	42

Sweden: Visit from mid-May to early October to take advantage of long days and warm nights.

rain	1.5	1	1	1	1.5	2	2.5	3	2.5	2	2	1.5
temp.	26	26	30	40	50	59	63	61	53	44	36	32

Switzerland: Lovely from late April to early October. Cold and gray in the valleys during the winter — go to the ski resorts for sunshine. Most mountain resorts open winter and summer only, despite temperate spring and fall weather — which is ideal for visiting the major cities.

rain	2.5	2	2	2	2.5	3.5	2.5	4	3	3	3.5	2
temp.	34	35	43	50	57	63	68	66	60	50	42	35

Yugoslavia: The coastline, the major attraction of this country, should be visited in the summer — not only because the weather is best, but also because many hotels and restaurants close in the off-season.

rain	1.5	1	1.5	2	3	3	2	2	2	3	2	2
temp.	33	39	43	53	62	71	70	71	64	49	41	36

The Best of Europe

Andorra

A lovely isolated mountain retreat with superb duty-free shopping.

Austria

In **Vienna,** you'll want to see the Spanish Riding School (closed Monday and from mid-June to August), the Boys' Choir (9:30 a.m. Mass from mid-September to late June), the Hofburg (free Sunday), the Imperial Treasury (closed Friday), the Museum of Fine Arts, and Schoenbrunn Palace.

In **Salzburg,** go to the Hellbrunn Palace and underground through the Hallein Salt Mine (hard hats and all).

On a clear day, take the **Grossglockner** Mountain drive from Lienz to Zell am Zee. Bring enough Austrian currency to pay the toll and for gas.

Seefeld (near **Innsbruck**) offers a lively casino and resort life.

Skiing in the Austrian **Alps** — don't go at Christmas or Easter.

Azores

For total isolation and stark beauty. Go in July when the hydrangeas bloom.

Belgium

Fabulous food, from fresh mussels to Ardennes ham.

In **Brussels,** visit the Grand' Place and Royal Palace.

In **Antwerp,** you'll find Flemish masters in the Museum of Fine Arts. Take in the House of Rubens, several of his paintings in the cathedral (they're covered until noon), and the Plantin House.

In **Bruges,** hear carillon concerts at the Basilica of the Holy Blood on Wednesday and Saturday at 11:45 a.m., January to September. The world-famous Procession of the Holy Blood takes place in late May.

In **Ghent,** visit the St. Bavon Cathedral.

Outstanding are the castles of **Beloeil** and **Chimay** and the Château of **Annevoie-Rouillon.**

Try to visit a rural inn in the **Ardennes** region.

Binche's Carnival on Shrove Tuesday is one of the great festivals of Europe.

Canary Islands

These offer excellent off-season weather, low prices, and varied scenery, from desert to tropical.

Corsica
Popular offbeat destination in summer with isolated bathing beaches. Rustic.

Crete
Forbidding and dry island famed for the ruins of **Knossos.** Good off-season weather from March to November and relatively low prices. Rustic.

Denmark
In **Copenhagen,** shop along the **Strøget;** go to the Tivoli Amusement Park (open May to mid-September and best at night), the Ny Carlsberg Glyptotek (impressionists; closed Monday), the Royal Theatre (September to May), Amalienborg Palace (changing of the guard at noon when the queen is in residence), Rosenborg Castle, and the suburb of **Dragør.**

In **Helsingør,** you'll find Kronborg Castle.

Stay in at least one country inn (*kro*).

Finland
Excellent trout fishing in summer.

France
Paris, with fabulous food, sightseeing, shopping, and sex. Here are the top 10 sights, followed by the most convenient métro (subway) stations:
- Arc de Triomphe (Étoile).
- Eiffel Tower (Trocadéro).
- Invalides and Tomb of Napoleon (Invalides).
- Louvre — closed Tuesday (Palais Royal).
- Musée d'Orsay (Chambre des Députés or Solferino)
- Notre Dame — 10 a.m. mass (Cité).
- Panthéon (St. Michel).
- Sacré Coeur (Abbesses).
- Sainte Chapelle (Cité).
- Versailles (Pont de Sèvres, then bus No. 171).

The château country of the **Loire** with *Son et Lumière* shows from May to September. Don't miss **Chenonceaux.**

The **Riviera** (Côte d'Azur), best in spring and fall. Most lively in summer.

The cathedrals of **Amiens, Chartres,** and **Reims.**

The wine road from **Mâcon** to **Dijon.**

Mont St. Michel in Normandy.

The medieval city of **Carcassonne.**

Skiing in the French **Alps** (don't go at Christmas or Easter).

Prehistory of the area around **Les Eyzies-de-Tayac.**

Stays in château hotels and *relais de campagne* (country inns).

Germany

Munich offers both sightseeing and beer halls. The technical museum is outstanding, as is the Oktoberfest from late September to early October.

A trip through the **Black Forest** with stays in *Romantik Hotels.*

A trip along the **Rhine,** using Koblenz as a base.
Neuschwanstein Castle in the South.

The medieval towns of **Rothenburg ob der Tauber** and **Dinkelsbühl.**

The Richard Wagner Festival in. **Bayreuth** from late May to September.

Sex and night life along **Hamburg**'s Reeperbahn.

A must — the cathedral of **Cologne** (Köln).

Stays in *castles* and *Romantik Hotels.*

The Wall in **Berlin.**

Gibraltar

The **Rock,** duty-free shopping for real bargains, and mild weather in spring and fall.

Great Britain

London, with terrific shopping, theater, and sightseeing. Here are the top 11 sights, followed by the most convenient tube (subway) station:

- British Museum, Great Russell Street (Holborn).
- Buckingham Palace — Changing of the Guard at 11:30 a.m. (Victoria).
- Houses of Parliament (Westminster).
- Madame Tussaud's Waxworks, Marylebone Road (Baker Street).
- National Gallery (Trafalgar Square).
- National Portrait Gallery, St. Martin's Place (Trafalgar Square).
- St. Paul's Cathedral, Ludgate Hill (St. Paul's).
- Tate Gallery, Millbank (Pimlico).
- Tower of London (Tower Hill).

- Victoria and Albert Museum, Cromwell Road (South Kensington).
- Westminster Abbey (Westminster).

Theater at **Stratford-upon-Avon** from May to January.

Great cathedrals: **Canterbury, Chichester, Winchester, York** — to name a few. The well-preserved Roman baths at **Bath.**

Stonehenge and **Hadrian's Wall,** for lovers of ruins.

Peter Scott's unique bird sanctuary at **Slimbridge.**

The college towns of **Cambridge** and **Oxford.**

Medieval gems like the town of **Chester.**

Scenic tours through **Cornwall** (spring), **Dorset** (fall), and the **Lake Country** (summer).

Stays in charming *historic inns.*

Salmon fishing and upland game shooting in **Scotland.**

Edinburgh's Royal Mile.

Greece

Athens, with a visit to the Acropolis and the National Archaeological Museum (pay the extra fee for the Santorini exhibit).

Make excursions to the temples at **Sounion** and **Delphi.**

The **Greek Islands** — all fascinating. If you're short on time, go to those just off the coast.

The monasteries of **Méteora** and **Mt. Athos** (men only) for Byzantine art.

Excellent weather from April to early November.

Greek Orthodox Easter (different date from our Easter).

Ruins in the **Peloponnesus,** the region southwest of Athens.

Theater at **Epidauros** in summer (exceptional acoustics).

Dafni wine festival from July to September.

Excellent value for your travel dollar.

Iceland

Fascinating geology: volcanoes, glaciers, faults (visit **Eldga**).

Lovely falls, including **Dettifoss** and **Gulfoss.**

Trout and salmon fishing — the latter requiring advance preparation.

Bird watching: **Eldey Rock** and **Thjorsarver.**

Ireland

In **Dublin,** visit:

- **Trinity College** Library and see the Book of Kells.
- The **National Museum** (closed Mondays).
- The lovely 18th-century architecture of **Merrion Square,** the **Abbey** and **Gaiety Theaters, St. Patrick's Cathedral** (where Jonathan Swift is buried).
- The **GPO,** headquarters of the 1916 Easter Rebellion.
- You can shop along **Grafton Street.**

Take a short trip south out of Dublin to the **Martello Tower** in **Sandycove,** site of the James Joyce Museum.

Make sure you visit the southwest of Ireland. Spend a day or two on the **Dingle Peninsula,** gazing out from **Slea Head** to the **Blasket Islands.**

The **Cliffs of Moher** in **County Clare.**

The **Aran Islands,** a three-hour boat trip out of **Galway.**

Yeats country in **Sligo** in the Northwest, including his famous burial site at Drumcliffe Churchyard under **Ben Bulben.**

Beautiful **Donegal** in the Northwest.

Italy

In **Florence,** a fabulous Renaissance city, visit the Academia (closed Monday) and the Baptistry.

- Duomo.
- Medici Chapels.
- Palazzo Vecchio.
- Pitti Palace.
- Ponte Vecchio.
- Santa Maria del Fiore.
- Uffizi Gallery.

Milan, famed for La Scala Opera from December to May. See its cathedral, the paintings by Leonardo da Vinci in the Pinacoteca Ambrosiana, and his *Last Supper* in Santa Maria delle Grazie (closed Monday).

Rome is a must on any itinerary. While there, see:

- Colosseum (closed Sunday).
- Forum (closed Tuesday).
- Pantheon.
- Trevi Fountain.
- Vatican with St. Peter's Basilica.

In **Venice,** best visited in spring and late fall, see:

- Bridge of Sighs.
- Doge's Palace.
- Grand Canal.
- San Marco.

Excellent and relatively inexpensive skiing in the Italian **Alps.**

Pompeii (near Naples) and **Paestum** — some of the most fascinating ruins in Europe.

Superb off-season weather in **Sicily.**

Elegant summer resort area — the **Costa Smeralda** in **Sardinia.** Very expensive!

The catacombs of **Naples.**

Stunning drives: **Amalfi Drive,** a tour of the **Como Lake** region, the **Italian Riviera** from the border of France south.

Famous festivals: the *Calcio* in **Florence** in June and the *Palio* in **Siena** in both July and August.

Liechtenstein

Famous for its colorful stamps.

Madeira

Lush island with good off-season weather.

Swimming is in pools only: the shore is rocky and off-shore currents are treacherous.

Shopping for handmade lace, wicker items, and varieties of the excellent Madeira wines.

Majorca

Hot and dry summer weather with excellent bathing areas.

Low off-season prices (winter weather mild but not warm).

Monaco

World-famous **Monte Carlo** Casino and world's largest aquarium.

Netherlands

Amsterdam: sightseeing and sex. Best sights:

- Anne Frank's house.
- Rembrandt's house.

- Rijksmuseum.
- Stedelijk museum.
- Van Gogh museum.

And the red-light district (fascinating and totally safe at night — with common sense and reasonable caution).

Keukenhof (near **Lisse**), with fabulous beds of tulips in full bloom from mid-March to early April — only a 45-minute drive from Amsterdam.

Twenty-one windmills spin on Saturdays in the summer at **Kinderdijk** (near **Rotterdam**).

Take in **The Hague**'s Gemeentemuseum, Mauritshuis Museum, and Maduradam (Holland in Miniature — open summers only).

Haarlem's Frans Hals Museum (check into candlelight music from April to August).

The ancient villages of **Volendam** and **Monnickendam.**

The cheese market at **Alkmaar,** each Friday from 10 a.m. until noon from late April to late September (take the Kaas-Express train from the central railway station — much less expensive than most organized tour buses).

Aalsmeer's Flower Auction at 8 a.m., Monday to Saturday. See the reclamation project at the *Delta Expo* on the coast.

Norway

Visit the great fjords from May to September — **Geiranger** is one of the best!

Take the train (*Bergensbanen*) from **Oslo** to **Bergen** — one of Europe's finest railway excursions.

Also stunning: a coastal trip on the Bergen Line's mail boat — make reservations months in advance

Pulpit Rock, east of **Stavanger.**

The Munich and Viking Ship Museums in **Oslo.**

The midnight sun from late May to late July at **Kirkenes** (far north).

Try **Lake Svela** in mid-June for trout fishing.

Superb cross-country skiing in March.

The ancient cathedrals of **Stavanger** and **Trondheim.**

Portugal

Not to miss in **Lisbon:**

- Alfama (old Moorish quarter).
- Coach Museum (closed Monday).
- Madre de Deus Church.
- Mosteiro dos Jéronimos.

• Torre de Belém.

Visit the hilltop town of **Sintra** (best in spring).

Excellent weather and swimming on the southern coast **(Algarve)** from late March to early November. Base yourself in **Albufeira** (lively) or **Praia da Rocha** (cliffs over the sea).

Don't miss the cathedrals of **Alcobaça** and **Batalha.**

Incredible religious processions of **Fátima** on the eve of May 13 and October 13.

Go to **Santarém** in June to see colorful bullfights.

Great resorts with lively social scenes: **Estoril** and **Caiscais.**

Ancient towns full of atmosphere: **Elvas, Estremoz, Évora, Obidos.** The Manueline architecture of **Tomar,** truly unique to Portugal.

The fish market in **Sines** (go in the morning).

Coimbra's world-famous library.

The colorful spectacle of fishing at **Nazaré.**

Stays in *pousadas*, charming country inns.

Port wine tasting in **Vila Nova de Gaia,** across the river from **Oporto.**

Rhodes

Mild off-season weather and fascinating architecture.

Sardinia

Luxury summer resorts on the **Costa Smeralda** — very fashionable and equally expensive.

Good weather from April to October.

Sicily

Excellent off-season weather.

Spain

Madrid's museums, with much time devoted to the Prado (closed Monday).

An excursion to **Toledo** (give it a full day or more).

Good swimming weather in resorts along the **Costa del Sol** from April to early November.

Bullfighting in **Madrid** and **Barcelona.**

Running of the bulls in **Pamplona** in early June.

The great tourist cities of **Córdoba, Granada** (The Alhambra), and **Seville** (Cathedral and Alcazar).

Duck hunting near **Valencia** by advance arrangement.

The ancient town of **Santiago do compostela** in the Northwest.

Wine tasting in **Jérez de Frontera** (go in September).

Las Fallas celebration in **Valencia** on March 19.

Tennis in **Fuengirola** (superb in spring and fall).

Stays in *paradores* (inexpensive country inns).

Sweden

Stockholm, for Drottningholm Opera from May to September. Interesting Wasa Museum (sunken ship faithfully restored).

The **Göta Canal** trip from Gothenburg to Stockholm, from mid-May through August. Reserve space weeks in advance.

Midnight sun at **Luleå** from late May to mid-August.

Salmon fishing at **Morrun** in mid-March.

Switzerland

A trip to **Zermatt** (the Matterhorn) or to the **Jungfrau.**

Stays in medieval towns like **Gottlieben** (tiny) or **Stein–am-Rhein** (a gem).

Outstanding high-mountain skiing in the Swiss **Alps** (avoid Christmas and Easter).

Stunning lake area in the South known as **Ticino** (go anytime from late April to late October).

Yugoslavia

One of the world's great scenic drives along a stunning and varied coastline.

Seven-hundred offshore islands for romantic retreats.

A stay in **Sveti Stephan.**

A trip to the inland lakes of **Plitvicka Jezera.**

A stay in **Dubrovnik** with plenty of time to walk.

The mosques of **Banja Luka, Mostar,** and **Sarajevo** (take off your shoes).

Free Things for Travelers

Dozens of other free things for travelers are described throughout this book. They'll save you hundreds of dollars if you'll make use of them, and so will these.

- Note that you can get a passport with more pages (and more room for visas, etc.) at no extra charge. It is ideal for extensive travel. Ask for it if you'll need it.

- Ask for free maps and brochures if you buy a Eurailpass. You can get them from the French, German, Italian, and Swiss railroad offices or from your travel agent.

- Check with WATS information to see whether or not there's a toll-free number before calling an airline or company. Dial 1-800-555-1212.

- Pick up a telephone credit card for free from the telephone company. Use it to make calls home from Europe and avoid the surcharges in many hotels.

- Ask about special incentives when booking a seat. Many tourist offices and airlines offer "bonus coupons" to foreign travelers. Some of these programs can save you a hundred dollars or more!

- Find out whether the international airline you fly on picks up the tab for a helicopter transfer from Newark or La Guardia if your connecting flight leaves from JFK. The best time to ask is when you're making reservations.

- Ask the airline you're flying on to book room reservations for you — many do so without charge. But ask as far in advance as possible.

- If you travel first class, you can get business cards made up for free in foreign languages. Tourist passengers pay only a nominal charge for such a service. Ask your airline whether this super bargain is available.

- If a plane's coach seats are filled, suggest to the airline clerk that you be placed in first class at no extra charge. Airlines "up-grade" passengers when economy class has been overbooked. If you're dressed well, it helps!

- If your flight arrives in a city too late to make a connection, you can get a night's lodging paid for by most airlines. But you have to ask for this bargain since the airline cannot advertise the service.

- Find out about the thousands of foreign-made items you can bring back into the U.S. duty-free. To learn which ones fall into this category, write for *GSP and the Traveler,* a publication of the U.S. Customs Service, P.O. Box 7407, Washington, DC 20044.

Share Your Favorite Tips With Us!

If they are used in future editions of
The Best European Travel Tips,
you will be notified and sent a free
copy.

Send to:
Best European Travel Tips
c/o John Whitman
P.O. Box 202
Long Lake, MN 55356

Index

Boldface page numbers indicate material in maps and charts.

Notes

Notes

Notes

ORDER FORM

Qty.	Book Title	Author	Price
_____	Baby and Child Medical Care	Hart, T.	$5.95
_____	Baby Talk	Lansky, B.	$4.95
_____	Best Baby Name Book, The	Lansky, B.	$3.95
_____	Best Baby Shower Book, The	Cooke, C.	$4.95
_____	Best Wedding Shower Book, The	Cooke, C.	$4.95
_____	Best European Travel Tips	Whitman, J.	$6.95
_____	David, We're Pregnant!	Johnston, L.	$3.95
_____	Dear Babysitter	Lansky, V.	$8.95
_____	Discipline Without Shouting or Spanking	Wyckoff/Unell	$4.95
_____	Do They Ever Grow Up?	Johnston, L.	$3.95
_____	European Customs and Manners	Braganti/Devine	$6.95
_____	Exercises for Baby and Me	Regnier, S.	$9.95
_____	Feed Me! I'm Yours	Lansky, V.	$6.95
_____	First-Year Baby Care	Kelly, P.	$5.95
_____	Grandma Knows Best	McBride, M.	$4.95
_____	Hi Mom! Hi Dad!	Johnston, L.	$3.95
_____	Mother Murphy's Law	Lansky, B.	$2.95
_____	Mother Murphy's 2nd Law	Lansky, B.	$2.95
_____	Practical Parenting Tips	Lansky, V.	$6.95
_____	Pregnancy, Childbirth and the Newborn	Simkin/Whalley	$9.95
_____	Successful Breastfeeding	Dana/Price	$8.95
_____	Successful Dieting Tips	Lansky, B.	$2.95
_____	10,000 Baby Names	Lansky, B.	$2.95
_____	Webster's Dictionary Game	Webster, W.	$5.95

Please send me copies of the books checked above. I am enclosing $_____ which covers the full amount per book shown above plus $1.00 for postage and handling for the first book and $.50 for each additional book. (Add $2.00 to total for postage and handling for books shipped to Canada. Overseas postage and handling will be billed. MN residents add 6% sales tax.) Allow up to four weeks for delivery. **Quantity discounts available upon request.**

Send check or money order to Meadowbrook, Inc. No cash or C.O.D.s, please.

For purchases over $10.00, you may use VISA or MasterCard (order by mail or phone). For these orders we need information below.

Charge to: ☐ VISA ☐ MasterCard Account # _____

Expiration Date _____

Card Signature _____

Send Book(s) to:

Name _____

Address _____

City _____ State _____ Zip _____

Mail order to:
Book Orders, Meadowbrook, Inc., 18318 Minnetonka Blvd., Deephaven, MN 55391, Phone orders: (612) 473-5400, or Toll-Free (800) 338-2232.